INDIGENOUS PEOPLES AND POLITICS

Edited by
Franke Wilmer
Montana State University

A Routledge Series

INDIGENOUS PEOPLES AND POLITICS

FRANKE WILMER, *General Editor*

INVENTING INDIGENOUS KNOWLEDGE
Archaeology, Rural Development, and the Raised Field Rehabilitation Project in Bolivia
Lynn Swartley

THE GLOBALIZATION OF CONTENTIOUS POLITICS
The Amazonian Indigenous Rights Movement
Pamela L. Martin

CULTURAL INTERMARRIAGE IN SOUTHERN APPALACHIA
Cherokee Elements in Four Selected Novels by Lee Smith
Kateřina Prajnerová

STORIED VOICES IN NATIVE AMERICAN TEXTS
Harry Robinson, Thomas King, James Welch, and Leslie Marmon Silko
Blanca Schorcht

ON THE STREETS AND IN THE STATE HOUSE
American Indian and Hispanic Women and Environmental Policymaking in New Mexico
Diane-Michele Prindeville

CHIEF JOSEPH, YELLOW WOLF, AND THE CREATION OF NEZ PERCE HISTORY IN THE PACIFIC NORTHWEST
Robert R. McCoy

NATIONAL IDENTITY AND THE CONFLICT AT OKA
Native Belonging and Myths of Postcolonial Nationhood in Canada
Amelia Kalant

NATIVE AMERICAN AND CHICANO/A LITERATURE OF THE AMERICAN SOUTHWEST
Intersections of Indigenous Literature
Christina M. Hebebrand

THE PRESENT POLITICS OF THE PAST
Indigenous Legal Activism and Resistance to (Neo)Liberal Governmentality
Seán Patrick Eudaily

THE ECOLOGICAL NATIVE
Indigenous Peoples' Movements and Eco-Governmentality in Colombia
Astrid Ulloa

SPIRALING WEBS OF RELATION
Movements Toward an Indigenist Criticism
Joanne R. DiNova

SPIRALING WEBS OF RELATION
MOVEMENTS TOWARD AN INDIGENIST CRITICISM

Joanne R. DiNova

NEW YORK AND LONDON

Portions of James Redsky, *Great Leader of the Ojibway: Mis-quona-queb* (McClelland and Stewart, 1972) are used with permission from McClelland and Stewart Limited.

Published in 2005 by
Routledge
605 Third Avenue, New
York, NY 10017

Published in Great Britain by
Routledge
4 Park Square, Milton Park,
Abingdon, Oxon OX14 4RN

© 2005 by Taylor & Francis Group, LLC

Routledge is an imprint of the Taylor & Francis Group, an informa business

First published in papperback 2012

ISBN 13: 978-0-415-97338-0 (hbk)
ISBN 13: 978-0-415-65190-5 (pbk)

Library of Congress Card Number 2005012399

All rights reserved. No part of this book may be reprinted or reproduced or utilised in any form or by any electronic, mechanical, or other means, now known or hereafter invented, including photocopying and recording, or in any information storage or retrieval system, without permission in writing from

Trademark Notice: Product or corporate names may be trademarks or registered trademarks, and are used only for identification and explanation without intent to infringe.

Library of Congress Cataloging-in-Publication Data

DiNova, Joanne R.
  Spiraling webs of relation : movements toward an indigenist criticism / Joanne R. DiNova.
     p. cm. -- (Indigenous peoples and politics)
  Includes bibliographical references (p.) and index.
  ISBN 0-415-97338-4
  1. American literature--Indian authors--History and criticism--Theory, etc. 2. Canadian literature--Indian authors--History and criticism--Theory, etc. 3. American literature--Indian authors--History and criticism. 4. Canadian literature--Indian authors--History and criticism. 5. Indigenous peoples--North America--Intellectual life. 6. Indians of North America--Intellectual life. 7. Indians in literature. I. Title. II. Series.

PS153.I52D56 2005
810.9'897--dc22   2005012399

Publisher's Note
The publisher has gone to great lengths to ensure the quality of this reprint but points out that some imperfections in the original may be apparent.

To

Mary (Jourdain) Mainville
(1910–1974)

and

Bernadette (Cassidy) DiNova
(1914–)

For the immeasurable gift of relations.

Contents

Acknowledgments — ix

Introduction — 3

Chapter One — 21
Academic Cowboys and North American Indians

Chapter Two — 49
When "I" Equals More Than "Me": Constructions of (Constructions of) Indigenous Identity

Chapter Three — 75
Critical Warriors and "Hang-Around-the-Academy" Indians: Toward an Indigenist Criticism

Chapter Four — 109
The Essential Métis: Being *Halfbreed*

Chapter Five — 139
Spirals, Maps, and Poetry: Re-Reading Joy Harjo

Conclusion — 173

Notes — 181

Bibliography — 195

Index — 209

Acknowledgments

Without the support and encouragement of many people, this book would simply not have been possible. To all, I wish to express my warmest gratitude. The project began life as a doctoral thesis, and generous financial support was received from the Social Sciences and Humanities Research Council of Canada (Doctoral Fellowship), the Michigan State University American Indian Studies Program (Pre-Doctoral Fellowship), and the Ontario Graduate Scholarship program. Thanks also to the Couchiching First Nation of Fort Frances, Ontario—Edna Lockhart and Joan Mainville of the Education Department in particular—whose support was always more than financial.

To Elaine Garner at the University of Waterloo and to Ginny Carney, thanks for the friendship and encouragement. Special thanks to Fr. Michael Brosnan for pointing me in the right direction. To my family, much love and warm thanks: my brothers Joe and Dan, my nephews (especially Pete, whose work coincides with my own), my niece, and the rest of my family. To Elaine DiNova, thanks for believing. To my parents, Rudy DiNova and Jayne Mainville, thanks for teaching us the importance of a social conscience. And to my daughter Taryn DiNova-Owl, a very special thank-you and a big hug for all your patience during every stage of this project.

To my thesis supervisor, Dr. Linda Warley, thanks for insisting on my best and for mentoring me through the unfamiliar terrain. To the rest of my dissertation committee—Drs. Kevin McGuirk, Victoria Lamont, Robert Needham, and Simon Ortiz—thanks for the careful readings and thoughtful suggestions that made this a much stronger work. And to all my teachers, in the many places we have met, Migwetch.

Seventh Fire

>
> For a time we forgot
> The sounds of ghost
>   dancers
> On the plains, the drums
> Ancestral, resolute
> Converging in the distance
>
> For a time we forgot
>   the Voices
> For a time we believed
> The tinny pulpit voices
>   instead
> Could see only their pink
> Fisted bibles
> Raised as if poised
>   to strike
> And for a time we were afraid
>
> But now I believe the sounds grow large
> And now I see the Northern Lights gone wild
> And between the shivering folds of pink paranoia
> I hear the Voices, softly now:
>   *Tear down their fences*
>   *They can't think without lines.*

                                                (DiNova 104)

Introduction

> Indigenous teaching mirrors thinking back to the learner.
>
> —Gregory Cajete[1]

My first course in Native literature was thought-provoking in several respects, but perhaps most intriguing was the story that our instructor related to us during the first day of classes, a story from her own experience as a graduate student. She told us that an otherwise knowledgeable friend had once asked why she was choosing to study Native literature because, the friend said, "it isn't any good." The story might have remained just a disturbing little anecdote and I might happily have gone on to discover the wonders of indigenous literature for myself, but over the years that this project has taken shape, I have come to the realization that such comments are not anomalous.[2] Throughout the academy, stated and unstated, the disparagement of indigenous literatures continues, sometimes even among those directly involved. There are, of course, exceptions too numerous to mention, but the inelegant furor over and dismissal of recent attempts by Native academics to obtain control of the study of their own verbal art suggests that the condescension is widespread and is not confined to considerations of literature.[3] The assumption that "it isn't any good," premised on a tacit presupposition that it could not be otherwise, is apparently applied to every aspect of Aboriginal thought and creativity. That is, the same premise accounts for the assumption that Native scholars "aren't any good," at least not good enough to govern critical approaches to the literature of their own people.

The present work persistently rejects the notion that the literature (or scholarship) of any given group, indigenous peoples in particular, can be inherently inferior. It rejects the unstated conclusion that, since Native people have had a written culture for a relatively short period of time, the literature must therefore be primitive, further back on some evolutionary scale.[4]

To begin, the evolutionary model, on which so much of the condescension rests, is just a story—and not a very convincing one. Like most stories, the evolutionary myth heavily favors its tellers. More to the point, however, the model is incapable of explaining the fact that some readers are truly captivated by indigenous verbal art. Presumably, some distinguished and astute scholars are among those who dismiss Aboriginal work as simplistic, undeveloped. Attributing the position to weak scholarship or widespread fatuity is, therefore, not tenable. The only acceptable conclusion is that such critics must be viewing the literature in a radically different way: from Eurocentric eyes. In other words, the Euro-based view of literature must be an aspect of a worldview which perceives contradistinctively to another possible worldview, the Aboriginal, and the vastly different evaluations of Native literature are attributable to the vastly different worldviews from which the texts are approached. What I refer to as "the Aboriginal worldview" can be seen to occur in variations among different tribes across the Americas. Moreover, the similarity in worldview occurs among indigenous peoples around the globe, including the indigenous people of northern Europe, the Saami. It will probably be objected that such a claim—that all Aboriginal peoples of the Americas share a similar worldview—is pan-Indianism. In a sense, it is; however, it can be countered that the Western worldview is an exception to a more widespread—diverse in manifestation though strikingly similar—worldview witnessed among indigenous peoples worldwide.[5] With this in mind, the fact that indigenous peoples in the Americas share a worldview is not surprising. What is surprising is that the Western worldview is so peculiar.

In order to illustrate the critical incongruity, I would like to oppose these two radically different worldviews—which, for lack of better terms, I designate "Western" and "Aboriginal"—in a somewhat contrived way. I will suggest (and develop the suggestion throughout this book) that the distinction is traceable to particular occurrences in European philosophy in the Middle Ages.[6] In short, two major breakthroughs can be seen to have occurred in medieval thought, for better or worse.[7] The first concerns Creation, which, in classical Greek philosophy, was not an issue of concern.[8] However, medieval philosopher-theologians (there was at the time no distinction between the two) were faced—due to the assertion that God created the world—with the possible non-existence of Creation. If God created the world, then the existence of the world is contingent, not necessary. The world could conceivably not exist. This raises the related question of whether God created the world once and for all: that is, whether the Creator endowed Creation with the capacity to go on existing independently, or whether the world needed the Creator's constant input in order to go on existing, to prevent the world from lapsing into the nothingness from which it presumably sprang. The Middle Ages, in general, began with an acceptance of ongoing creation and ended with the adoption of a once-and-for-all creation (Marías 131–33). This may not seem in the least related to Native literature, and indeed the connection is centuries apart. The important point to take from the discussion is that if God made the world and then left it to carry on independently, then the Creator is not part of, or ultimately accessible to, Creation. Thus, by the end of the medieval period, the Creator had been effectively separated from Creation. Since Native literature so frequently depicts a spiritualized Creation, some relation to the present discussion should already be evident.

The second issue concerns the universals: Aristotle's secondary substances, the general classes and species that relate to his primary substances, or individual instances of objects. In the Middle Ages, the question of the ontology of the universals came into prominence. Recall that Plato's Ideas exist in a separate, though supreme, reality, while Aristotle's universals inform the matter that constitutes this reality. For Aristotle, the universal is a necessary and intrinsic feature of the individual; it is that which makes the thing what it is. Generally speaking, thinkers at the beginning of the Middle Ages held that the universals were real, physical components of actual things, while at the end of the period, the universals were taken as nothing more than symbols, mental constructs (133–36). The concept of, for example, "dog-ness" (the universal dog) no longer related in any physical way to particular and actual dogs. The concept was nothing more than a conventional but arbitrary way of referring to a class of objects. The (possibly) positive side to the move was that classes of objects could then be subjected to more and more refined distinctions. The symbols referring to reality could be deftly manipulated, having been released from their clumsy physicality, and an explosion in mathematics and modern physics could occur, which would lead in turn to the amazing technological advances that characterized the Renaissance and later periods. However, since the concepts were no longer inherently connected to the physical realm, the conceptual realm was all humanity had access to after this move in medieval European thought. That is, the thinking-being had become isolated from Creation and, as mentioned previously, the Creator.

Given the technological advances that followed, it is not surprising that the earlier position, which saw all of Creation as connected to the Creator and to other aspects of Creation, would be deemed primitive. The refined distinctions, or increasing fragmentation, came to be seen as evidence of advanced thinking, giving rise to a kind of evolutionary model of epistemology. At the same time, a corresponding rejection of the tradition (that is, of medieval thought) which had produced the epistemological shift that had enabled such advances also occurred. Aboriginal thought, when it was afterwards encountered, was likewise dismissed by European thinkers as primitive. This is not to suggest that Aboriginal thought and medieval thought are identical. There are vast differences, and Viola Cordova (Mescalero Apache) suggests that we would have to look to Classical Greece and Rome to find something that truly approximates Aboriginal thought in Europe ("European Concept" 31).[9] What I am suggesting is that, during the medieval period, Western thought abandoned fundamental connectedness for the lure of fragmentation, and that this abandonment is not a feature of classical Aboriginal thought or the literature that springs from such thought.

The Aboriginal worldview, as often noted, is characterized by an emphasis on connectedness, the idea that all of existence is connected and that the connectivity encompasses, infuses, and constitutes everything. This connectedness is called *manitou, wakan tanka, usen*, etc., and, as Willie Ermine points out, it forms the basis for Aboriginal thought (103).[10] Since connectedness is highlighted, community (in a very wide sense) is of utmost importance in classical Aboriginal thought. In contrast, later European (Western) thought is characterized by a thrust toward isolation and fragmentation. With the thinking-being now isolated from the Creator and Creation, and with an orientation towards fragmentation (pronounced isolation) the emphasis settles implosively on the self. The claim is sometimes made that in the Western view individualism prevails; however, while the focus may be on the self, the celebration of individuality in the West is a cultural myth. The thrust in Western culture is, paradoxically, towards the elimination of individuality. The process of individuation, carried to its extreme as is unavoidable once begun, may end in a distinction of the self from each and every other individual and even from different periods and aspects of the self; however, the paradoxical end result is a grey and indistinguishable mass of infinitely individuated humanity. Highlighted individuality becomes paradoxically indistinguishable from the mass. As a result, actual individuality is shunned while extreme normalcy (the mean) is celebrated and misrecognized as paramount individuality. Conversely, in the Aboriginal worldview, in which the emphasis is on the community, the individual is simultaneously crucial. That is, if the community is important, then each individual is also crucial, because the diverse gifts of individuals are integral to the functioning of the community. The community is immeasurably weaker if the unique gift of any of its individuals is erased. In the Aboriginal worldview, while the community governs the orientation, the individual is also paradoxically celebrated.

Introduction

These divergent worldviews get expressed in radically different approaches to art and literature.[11] In order to illustrate the point, I will give a brief and admittedly simplistic description of, by turns, Western and Aboriginal visual art and poetry. A binary will emerge that, throughout the course of this book, I will work to erase. Note that Western philosophy is an elite discourse and that remnants of the cohesive worldview which characterized early European thought, as well as contemporary Saami (European indigenous) thought, continue to be evident in Western culture. Furthermore, the fragmentation that I will suggest characterizes Western thought is becoming increasingly evident in North American Aboriginal communities. However, in order to unravel the seemingly widespread dismissal of indigenous art and literature, I will begin by emphasizing the binary, by examining and highlighting the differences on which the dismissal of Native literature is based.

To begin, the early twentieth century was marked by the emergence of the modernist and abstract movements. Features of modernism include a rejection of tradition that becomes more and more pronounced, an increasingly pronounced focus on the artist, and an increasingly pronounced focus on the process of painting. To quote Canadian modernist painter John Lyman: "The real subject of a painting is how you paint it, not what you paint." Abstraction in painting has been described as a liberation of action from the colored form (*Modern*); however, I find it more useful to think of the term etymologically: *to drag, draw, or pull from*. Abstract art, then, is that in which some certain aspect is pulled, or abstracted, from the whole. In later *avante garde* works, the same trends are pushed further still; the renunciation of tradition and the focus on artist and process become more extreme. I think here of Orlan and of Andres Serrano. Serrano's work received an unanticipated amount of attention when his *Piss Christ* (1987) was exhibited. The work is an edition of four large and luminous photos of a wooden crucifix immersed in the artist's own urine. His intent was to raise questions about the marketing of Christianity, the Church's stigmatization of normal bodily functions, the aestheticizing of the crucifixion *vis-à-vis* the horror of execution, and so on. What was aroused among politicians and the public, however, was shock and outrage. Serrano has the artistic distinction of having had his work discussed in the United States Congress, since he was working under a National Endowment for the Arts (NEA) grant at the time the work was produced (Weintraub 159–64).

Orlan is a French artist who began the process of altering her own identity when she was fifteen. Strongly influenced by Lacanian psychoanalysis, the artist works with psychotherapists to permanently change her personality.

At the same time, she has been physically altering her identity through successive cosmetic surgeries, which become artistic performances. Her hope is, following the masters of European representation, to achieve "the chin of Botticelli's Venus, the nose of Gérôme's Psyche, the lips of François Boucher's Europa, the eyes of Diana from a sixteenth-century French School of Fontainebleau painting . . . [and] the forehead of Leonardo da Vinci's *Mona Lisa*" (Wientraub 79). As such, she is herself a work of European art in progress. She is also a saint, having canonized herself in 1971, and sells her own relics: her fat, her flesh, and the blood-soaked gauze from her surgical performances.[12] Orlan's work emphasizes the artist to the extent that the artist literally becomes the artwork, while Seranno's work emphasizes the process and medium. In both cases, the rejection of tradition is pronounced. However, while the theory behind such works becomes increasingly complex—both raise significant questions about the meaning of art, identity, religion, etc., in contemporary culture—the discussion becomes accessible to an increasingly limited (and elite) audience.

Less provocative works include Barnett Newman's *Voice of Fire* (1967). Purchased by the National Gallery of Canada in 1989 for $1.76 million, a public outcry not unlike that surrounding Serrano's work was raised over the use of public funds to buy the starkly minimalist work: a sixteen-foot painting of a red stripe between two blue stripes.[13] The gallery insisted it was a bargain, and, given the complex theory informing the work, it was. The public, however, was not impressed. The overall effect of much recent art on "the public," which is in many ways "the community" of contemporary mass culture, has been a sense of revulsion. The severing of the contemporary from tradition, of certain aspects of the subject from the whole (abstraction), of the artist and of certain features of the artistic process from the art has been carried to such startling extremes that the community has become radically disconnected from the art as well.

Note that by "theory," I am referring to the mental models by means of which we make sense of the world. These models usually operate beneath the level of consciousness, present only as tacit beliefs or common sense assumptions. Raised to the level of consciousness, a theory can itself become the object of art or literature, in addition to the means of interpreting art or literature. Furthermore, this theoretical objectification of the means of interpretation can again become the object of expression or the subject of interpretation. Obviously, the analysis or expression will be complicated exponentially with each inversion. In the discourse of literary criticism, "theory," often called "methodology," is somewhat interchangeable with "philosophy." In the discourse of literary criticism, "theory" also refers in most cases to the post-structuralist variety. A tacit belief or common sense assumption attached to this usage is that only Western scholars do theory: Others don't. I reject that assumption in this book and put forth Aboriginal theory, sometimes called the Aboriginal worldview, as a compelling alternative to post-structuralism. The alternative theory becomes as important to human survival as it does to the criticism of literature.

Visual art produced from the Aboriginal worldview generally shows some characteristic features: a sense of connectedness, in which one thing fuses seamlessly into another and constitutes a whole. Inuit sculptor Manasie Akpaliapik's *Respecting the Circle* (1989) is one such example, comprising several conjoined figures sculpted of whalebone, ivory, dark grey stone, antler, baleen, rust stone, and horn, and forming a unified and seamless whole. To quote Akpaliapik on the cosmology which informs his work, "Everything in the world is connected, people and the animals and the entire food chain. When you disturb the circle, the chain, you disturb everything" (qtd. in Newlands 15). Contemporary sculpture by Aboriginal artists has received considerable attention in recent years because it bears some similarity to Western abstract art. However, a major difference is that whereas Western abstract art works against tradition (in many respects, it makes a tradition of rejecting tradition), Aboriginal art works within tradition—even when the art incorporates Western postmodern influences.

Tlingit/Tahltan artist and instructor Dempsey Bob, for example, produces contemporary pieces within the heavily prescribed artistic tradition of his people. His work seeks a return to and revitalization of the artistic tradition that was all but lost with the banning of potlatch ceremonies by the Canadian government and the resulting confiscation of works of ceremonial art (Dickason 261, 301). At the same time, Bob infuses his recognizably traditional pieces with contemporary elements. In *Eagle Woman* (2001), for example, he works with contemporary media: bronze and horse hair. The piece depicts two fused figures, eagle and woman, rendered in two fused styles, traditional Northwest Coast iconography and a contemporary and stylized naturalism. However, the fusion of dichotomies is seamless, making it impossible to locate where one ends and the other begins. The naturalism of the woman figure is so highly stylized (an abstraction of form) that it moves toward a revitalized iconography and a revitalized artistic traditionalism. Simultaneously, the more traditional iconography of the eagle figure is rendered contemporary. Tradition, in Bob's work, resists ossification and becomes relevant in a contemporary context.[14] Like Akpaliapik, Bob seeks to bring into his work the connections that exist among the land, the people, their culture, and their spirituality. He sees his art as literally having a life its own, a life to which he is closely related. He refers to the pieces as his children and is often surprised at how they turn out (*The Smart One*).

A similar set of distinctions is evident in poetry. Abstraction, in this case of language from representation (signification), becomes especially pronounced with Western modernist poets, as evident in Ezra Pound's classic imagist poem "In a Station of the Metro":

> The apparition of these faces in the crowd;
> Petals on a wet black bough. (lines 1–2)

Here the image is disconnected (abstracted) from meaning, in accordance with Pound's desire for "Direct treatment of the 'thing'" ("A Retrospect" 3). The modernist urge to dispel connective tissue is pronounced in his severing of the "thing" from signification beyond itself. Gertrude Stein's abstraction with words is more pronounced still. For her the word itself is abstracted from meaning, rarely building so far in its connections to reality as the image. A short example from her larger work *Tender Buttons* illustrates:

> A PIECE OF COFFEE
>
> More of double.
>
> A place in no new table.
>
> A single image is not splendor. Dirty is yellow. A sign of not more in not mentioned. A piece of coffee is not a detainer. The resemblance to yellow is dirtier and distincter. The clean mixture is whiter and not coal color, never more coal color than altogether.
> The sight of a reason, the same sight slighter, the sight of a simpler negative answer, the same sore sounder, the intention to wishing, the same splendor, the same furniture.
> The time to show a message is when too late and later there is no hanging in a blight. (463)

Here, Stein evades conventional meaning and explores alternative avenues of signification in the "struggle with the ridding of [her]self of nouns" (460). She attempts to liberate the word from fixed signification, from conventional connection to reality, in her own exercise in making it new. Stein's work experiments with language much as a painter does with color and form. She manipulates the sounds of words—the rhythms, rhymes, and plasticity thereof—in isolation from meaning and engenders a radical

Introduction

resistance to fixed meaning. Interestingly, her work signifies nevertheless. As F. W. Dupee notes, "Poets have found her work exciting, however inexplicably so, as if words in themselves might in certain circumstances appeal to some receptive apparatus in man [*sic*] that is comparable to what people call extrasensory perception" (xiv). In evading the signifying aspect of language, Stein simultaneously emphasizes its musical aspects (rhythmic, rhyming, alliterative, assonant, and so on) and, as musicians are well aware, meaning can be made without words.

As important as Stein's work is in a theoretical sense, it also parallels the rejection of both tradition and connection to reality that is evident in the visual arts discussed previously. Similarly, her moves toward radical fragmentation are carried to further extremes by later poets. Language poet Lyn Hejinian, for example, works in a distinctly Steinian tradition, while dispensing with some of Stein's musicality and musical signification:

>   spice quilt mix
>
>   know shipping pivot
>
>   sprinkle with a little melody
>
>   nor blot past this dot mix
>
>   now for a bit and fog of bath rain
>
> do dot goats
>
>   swift whipper of rice (lines 10–16)

Ron Silliman in *Tjanting* also resists closure, abstracting language from meaning, but at the narrative level. He severs his work from such traditions as conventions of spelling, of grammar, and of narrative technique:

> Not this.
> What then?
> I started over & over. Not this.
> Last week I wrote "the muscles in my palm so sore from halving the rump roast I cld barely grip the pen." What then? This morning my lip is blisterd.
>   Of about to within which. Again & again I began. The gray light of day fills the yellow room in a way wch is somber. Not this. Hot grease had spilld on the stove top.

> Nor that either. Last week I wrote "the muscle at my thumb's root so taut from carving that beef I thought it wld cramp." Not so. What then? Wld I begin? This morning my lip is tender, disfigurd. I sat in an old chair out behind the anise. I cld have gone about this some other way. (134)

As with the visual art discussed earlier, the focus on the artist and on the artistic process intensifies. An increasing tendency to abstract words from meaning is evident, and the audience, aside from the elite audience, is alienated. Such literature, since it proceeds from a Western worldview, is governed by a principle of fragmentation. From a Western perspective, the works are significant and worthy of serious scholarly attention; however, the work is once again disconnected from the public, which, as mentioned, might be understood as the community. Again, the critical shift in Western epistemology occurred within an elite discourse and, as suggested, governs elite Western contemporary art and poetry. Interestingly, such fragmentation increasingly governs advertising, the most pervasive venue for contemporary art.

An example of poetry which is governed by an Aboriginal worldview, on the other hand, is Joy Harjo's "Creation Story" from her collection *The Woman Who Fell From the Sky:*

> I'm not afraid of love
> or its consequence of light.
>
> It's not easy to say this
> or anything when my entrails
> dangle between paradise
> and fear.
>
> I am ashamed
> I never had the words
> to carry a friend from her death
> to the stars
> correctly.
>
> Or the words to keep
> my people safe
> from drought
> or gunshot. //
> If these words can do anything
> I say bless this house
> with stars
>
> Transfix us with love. (lines 1–15, 22–25)

A major theme in Harjo's poetry is love, but this is not simply the narrowly defined emotional experience of "love poetry." Rather, Harjo's use of the term suggests the vast connectedness that encompasses and infuses and constitutes all that is. Love is her term for what others refer to as *manitou* and what I will call "the principle of connectedness." Love concerns (is) the relationships with and among everything that is. It involves not only the relationships among lovers and loved ones, but all relationships with all of existence and all of eternity. Fear, another major theme of Harjo's poetry, is the inverse of love. It is that which disconnects and fragments relationships. Despite the importance of keeping relationships (connections) alive and stable, the contemporary world is riddled with imbalance and fracture. Thus, Harjo's work prays love into being and dispels fear. While distinctly euphonious, its primary social function is not aesthetic.

The nature and function of language is yet another theme in Harjo's poetry, as it is for the language poets. However, as with the similarity between Dempsey Bob's work and Western abstract art, the similarity between Harjo's work and Western abstract poetry is superficial. For Harjo, words carry friends to the stars, they keep one's people safe, and they constitute our being. That is, rather than causing the language to collapse in on itself, simultaneously (if inadvertently) turning the focus on the poet and the poetic process, Harjo uses language as an instrument of actual change in the world.

Recall that in the late medieval period, the universals were disconnected from reality. All that remained were the names, *flatus vocis* (puffs of [spoken] air), which had no necessary relation to reality, much less any ontological significance in themselves. The connection between language and reality was severed at that point in Western epistemology, and the stage was set for an arbitrary and endless play of signification—though Saussure and Derrida were a long time coming. Had the severance of language from reality not occurred, words would retain their transformative potential, and prayer would remain something more than wishful thinking. In the classical Aboriginal worldview, however, which informs Harjo's work and much of Aboriginal literature, language continues to assume transformative potential. For such writers, the relationship between words and Creation continues to be vibrant and physical. More to the point, it is only from a contemporary Western epistemological perspective that such thought and such deployment of art and language is naïve, simplistic, or primitive.

Harjo's work will be covered in greater detail in Chapter Five, and contemporary, medieval, and Aboriginal understandings of language, in Chapter Two. What is important to note at this point is that such radically different worldviews explain not only the differences between Aboriginal and Western literatures, but also the differences in evaluations of the two bodies of material. While indigenous literature is, in most cases, produced from an indigenous worldview, the assessment of the literature has proceeded, oddly enough, predominantly from a Western worldview. The reason, in other words, that Aboriginal literature has been perceived as not "any good" is quite simply because it has been examined according to Western paradigms. From the Western worldview, art and literature are more highly valued, perceived to be more sophisticated, when more fragmented and elusive of meaning. The fundamental connectedness evident in the early medieval period is perceived as primitive, and a similar assessment has been applied to Aboriginal literature for the same reason. Not only is such an approach "ethno-critically" inappropriate, it also misses the full significance of movements in indigenous literature, which have scarcely been revealed.

The present work, then, does not seek to situate itself among the mainstream of Native literary criticism; for the same reason, it does not rehearse annotated bibliographies of the writer's own reading in the field. In most cases the practice would simply require my pointing out *ad nauseam* the recurring fundamental flaw in orientation outlined above. Rather, I select several works as indicative of wider trends in the prevailing scholarship and then situate my own work among the growing body of (sometimes lesser known) indigenist works. In other words, the present work builds upon and describes, at the same time as it attempts to perform, an inexorable movement towards an indigenist criticism. As Gloria Bird writes, "the master trope of Native American literature [is] the interconnectedness of all things—of people to land, of stories to people, of people to people" ("Decolonization" 4). An indigenist criticism not only recognizes this fundamental connectedness in the literature, but also itself participates in "the interconnectedness of all things." That is, an indigenist criticism recognizes and works to ameliorate social, political, and environmental conditions, even while addressing literary and scholarly concerns. For an indigenist critic (as for the indigenist author), the social, political, ecological, literary, scholarly, economic, and more are inseparable. To proceed as if they were (separable) would be to dismiss "the interconnectedness of all things," which Bird describes as "the master trope of Native American literature," and (the more egregious error) would turn the focus toward the critic and the criticism and away from the literature she addresses.

As mentioned, this book examines selected works by selected writers of (or about) Aboriginal literature, and many of the themes touched upon in the preceding discussion will be developed in more detail. The selected works have been drawn from several genres—critical essay, autobiography, fiction, and poetry—and from both sides of the Canada-U.S. border.[15] Selected texts are considered in order to support the suggestion that indigenous literature springs from a worldview that emphasizes connectedness. The corresponding note will also emerge: that to view the literature from a Western worldview is to miss the mark entirely. Each of the literary texts examined will be seen to be part of a collective impetus that involves the unified (interconnected) efforts of Native people in widely divergent fields of pursuit. Some of the critical works examined, on the other hand, will be seen to be part of a countering impetus that seeks to wrest the literary texts from their functional (interconnected) context and re-inscribe them as mere and isolated objects for scholarly dissection. In response, this book is more meta-critical than critical and in no way seeks to present an exhaustive critical examination of even a single text. Instead, it suggests the need for and engages in a re-examination of approaches to Native literature, while making its own tentative approaches to selected works from an indigenist position.

What has continually occurred to me during the writing of this book is the fact that, despite its sometimes "radical" nature, very little of what I say is new. Most of it has been said before, many times, as I hope will become evident. It is not my hope, therefore, or delusion, that this will be a groundbreaking work, but rather that it become part of the unified effort that is evident in many of the texts I examine. My contention is that the reason for reading Native literature is not simply to "understand" Native people, or to "help" them and their literature "catch up" with the mainstream. The reason for reading, and my reason for studying, Native literature is that these texts are of immense contemporary importance. The worldview that disparages Native literature is also the worldview that has given rise to nuclear arsenals, global warming, and "Third-" and "Fourth-Worlds." It is becoming increasingly evident that this worldview is inherently unsustainable. It is, therefore, becoming increasingly important to examine other ways of viewing the world, to examine diverse ways of imagining a difference, perhaps even to imagine the re-connection of the Settler Nations to the lands they exploit. My contention, then, is that Aboriginal literature is part of an emerging vision of a different world, and my desire is to clear away some misconceptions in order to allow the literature to be examined on its own terms: according to the worldview from which it was produced.

The first three chapters discuss prevailing criticism in order to situate my work in the existing scholarly context. For the most part, this will amount to pointing out what this book is not. In Chapter One, I give special attention to Arnold Krupat's ethnocritical approach, with some mention of Walter Ong's evolutionary model of language use and of Terry Goldie and the study of the indigenous image in Canadian literature. Chapter Two is an examination of dominant theories concerning the construction of the self in Native autobiographies, since the understanding of the self determines the notion of identity. This chapter will discuss the fracture in medieval philosophy in more detail, relating it to the fractured image of self that characterizes Western thought, and will cover the autobiography of Wilma Mankiller, former Principal Chief of the Cherokee Nation of Oklahoma. I suggest that Mankiller cannot extricate her own story from that of her people. Her book is as much a Cherokee history as it is a personal one, as much about Cherokee political struggles as about the writer's own. Chapter Three looks at some dominant approaches to indigenous literature by indigenous critics, pointing out some inadequacies in these, while at the same time implying that Aboriginal ancestry is no guarantee of a critic's proceeding from an Aboriginal worldview. Chapter Four treats *Halfbreed*, the autobiography of author-activist Maria Campbell (Métis). The chapter discusses issues of Métis identity and essence, distinguishes between First and Settler Nations, and highlights the emergence of indigenous thought in literature as presented so forcefully in Campbell's work. Chapter Five examines the poetry of Joy Harjo (Muscogee Creek), uncovering the implicitly political message her poetry conveys and the complex metaphysics woven into her verse. My primary purpose is to conduct an indigenist reading—the groundwork of which is provided in preceding chapters—of Harjo's poetry.

A word about terminology: throughout this work, I use various terms to refer to the original people of North America. The preferred term, of course, is always the respective people's name for themselves in their own language—Anishinaabe, Tsalagi, Haudenosaunee, and the like. Frequently, the terms simply mean "people," or "principal people," and I likewise use the term "people" on occasion. The need for a term that includes all people of the hundreds of First Nations but excludes all others, however, is a fairly recent problem and not one that will be easily solved. With this in mind, I have tried to avoid privileging a single term, recognizing that each has its problems. "Indian" is a European blunder; "Native" is too often used to describe people of the Settler Nations born in this land; "indigenous" is troubling because of its scholarly connotations and because etymologically it simply means "native."[16] "Aboriginal" evokes linear temporal assumptions etymologically, which is to say it suggests that what makes Native people distinct is that they were "here first," as if that were their only claim to sovereignty. More to the point, they are still here, have always been and will go on being here, living Aboriginally. Finally, "First Nation" is a term used almost exclusively of the people in Canada, although the expression is becoming more common in some places in the United States. Since no term is truly adequate, in this work I move among them and settle on none. (Perhaps I favor "Native" as a kind of terminological middle ground.) One term I avoid, however, is "Native American." I think of Gloria Bird and Joy Harjo's introduction to *Re-inventing the Enemy's Language,* in which they suggest, "*Native American* is a term invented in academe and is the term of the moment. It was invented to replace the term *American Indian*. This is a serious misnomer. In our communities we first name ourselves by tribe, but the general term commonly used is *Indian* in the United States and *native* in Canada" (20). An exception to my general rule of terminological diversity occurs in Chapter Four. In this chapter, I will find it necessary to use the term "Indian" much more frequently, since I must distinguish, for the sake of discussion, between Métis and Indian people. "Tribe" is another term I use sparingly throughout this book. Originally used in English to refer to the three original tribes of Rome and the twelve tribes of Israel, the term acquired and has not escaped pejorative connotations in reference to indigenous peoples. However, "tribal" has more recently been redeployed by Native people themselves as an affirmation of sovereignty and an expression of solidarity with indigenous peoples worldwide.

A thornier issue, strangely, is how to refer to people of the Settler Nations. In this case, the preferred academic term is "dominant," against which everyone else is deemed "subordinate," "oppressed," or simply "Other." While there is certainly a lot of oppression going on and certain social groupings have been privileged with the opportunity to prevail in the oppressing, Gloria Bird's contention that the term "dominant" gives the impression of strength and implies weakness on the part of the "Other" is also worth noting: "Each time we use 'the dominant culture,' or speak of ourselves as 'minorities' we are perpetuating notions of our own inferiority and domination. In order to move out of colonizing instances of interiorized oppression, we first have to identify those moments in which we reinforce those useless paradigms and search for new approaches to the way we speak of ourselves in relation to our histories and stories" ("Decolonization" 6). The difficulty with "non-Native" is that the discussion frequently does not refer to all non-Natives, but rather to a particular branch. The term "white" has been objected to, mostly by white people, as racist. The objection is supported by a wholesale rejection of race as biologically unsupportable and essentialist.

Chapter Four discusses essentialism in much detail, so I will defer the fullness of my response until then. Instead I will recall Jace Weaver's note with reference to such discussions:

> Putting aside for the moment the diasporic nature of much of modern Native existence, one must nevertheless admit that there is something real, concrete, and centered in Native existence and identity. Joseph Conrad can become a major figure of English letters and Léopold Sédar Senghor a member of the French Academy, but either one is Indian or one is not. And certain genuine consequences flow from those accidents of birth and culture. ("I-Hermeneutics" 14)

It may also be the case that "either one is [White] or one is not. And certain genuine [benefits] flow from those accidents of birth and culture." Furthermore, as Viola Cordova points out, the frequent use of the term "Western" by non-Native people suggests the tacit acceptance of similarities:

> [T]he European has invented the term *Western* to signify the shared notions that set off European, or 'Western,' peoples from all of the other of the planet's peoples. The term indicates, through its prevalent use, that there are some agreed-upon ideas, a matrix, if you will, that are held—in general—that would allow such a designation to carry any meaning for Westerners and non-Westerners alike. ("European Concept" 26)

The entire discussion seems to wend from the fact that some members of the dominant group, while they may like to dabble in the literatures and cultural studies of the Other, may become uncomfortable when the gaze of the Other is turned upon them, when the subaltern "researches back," to use Maori researcher Linda Tuhiwai Smith's term (6).[17] Too often, dominant researchers have preferred to occupy the position of non-ethnic, non-racial, default social grouping against which all Others are measured deviations. With this in mind, I will resist becoming mired in discussions of what to call people of the collective nations that have systematically dispossessed the indigenous peoples of the world. At times I will use the term "White"; at other times, "Western" or "European"; and at still others, "non-Native." Although such questions as terminology may be important in some arenas—especially those in which the terms have been forcibly imposed on "Others"—objections to the present work will likely be more to the subject matter than to its terminology. Too often such questions have been used to detract from more important issues. Arguably, the less important issue is how to refer to the dispossessed and their dispossessors, and

Introduction 19

the more important, to understand how dispossession functions and how ultimately to put an end to it.

Ten years ago, Kimberly Blaeser (Ojibwe) proclaimed the need for a "tribal-centered criticism," one that would seek "a critical voice and method which moves from the culturally-centered text outward toward the frontier of 'border' studies, rather than an external critical voice and method which seeks to penetrate, appropriate, colonize or conquer the cultural center, and thereby, change the stories or remake the literary meaning" ("Native Literature" 53). More recently, Renée Hulan and Linda Warley have repeated Blaeser's call: "The complexity and sophistication of Native literary texts . . . can only be fully apprehended if we learn to read them from the inside out" ("Comic Relief" 141). That, a decade later, it would still be necessary to remind colleagues of the need for a tribally centered approach to Native literature suggests that the movement toward an indigenist criticism has for the most part been skeptically regarded. As Hulan and Warley point out, however, since indigenous literature proceeds from a distinct worldview, the radical re-thinking of critical approaches is nevertheless crucial:

> Teachers and critics can also draw readers' attention to the epistemological, philosophical, and formal differences that undergird Native texts, and, in so doing, they must be [self-conscious] about the analytical models they bring to bear on them. Yet too often critical analyses are shaped either by preconceived ideas of what Native texts are about or by imported critical paradigms. (140)

While the present work does occasionally proceed from imported criticisms, finding some discourse analysis and materialist models especially useful, it is primarily interested in taking up the challenge issued by Blaeser and by Hulan and Warley to seek out a tribal-centered, or indigenist, approach. Post-structuralist and psychoanalytic methodologies will, for the most part, be notable by their absence. While the following chapter will outline some difficulties associated with relying too heavily on imported paradigms, the entire book is a re-affirmation of the suggestion that, due to the "epistemological, philosophical, and formal differences that undergird Native texts," the indigenous literary and scholarly corpus itself yields the ideal critical methodology with which to approach indigenous literature.

Chapter One
Academic Cowboys and North American Indians

> We can make the trail like our ancestors did for us. Make medicine, put the stories forward along with the energy so another generation can carry them into our future. To hell with feeling marginalized.
>
> —Maria Campbell[1]

As noted by Renée Hulan and Linda Warley, "The complexity and sophistication of Native literary texts . . . can only be fully apprehended if we learn to read them from the inside out" ("Comic Relief" 141). The statement may raise some questions. For example, it might be argued that it is not possible for the Euro-based reader to avoid bringing preconceptions to the text, to arrive without some colonial baggage. However, Hulan and Warley's contention, as elaborated in their earlier article "Cultural Literacy, First Nations and the Future of Canadian Literary Studies," is not a naïve assumption of the possibility (nor even of the desirability) of the reader's becoming a literary *tabula rasa:* " . . . we are always determined by our own cultural traditions and epistemological systems and we cannot simply set them aside through an act of will" (76). Rather, they argue "that there is a direct relationship between classroom study of First Nations literature and the transformation of mainstream culture . . . and [that] it cannot be the exclusive burden of the colonized to end colonialism" (81). Nevertheless, Hulan and Warley's suggestion that indigenous texts be read "from the inside out" is likewise crucial. Perhaps more than any other group, North American Indians have been subjected to erroneous, degrading, and startlingly persistent stereotypes, as the ongoing sports mascot controversy makes evident, and such persistence may be attributed to an equally persistent tendency to read "from the outside in."[2] The present chapter suggests that the biases that give rise to the distorted image of indigenous persons in the popular mind, while grossly misinformed, also pervade scholarly literature on Native people. That is, the fictitious indigenous image not only persists in the derogatory stereotypes of popular film and sports team mascots, it also infects literature by non-Natives and, albeit in a more subtle way, critical texts about Natives and their literature.

Since this mistaken image pervades even the scholarly world, any uncritical reading (from the outside in, as it were) of Native literature, including any that rely without discernment on Western methodologies, risks importing the derogatory image of the Indian, of which a distorted perception of the indigenous person's capacity for artistic and theoretical sophistication is one aspect. In such cases, the social function of Western criticism is not so different from that of the offensively ridiculous mascot prancing across the sports field, re-instantiating a fictitious justification for colonization. Reading from the inside out, on the other hand, requires an ongoing (sometimes painful) self-reflexivity and social awareness to avoid importing the immensely pervasive but immensely damaging popular image of Native people. Much has been written on this indigenous image, and, while I will add little to the discussion, a brief outline of some of the issues and writers will help to contextualize the remainder of my discussion. Of necessity, the discussion is limited to selected texts by selected writers. I begin by considering selected historical and contemporary representations of Native people in mainstream literature and situate this literary image among contemporaneous discourse of other types. I also suggest that mainstream discourse (particularly scholarly discourse which treats the indigenous image and indigenous literatures) is linked to the social order that continues to oppress actual indigenous people. That is, the scholarship concerning Native people, while ostensibly working against oppression, often (sometimes unwittingly) reinforces it.

Since I take something of an object-text approach to my readings, I do not provide an exhaustive survey of the field (assuming that were possible). Rather, I simply provide evidence of some difficulties in the literature and leave the reader to make the obvious connections elsewhere. I also try to avoid sweeping generalizations, though I do make the suggestion that the problems uncovered here are to some extent indicative of wider trends. With that in mind, the governing principle in my selection of texts and writers has been an attempt to attain breadth in brevity by covering both sides of the Canada-U.S. border and by selecting widely published and respected writers. If problematic tendencies are evident in the work of such respected writers, then the suggestion that the tendencies are widespread is easier to sustain than if works (perhaps more troubling ones) by more obscure writers had been chosen. Texts from both sides of the Canada-U.S. border were selected in order to demonstrate that cross-border differences are incidental, that the fundamental problem on either side is a widespread, if sometimes tacit, acceptance of the fictitious idea of indigeneity. For the same reason, I briefly examine some early encounter narratives in order to suggest the historical pervasiveness of the problem. My intent in this chapter, then, is to demonstrate that the indigenous image, which pervades the Western consciousness and manifests itself in popular culture (and fine literature), is also, not surprisingly, sometimes evident in criticism by Western scholars of Native literature.

* * * *

Robert F. Berkhofer, Jr.'s *The White Man's Indian* (1978) established him as a pioneer in the study of representations of Native people in Euro-American literature.[3] Several excellent studies have followed Berkhofer's, among them Lucy Maddox's *Removals: Nineteenth-Century American Literature and the Politics of Indian Affairs*, Gordon Sayre's *Les Sauvages: Representations of Native Americans in French and English Colonial Literature*, and Terry Goldie's *Fear and Temptation: The Image of the Indigene in Canadian, Australian and New Zealand Literatures*, which was later summarized for a Canadian context in "Semiotic Control: Native Peoples in Canadian Literature in English."[4] Proceeding from Edward Said's *Orientalism*, Goldie looks at the disjuncture between the signifier and the implied signified, between the indigenous image in Canadian literature and actual Native people in Canada. Goldie accepts that the ideology of oppression is tied to real-world oppression and notes that the indigenous image in literature is not significantly based on real-world events at all. Furthermore, as Goldie notes, since control of the indigenous image in literature has not been in the hands of those whom the image is supposed to represent, the study of texts depicting First Nations people is not in any way a study of the people themselves: "History awarded semiotic control to the invaders. Since then the image of native peoples has functioned as a constant source of semiotic reproduction, in which each textual image refers to those offered before. The image of 'them' has become 'ours'" ("Semiotic" 111). Goldie is surely correct in this; however, the argument does sidestep the issue of the real-world effects of actions in the discursive landscape. The indigenous image may not be based in reality, but it is part of a discursive landscape which is controlled by invaders, and while it may not be possible to locate any real-world signified for the indigenous image, the linguistic construct does have devastating consequences in the real world since it is misrecognized as legitimate. When literary consumers of the indigenous image enter into real North American space, that is, real Native people are misrecognized as the indigenous image of literature. Furthermore, in print-based cultures, the inscribed image, while not based in reality, is granted authenticity by simple virtue of its inscription. As a result, actual indigenous people are judged as more or less authentic, more or less real, to the extent that they live up or down to a fictitious representation.

Goldie assesses the ontology of the indigenous image, correctly questioning its real-world existence. Olive Dickason notes further, in *The Myth of the Savage and the Beginnings of French Colonialism in the Americas*, that a Wild Man figure existed in the European imagination long before Columbus ever sailed. The Wild Man (*l'homme sauvage*) was a Christianized blend of various folkloric figures, combining the satyr, faun, ogre, and offspring-devouring Saturn, and survives perhaps in our own Neandertals and "missing links." The Wild Man, a stock figure in medieval mystery plays and Carnival and Twelfth Night pageants, also had a gentler manifestation (74). This "noble savage," as Dickason points out, is equally ancient, predating Rousseau by centuries at least. The composite notion of the Wild Man—hairy, uncivilized, cannibalistic, and given to unrestrained sensuality—arrived in the Americas as part of the mental cargo of early explorers and was almost immediately transposed onto indigenous peoples. The mapping of this ancient European mythic figure onto indigenous peoples persisted, despite numerous attempts by informed missionaries and officials to correct it (77–78). The point is, as Goldie and others suggest, that the idea of the Indian was and is of Western origin.

Jonathan Hart examines such conflation of myth and reality in Columbian discourse and other early encounter narratives. He argues that these narratives worked to build and perpetuate an image of indigenous peoples as treacherous, cowardly, and idolatrous, as disturbers of gender and the embodiment of anti-Christian values. Hart does not interrogate the relation of this fiction to fact, but points out that such narratives were widely available. That is, encounters with the indigenous image preceded any encounter with actual Native people: "[R]eligious and secular narratives did not allow Europeans enough wonder and openness to see the world entirely anew. They brought expectations with them that helped to judge the Natives before the actual encounter. History as writing brought with it an encounter before the encounter became a historical event" (71). Aboriginal people in the Americas, then, were read only within the framework of the pre-existing European image. Furthermore, the image and its later more subtle permutations remains present in later EuroAmerican and EuroCanadian discourse.

In the same tradition as Christopher Columbus, Alexander Mackenzie writes in his *Voyages from Montreal* of accounts with First Nations people in the western regions of what later became Canada. Born in Scotland, Mackenzie was the first non-Native person to reach the Pacific coast north of Mexico traveling from the east. The Pacific coast had been generously inhabited from time immemorial, and countless numbers of people had been traversing the same route with less difficulty, but Mackenzie is still regarded and renowned as a first. This is due, in part, to the limitations of the indigenous image, which did not allow for any meaningful cognizance by indigenous peoples of the rivers and trade routes they frequented and guided European newcomers across. In addition, the EuroCanadian privileging of text rendered Mackenzie's travels more important. Mackenzie recorded his travels in written text and cartography and was, therefore, able to enter into the ongoing and sanctioned discourse of encounter and exploration narratives.

Parker Duchemin, in "'A Parcel of Whelps': Alexander Mackenzie among the Indians," examines the strategies of domination inscribed in Mackenzie's text (60). Duchemin points to the skillful combination of fact and opinion used by Mackenzie to construct a subject position for the people he encountered, a subject position based largely on the pre-existing, linguistically constructed, and Western-based indigenous image. Mackenzie was apparently not unaware of the precarious nature of the images he endorsed:

> I was very much surprised by the following question from one of the Indians: 'What,' demanded he, 'can be the reason that you are so particular and anxious in your inquiries of us respecting a knowledge of this country: do not you white men know every thing in the world?' This interrogatory was so very unexpected, that it occasioned some hesitation before I could answer it. At length, however, I replied, that we certainly were acquainted with the principal circumstances of every part of the world; that I knew where the sea is, and where I myself then was, but that I did not exactly understand what obstacles might interrupt me in getting to it; with which, he and his relations must be well acquainted, as they had so frequently surmounted them. Thus I fortunately preserved the impression in their minds, of the superiority of white people over themselves. (Qtd. in Duchemin 54)

What becomes evident is that Mackenzie believed the images to be accurate representations of reality, despite the convoluted logic necessary to maintain the integrity of the social order constructed around the representations. Mackenzie was knighted in 1802 and elected to the Legislative Assembly of Lower Canada in 1804 before retiring to his native Scotland in 1812. Further, despite the incredulous and magnanimous nature of his narrative, Mackenzie's descriptions were, and probably continue to be, regarded as historical (i.e., objective) documents. Duchemin points out that Mackenzie's "caricature of native life . . . lent strong support to traders, settlers, and administrators for their policies of intervention and control" (69). That is, colonization depended in large part on Mackenzie's assumption and affirmation of "the superiority of white people over [Native people]."

Mackenzie was not the first European to import a preconceived indigenous image (and a corresponding European image *vis-à-vis* the indigenous), nor was his the only written affirmation of the social order. With the indigenous image—that is, a pre-existing myth of the savage inscribed onto indigenous peoples—firmly rooted in the European imagination, the extension of the same image into literature was predictable. The indigenous image that informed Mackenzie's narrative is also embedded in Canadian poetry of the same period. D. M. R. Bentley, for example, discusses the prevalence of the "four stages theory" of economic development in Georgian (1759–1825) poetry. Ethnocentrically perceived as "hunters and gatherers," Native people in this theory are assigned the primal stage of economic development (77). J. Mackay's *Quebec Hill* provides a poetic enactment of this economic theory:

> . . . view the slope on yonder hill . . .
> There, tam'd and staid, the Indian seeks repose,
> Nor still imagines all the world his foes;
> With art and care, he cultivates his lands,
> And gathers in their fruits with willing hands.
> Yet 'mong the few who shun the forest's gloom,
> And Europe's garb and languages assume,
> Still sloth and ignorance our pity claim. (lines 225–35)

The indigenous figure here is depicted as having risen (thanks to the arrival of Europeans) to the second and third economic stages of herding and cultivating. However, the figure remains tainted by an innate and pitiful backwardness. What is always neglected in this social-Darwinian view of the means of production, of course, is the fact that numerous indigenous nations have farmed the land for countless generations. Similarly forgotten are the huge (in relation to European cities of the same era) and thriving cities of the Inca, Aztec, and Mayan nations.[5] This notion of racially determined economic evolution still seems pervasive. For this reason, the contemporary "hunting and gathering" activities that currently dominate much of the Canadian economy—strip mining, clear cutting, and "sport" hunting and fishing, for example—are recast as parts of the ultimate stage of economic development, in spite of the Mackenzie-esque logic necessary to reaffirm the myth of Western economic superiority.

The imported indigenous image—pitiful, backward, and imaginary—was carried into later Canadian writing. The presence of the image is especially interesting in the writing of Duncan Campbell Scott (1862–1947), since he produced prominent political as well as poetic texts. Scott worked as a civil servant for the Canadian government, acting as superintendent of Indian education from 1909–13 and occupying the post of Deputy Superintendent General of Indian Affairs from 1913–32. In that post, he was responsible for many of the most brutal assimilationist policies of the Canadian government. His stated interest was to treat Indians as inept wards of the state until such time as "there is not a single Indian in Canada that has not been absorbed into the body politic" (qtd. in Napier *v*). A disparity between Scott's poetic and official attitudes towards First Nations has sometimes been noted, since his poetry depicts Native people in a highly romanticized light (Weis 27). However, the discrepancy is only superficial and is suggestive of the two sides of the same indigenous image: noble and ignoble savage. Neither aspect is at all related to the implied signified, but the former renders poetry Romantic, while the latter renders extermination policies politically expedient. The quality that binds positive and negative sides of the indigenous image is imminent disappearance. The negative side of the indigenous image describes the quintessence of evil, and Scott's official policies thus attempt to enforce the disappearance of Aboriginal people, who are misrecognized as the embodiment of the indigenous image.

While the Romantic side of the indigenous image may be presented more sentimentally, it is no less derogatory and no more tied to reality. The noble savage is simply a recasting of the same image, and this romanticized version is likewise disappearing:

> She stands full-throated and with careless pose,
> This woman of a weird and waning race,
> The tragic savage lurking in her face,
> Where all her pagan passion burns and glows;
> Her blood is mingled with her ancient foes,
> And thrills with war and wildness in her veins;
> Her rebel lips are dabbled with the stains
> Of feuds and forays and her father's woes.
> ("The Onondaga Madonna" lines 1–8)

Scott's various representations, as incompatible as they sometimes appear, manifest a single vision. "The Onondaga Madonna" is interesting in that the poet-diplomat makes the conflation of noble and ignoble savage glaringly obvious: the woman of the poem "thrills with war" but is of a "waning race." Taken together, his imperious official documents and his sentimental verse point to the deleterious nature of both sides of the indigenous image and suggest the danger of permitting semiotic control to remain in the hands of the invaders (Goldie, "Semiotic" 111).

The indigenous image is variously represented in Canadian poetry, but one of the more subtle, yet detrimental, images is the "absent Indian," the presence in poetry of no Indian at all. D.M.R. Bentley documents the curious addition eight years after initial publication of a preface to Mackenzie's *Voyages from Montreal*. In the appended preface, Bentley notes, "Mackenzie gives the impression of a vast and nearly empty country, peopled only by scattered and insignificant 'tribes'" (69). The narrative that follows, however, belies his assertion of vacant space. Such curious later additions are also evident in the reconstructed narratives of Columbus, often serving to protect the legal interests of (in this case) Spain (Hart 64). Quite likely, the confiscation of a continent is more legally and morally justifiable when the original inhabitants are sub-human and few in number. Goldie terms such discursive action a "negative presence," following Machery's contention that "an ideology is made of what it does not mention; it exists because there are things which must not be spoken of" (114). The same absent Indian, present in the poetry of E.J. Pratt (1882–1964) and F.R. Scott (1899–1985), can raise no conscience-searing objections to the invasion of her space. Pratt, in his poem "Newfoundland," speaks of the "unpeopled shores" and the "untrodden shores" that the waves beat upon, neglecting any mention of the concerted governmental effort required to rid Newfoundland of its Beothuk inhabitants and render it "unpeopled" for the newcomers. F.R. Scott, in "Laurentian Shield," carries the vacant land motif even further. The land is depicted as hungry (wanton) for language, deprived of history and the means to write it:

> Inarticulate, arctic,
> Not written on by history, empty as paper.
> . . . .
> This waiting is wanting.
> It will choose its language
> When it has chosen its technic,
> A tongue to shape the vowels of its productivity. (4–5, 8–11)

Academic Cowboys and North American Indians

Not only is the land empty of people, but (worse) it lacks language. It is barren and unformed, linguistically, demographically, and economically, until the arrival of Europeans and their language, after which progress inexorably enters. In this social Darwinian model, European (written, therefore, evolved) language must enter in order for the country to develop and produce children from stone:

> This land stares at the sun in a huge silence
> . . . .
> Now there are pre-words,
> Cabin syllables,
> Nouns of settlement
> Slowly forming, with steel syntax,
> The long sentence of its exploitation. (2, 13–17)

Goldie also deals with this attempt in discourse to erase indigenous Peoples from the Canadian landscape. As he points out, the existence of "Other" people in Canada who are simultaneously Native implies the alien-ness of the Canadian. One response is, as in "Newfoundland" and "Laurentian Shield," to erase the First Nations: "The white culture might reject the indigene, by stating that the country really began with the arrival of the whites . . ." ("Semiotic"113). Goldie suggests that the only other alternative is to try to incorporate the Other through some form of appropriation. A third possibility also exists: the propagation of the image of a "weird and waning race" whose deterministic erasure is forthcoming, that which is evident in Duncan Campbell Scott's poetry and discussed earlier.

George Bowering's (1935—) "Indian Summer" includes a more recent re-working of the absent Indian:

> The Indians I think
> are dead, you cant
> immortalize them, a
> leaf prest between
> pages becomes a
> page. (7–12)

Here, the indigenous image is present only in the pages of dead history, a figure who once was but no longer is. The nostalgic longing for the indigenous image is treated as unrealistic, not because actual indigenous people never were, but rather because they no longer are.

Only slightly altered is the nostalgic longing in A.M. Klein's (1909–72) "Indian Reservation: Caughnawaga," in which the speaker laments the failure of contemporary indigenous peoples to conform to the pre-existing image:

> With French names, without paint, in overalls,
> their bronze, like their nobility expunged,—
> the men. Beneath their alimentary shawls
> sit like black tents their squaws; while for the tourist's
> brown pennies scattered at the old church door,
> the ragged papooses jump, and bite the dust. (16–21)

The speaker of Klein's poem recognizes the disjuncture of signifier and implied signified, but the indigenous image is nostalgically recalled while a superimposed image of supposedly actual indigenous people is disparagingly pitied. Rather than rejecting the image, the speaker rejects the people.

The degenerate element of *l'homme sauvage* is often portrayed even in contemporary Canadian poetry, and, when combined with misogyny, produces an especially nefarious manifestation of the indigenous image. In "The Cariboo Horses," Al Purdy (1918—) metaphorically depicts indigenous women as whores and horses:

> At 100 Mile House the cowboys ride in rolling
> stagey cigarettes with one hand reining
> half-tame bronco rebels on a morning grey as stone
> —so much like riding dangerous women
>   with whiskey coloured eyes—
> such women as once fell dead with their lovers
> with fire in their heads and slippery froth on thighs
> —Beaver and Carrier women maybe or
>   Blackfoot squaws . . . (1–9)

Misogyny here is thinly veiled by racism, and racism is thinly veiled by misogyny. Note also the continuing acceptance in Canadian poetry of the term "squaw," despite the highly offensive nature of the usage. Robert Kroetsch (1927—), in "Seed Catalogue," also displays blatantly racist misogyny:

> the absence of a condom dispenser in the Lethbridge Hotel and
>   me about to screw an old Blood whore. I was
>   in love. (32–34, sec. 4)

Kroetsch's misogyny is not limited to First Nations women, nor is his racism. However, despite the ferocity of his imagery, he continues to be celebrated in the scholarly community as he perpetuates and exacerbates a particularly detestable version of the indigenous image, since his poetry is inherently theoretical. His attacks are difficult to locate behind semiotic disclaimers like "the absence of" and theoretical fiats like the death of the author. As Kroetsch notes, conveniently, "We silence words / by writing them down" ("Seed Catalogue" 1–2, sec. 8). Unfortunately, such words are never silent enough, and the wide acceptance of Kroetsch's poetry points to a certain danger involved in postmodern treatments of the indigenous image. If the poetic act is able to excuse or mitigate overt racism, the same may occur with postmodern discussions which assert the divorce of language from reality. The amelioration by literary theorists of the oppression of Native people in Canada functions in word and image only. In isolating the discussion within the world of words, critics may avoid assuming responsibility for actual changes in the lives of actual people. As Bentley points out,

> In our own day, several poets and critics have attempted to penetrate the stereotypes and abstractions that have occluded the indigenes in Canada, but have any of them done more . . . than assemble archives of misrepresentation? With all their emphasis on deconstructing metaphysical assumptions, have the practitioners of post-modernism and post-structuralism helped to reify the native peoples of Britain's ex-colonies, or have they once more denied them a real presence in the world that matters—the world, now, of words, and words, moreover, in the great imperial languages of the modern age? (88)

Thus, theoretical interrogations of the causes of racism may themselves come to participate in the oppression they ostensibly challenge.

Norman Fairclough, following Foucault, defines "language as a social practice determined by social structures" (17), such that actual instances of discourse are determined by an order of discourse. Actual discourse and the order of discourse function in an interdependent (dialectical) relationship with actual practice and the social order (28–29). That is, while a discourse may not be an accurate representation of some real world entity, it is nevertheless determined by and determining of the actual social order in which it operates. As such, literary criticism that examines the indigenous image can nevertheless be part of an order of discourse which privileges certain types of discourse (Western poetry and Western literary discussions, for example). Literary criticism may unwittingly participate in the re-affirmation of a social order that historically excludes indigenous peoples, and interrogations of the indigenous image may easily participate in the oppression they interrogate. For as Gordon Johnston points out, "Indian figures have been interesting not in themselves but as symbolic referents in a discourse about European civilization's virtues and vices, triumphs and failures. The nature and force of images of Indians have been derived from the symbolic code or language of this debate rather than from any understanding of the Indians themselves" (50).

Ginny Carney, in her article on American Indian loanwords, points to an enlightening corollary. She suggests that the interest in things Native has always been an issue of self-interest, an interest reflected in the words borrowed. When EuroAmericans have needed indigenous people for their own survival, as well as during periods when liberal guilt needed to be assuaged, hundreds of Native loanwords became part of the English vocabulary. During the 18th and 19th centuries, however, when the Native people were being reduced to squalor, racial insults became embedded in the English vocabulary: *half-breed, Indian giver, warpath, war paint,* and so on (193). The same may well be true of scholarship. For example, Terry Goldie's *Fear and Temptation* is notable in that, among other things, it includes contemporary texts, whereas many other treatments of the indigenous image concern only pre-twentieth century texts.[6] At the same time, however, while his discussion builds on the work of numerous mainstream theorists (Bakhtin, Barthes, de Man, Derrida, Eagleton, Fanon, Lévi-Strauss, Said, Sartre, Todorov), Goldie rarely invokes indigenous theorists in his treatment of the indigenous image, making only two brief references to indigenous thinkers, one to George Copway (Ojibwe) and one to E. Pauline Johnson (Mohawk). Both references are accompanied by derogatory assessments: Copway's is deemed to be an "unsophisticated approach to relative theology" (129) and Johnson "present[s] a strong although ideologically undeveloped support of native people" (62). These two tendencies—the tendency to neglect contemporary texts and the tendency to neglect indigenous thought—are fairly widespread and suggestive of difficulties in Native studies. In particular, they suggest that the false indigenous image, despite assertions to the contrary, continues to prevail even in the academy. This preference for historical Indians and avoidance of indigenous thought recall the vanishing and primitive qualities of the fictitious indigenous image that so many scholars claim to struggle against. Furthermore, while it may be true that the indigenous image is only ever textual, restricting discussions to "not the reality the works seem to represent . . . but the reality of the texts and their ideology" (Goldie, "Semiotic" 111) permits scholarly interest to stop short of the real world. The scholar is thus able to profit from the fact of oppressive social conditions and to profit again from ostensible attempts to struggle against the conditions, while solidifying the conditions for scholarly profit. The discussion is only textual and the critic invariably avoids implication in and amelioration of the actual.

* * * *

Scott Lyons recently issued a call for "rhetorical sovereignty," which he defines as "the inherent right and ability of *peoples* to determine their own communicative needs and desires in this pursuit, to decide for themselves the goals, modes, styles, and languages of public discourse" (449–50). Since sovereignty over discourse is very much related to tribal sovereignty, it is crucial that it be secured. However, like the legal and political aspects, such calls for Aboriginal sovereignty over Aboriginal discourse have been met with resistance. Rhetorical colonization persists in Native studies, making evident the very reason rhetorical sovereignty is necessary. With respect to the study of literature, the absence of sovereignty over discourse has led to the prevalence of such rhetorically colonizing gestures as the theoretical destabilization of Indian identity and the imposition of anthropological myths onto Aboriginal peoples and their literature. Theoretical destabilizations of Indian identity have taken the form of quibbles over signification and accusations of essentialism. For instance, given the mixed ancestry of the writers, and given also their adoption of Western form and language, some have challenged such terms as "American Indian literature" (Krupat, *Turn* 17–22). The argument is based on the destabilization of the concept of race. Walter Benn Michaels, for example, suggests that race is a social construct and that culture is merely the doing and believing (or not) of a certain set of practices and beliefs—practices and beliefs which could just as easily be rejected. According to Michaels, any assertion of racial identity is a misguided reification of cultural practice, and, therefore, both logically flawed and predicated on racialist assumptions: "The modern concept of culture is not, in other words, a critique of racism; it is a form of racism" (129).

Applied to literature, Michaels' argument would imply that the identification of a work as "American Indian" or "First Nations" is racist, since any body of works so identified is not tied to any necessary or defining characteristics. The act of establishing a canon of Native literature, in this view, whether within or without the canon of American (or Canadian) literature, is always an arbitrary move—beyond the obvious and pertinent critiques of canon formation itself. What emerges, then, as "American Indian literature" is not a body of works selected by the definition of their writers as "American Indian," but a simple demarcation or delineation for the purposes of convenience. As with the equally unfixable boundaries of nationality, period, and genre, the lines of inclusion and exclusion for Native literature are drawn simply in order to limit the field and facilitate advanced study. However, while such deconstructions of identity categories are presented as anti-racist moves, they nevertheless serve the purposes of actual and rhetorical colonization.

At this point, my emphasis necessarily shifts to American Indian literature and the American scholarly context. Although some recent collections published in Canada—notably Renée Hulan's edited collection, *Native North America: Critical and Cultural Perspectives*, and Jeannette Armstrong's edited collection, *Looking at the Words of our People: First Nations Analysis of Literature*—have emphasized, as does the present work, a North American context for examinations of Native literature, American collections have tended to follow colonially imposed national boundaries.[7] Consequently, my shift in emphasis to American scholarship will necessitate a simultaneous shift in emphasis to American Indian literature. Renate Eigenbrod and Jo-Ann Episkenew suggest as a rationale for the strictly Canadian emphasis of their own edited collection, the "different patterns of colonization" and the fact that "national boundaries do provide the context for our teaching and researching of Aboriginal literatures in this country" (8). However, I find the differences in patterns of colonization to be incidental and university teaching templates to be irrelevant. Eigenbrod and Episkenew point to (extra-literary) comparative studies by Roger Nichols and Jill St. Germain to support their suggestion of fundamental American-Canadian Aboriginal differences and also obtain support from Emma LaRocque's suggestion that "There is an Aboriginal experience unique to the Canadian context" ("Teaching" 224). LaRocque writes in an endnote: "At the risk of 'going against the grain' in the recent emphasis on 'Native North America' (ie in the Hulan anthology) [sic], I argue for a number of significant cultural and national differences between Canadian and American Native intellectuals" (231). However, while distinct differences certainly exist on either side of the Canada-U.S. border (at the most basic level, Indian status is determined by the particular tribe in the United States, while in Canada status is determined by the Canadian government), I would argue that these differences are not as deep-rooted as the similarities among Aboriginal people (*vis-à-vis* non-Aboriginal) and the similarities in patterns of colonization. Furthermore, the lived experience (regarding patterns of colonization) of a Native person in Saskatchewan will probably have more in common with the lived experience of a Native person in South Dakota than either will have with that of a Native person in New

York City or Toronto. At any rate, the entire question illustrates the difficulty of examining indigenous literatures according to Western atomistic paradigms. Such atomism is inadvertent fuel for theoretical destabilizations of Indian identity, as evident in the work of Walter Benn Michaels and Arnold Krupat, and unwittingly permits postmodern re-fabrications of colonization.[8]

The destabilization of racial identity may be valid in biological discourse, but the argument ironically reveals a racialist motivation when transposed into other fields, even as it purports to work against racist assumptions. In the field of literature, for example, Arnold Krupat critiques what he calls "the problem of essentialization . . . in Native American literary studies" (*Turn* 3).[9] Following Michaels, Krupat admits that some generalization is needed in order to avoid the confusion and triviality that would result from infinite particularity. That is, speaking of "American Indians" and of "Euramericans" is acceptable insofar as the generalizations (what he sees as essentializations) permit discussion and avoid confusion. What is not acceptable to Krupat is the assertion of some essential traits or capabilities of a people: "There is no *essence* of America that Native people automatically incarnate, just as there is no *essence* of Europe (or elsewhere) inherent in people or groups with near or distant ties to those places" (5). The point he wishes to emphasize is that being Indian does not guarantee better or more correct stories of or about Indian life and literature than is possible for non-Natives. Defenses of essentialism, Krupat argues, rest on illogical argumentation and result in a double bind—the non-Native scholar is condemned either for speaking inappropriately if she deals with Native literature, or for ignoring Native works if she does not. To resolve this "problem of essentialization," Krupat forces his opponents' arguments into the confines of an excessively rigid brand of Western logic. He invokes Kant (via Satya Mohanty) to defend the universal right to knowledge (and literature) of all rational beings (12). Finally, he issues a radical challenge to Native identity claims.

While Krupat's arguments seem reasonable, even at times collegial, they raise serious concerns for American Indians and American Indian literature. First, his argument for the universal right to knowledge, if accepted, can be extended to justify any and all acts of cultural appropriation. More important, his challenge to American Indian identity not only devalues identity as a recurring theme in Native literary works; the dismissal of artistic and critical distinctiveness also undermines the validity of tribal sovereignty claims. For if there is no *Indian*, there can be no Indian land, culture, literature, or anything else.

Numerous Indian writers have assumed identity issues to be important enough to center entire works around the question. Sherman Alexie (Spokane/Coeur d'Alene), for example, examines the issue from multiple perspectives in *Indian Killer*. John Smith, a major character in the novel, loses his Indian identity through adoption and is never, despite the best intentions of his affluent, white parents, able to recapture it. Jack Wilson, another character, appropriates an Indian identity, then markets the assumed identity by means of popular "Indian" fiction. Other characters deal with real and assumed Indian identity in other ways. The novel functions as a far-reaching and perceptive examination of the question of authenticity in Indian identity and suggests, among other things, that identity killing is a particularly effective means of Indian killing. Not surprisingly, the novel is set in part in the Native Studies department of a major university, where the "Introduction to Native American Literature" course is taught by "Dr. Clarence Mather, the white professor, [who] supposedly loved Indians, or perhaps his idea of Indians" (58).

The importance of identity as a theme in Indian literature is understandable given the history of Native/non-Native interactions in North America. Indian identity may not have been an issue of concern prior to the arrival of Europeans, but it rapidly came to be interrogated and defined according to standards set by the invading peoples. The Allotment (Dawes Severalty) Act of 1887, for example, one of numerous recurring attempts at assimilation, provided for the division of tribally held Indian lands into individual allotments and made blood quantum the sole basis of allotment.[10] While the act was allegedly designed to hasten assimilation, inculcating in its subjects Western farming techniques and a private property mentality, the tangible result was the loss of ninety million acres (almost two-thirds) of Indian land in the less than fifty years that the act was in effect. Predictably, "excess" land after allotment was made available to white homesteaders (Mankiller 134–35). A more recent incarnation of the same policy was U.S. Supreme Court case #96–1581, SOUTH DAKOTA vs. YANKTON SIOUX TRIBE, in which the court ruled on January 26, 1998, that lands ceded to the Sioux tribe in 1894 did not retain reservation status and must be restored to public domain.

Since land allotment depended on Indian identification according to EuroAmerican standards, the psychological results of the Dawes Act were equally devastating. For the purposes of allotment, U.S. Congress had instituted a blood quantum standard requiring documented proof of at least one-half Indian blood (Livesay). Tribal rolls had originally been compiled by the U.S. government in a haphazard, often arbitrary, fashion. However, under the Dawes Act, land and other increasingly scarce resources could only be obtained by demonstrating one's Indian identity according to the records maintained and standards set by the same government. Faced with rapidly depleting resources and an identity-based system of allotment, infighting occurred. More recently, the Indian Arts and Crafts Act (1990), by insisting that Native artists prove their Native ancestry, caused similar infighting as Native artists struggled against each other to prove their heritage to an increasingly skeptical colonizer. Meanwhile, non-Native art investors secured an increased value for artworks in their possession, since the number of artists producing such works had been legislatively diminished (Bird, "Breaking" 27–28). Thus, identity has been a major issue in Indian literature (as in Indian life) precisely because the colonizer has made it an issue. The de-stabilization of Indian identity has likewise proven profitable, such that, by problematizing the identity of his critical subjects, a critic is able to acquire a controlling interest in the criticism and definition of an Other's literature.

Indian identity in the field of literature has also been destabilized by critiques of "memory in the blood," a phrase made current by N. Scott Momaday (Kiowa) but alluded to by numerous thinkers and writers in various Native communities. Memory in the blood, if accepted, establishes a solid claim to rhetorical (and other forms of) sovereignty for American Indians. Arnold Krupat has dismissed Momaday's thoughts on the matter entirely by invoking Western science and suggesting that, since the concept does not hold up to Western scientific scrutiny, it should therefore be rejected. (He likewise invokes the dictates of Western science to suggest that a non-Native perspective is needed in order to arrive at a truer picture of Native American literature, further suggesting that the Native critic's nearness to her subject obscures her objectivity.) In doing so, however, he departs from his self-imposed requirement for an "ethnocritical approach," one which "recogniz[es] the differences between Native American and Western conceptions of art, information, and culture in general and attempt[s] . . . to find some language that might mediate between the two" (*Turn* 21). He also fails to recognize the story-basis of Western science and philosophy, which are as rooted in story as Native conceptions of truth and knowledge.

This forceful implementation of Western reason against the arguments of Indian writers mirrors the historic and ongoing imposition of American laws, beliefs, systems of governance, and ideas of nationhood upon sovereign Indian nations. On occasion, Krupat acknowledges the need for sovereignty in Indian-American relations: "It is nation-to-nation relations as people-to-people relations," he writes, "that are thus particularly meaningful to Native Americans" (14). More often, however, he defuses the claims he allegedly supports by casting them within an analogue model (16). That is, he suggests that sovereignty issues should be understood as having been more or less achieved, rather than (as in a digital model) having been either achieved or not. This sounds reasonable enough: that sovereignty over literary production and criticism be understood with reference to a sliding scale of attainment. The predictable result, however, is that non-Native critics are able to engage in critical homesteading, with unproblematic access to and control over American Indian literary production, while futile arguments are waged over the relative degree of sovereignty attained and required.

Such attempts to bring Indian literature within the confines of the American canon and under the jurisdiction of American critics have a long history and are part of what Lucy Maddox calls "white America's efforts—official and unofficial—to include [Indians] within the discourse of American nationalism and, concomitantly, within the structure of the country's laws and institutions" (7). The ensuing frustration over the "Indian problem," political and critical, has been the result of failures to find "a master narrative, a discourse that would eliminate or submerge oppositions through new rhetorical arrangements and new definitions" (Maddox 8). Thus, Krupat's frustration with the persistent reproaches of Native writers is a frustration over their refusal to be read into the American master narrative to which he is a contributor.

Nevertheless, America is only an idea: an idea that finds expression in a rather spurious story (or master narrative) about (among other things) having been founded on principles such as "that all Men are created equal, that they are endowed by their Creator with certain inalienable rights, that among these are Life, Liberty and the Pursuit of Happiness." In order for the "Indian problem" or "Indian question" to be resolved, therefore, the anomaly must be written into the story. Methods of resolving this aspect of the story of America have included removal, assimilation, and extermination. All three have been practiced, separately and together, at various times and with varying severity—that American Indians have the lowest life expectancy and the highest suicide rates of any population in the United States suggests very strongly that extermination remains in effect, albeit with increasing subtlety. The annihilation of American Indians is required if the story of America is to be substantiated. That is, the myth of the vanishing Indian needs to be confirmed in order for the myths of universal life, liberty, and happy pursuits to remain intact, whereas sovereignty, the antithesis of extermination, underscores the fraudulent and constructed nature of the story of America. If we recall earlier discussions of the "weird and waning race" of Canadian literature, we sense that cross-border similarities may outweigh the differences.

Solutions to the "Indian problem" can be worked out symbolically, as well as physically, either by attempting to erase the concept of Indian identity altogether, or by dividing contemporary Indians (and their discourse) from (that of) their ancestors through an imposed discourse of anthropological determinism. By erasing the concept of identity, a concept imposed in the first place, actual Indian people and valid claims to sovereignty are symbolically erased. In this way, contemporary American Indians are forced into symbolic assimilation. The symbolic assimilation of American Indians permits the story of America to remain intact and reduces EuroAmerican-Indian relations to a sad, but early, chapter. This form of symbolic annihilation is complemented by the deterministic anthropological version, in which Indians were a defective (since primitive) race, doomed to extinction or assimilation. In this version of the story, extermination, removal, and imposed assimilation are justified by asserting the inevitability of extinction through what is called "evolution." Both versions function to justify genocidal practices and to assuage the national conscience. The one version justifies extermination based on the supposed inevitability of extinction; the other erases any need for justification.

Deterministic anthropology is equally destructive when applied to literature. For example, Walter Ong's *Orality and Literacy: The Technologizing of the Word* plots the economy of language on an evolutionary continuum. Although he does not deal specifically with Native literature (aside from the occasional reference), Ong's text has, like Krupat's, been an influential one in the study of American Indian literature. Although well researched, bolstered as it is with references to the classics and to more recent theoretical works, Ong's work is not self-reflexive in any way. He does not question the position from which he works but accepts, and thereby tacitly endorses, the political designs of the story of America. As Norman Fairclough has pointed out, all discourse is inherently political. Insofar as it either affirms or disrupts the social order in which it operates, discourse is always political (28–29). Fairclough, as mentioned earlier, defines language as "a social practice determined by social structures" (17). That is, the social order determines and is determined by certain sets of social practice, discourse being one such practice. Since the current social order in America is hierarchical, American (and Canadian) discourse types are also structured hierarchically, forming the current order of discourse.

Since academic discourse ranks fairly high in the current order of discourse, it is in the best interests of practitioners of this discourse type to affirm, even while appearing to disrupt, the social order. The illusion of dissent, so common in academic discourse, is consistent with a social structure based on an illusion of liberty and equality. Actual dissent in academic discourse, that which troubles the actual social order on which the academy is based, is marginalized into silence, dismissed as illogical, or re-fashioned to better fit with academic best interests.

Walter Ong's work, then, implicitly (if not overtly) participates in the re-affirmation of a social order which historically (and currently) works to annihilate the First Nations of the continent. It does this primarily by accepting as a given certain myths that contribute to the Western story—the correlated myths of progress and evolution. According to these deterministic myths, orality is a primitive precursor to literacy. Oral cultures, highly romanticized though they are, necessarily fade away due to the inevitable survival of the linguistically most fit: the literate. Since the extinction of oral cultures or their gradual assimilation with literate cultures (that is, their loss of linguistic distinction) is perfectly compatible with the story of the West, it is not surprising that Ong's work has been well received. Since it is based on the myth of evolution (that is, that humans evolved from apes and through tribal societies to the perceived apex of humanity, the western hu[man]), the anthropological understanding of literature will continue to assign to American Indian writers and literary works a primitive status (unless the writers are fully assimilated) and will continue to measure the "level of progress" along the evolutionary line by the ability to parrot mainstream writing styles and content.

This anthropology-based understanding of orality implicitly valorizes Western thought and literature: "[W]ithout writing, human consciousness cannot achieve its fuller potentials. . . . Literacy . . . is absolutely necessary for the development not only of science but also of history, philosophy, explicative understanding of literature and of any art, and indeed for the explanation of language (including oral speech) itself" (14–15). Since some influential adjudicators of literary progress—those critics who use Ong's ideas to understand American Indian literature—will presuppose the advanced position of their own culture, it is unlikely that, with few exceptions, Indian writers will ever be perceived to have "caught up." Likewise, given the privileged status of literate thought in this model, and given its continuing (if not overt) influence, the words of Indian writers, since less "evolved," will continue to be reduced to the status of museum pieces, valuable only in that they evince "disappearing" vestiges of "primitive" thought.

This is not to suggest that an understanding of orality and oral culture is unimportant to the study of American Indian literature. As Momaday has noted,

> . . . in the oral tradition one stands in a different relation to language. Words are rare and therefore dear. They are jealously preserved in the ear and in the mind. Words are spoken with great care, and they are heard. They matter, and they must not be taken for granted; they must be taken seriously and they must be remembered.
>
> With respect to the oral tradition of the American Indian, these attitudes are reflected in the character of the songs and stories themselves. Perhaps the most distinctive and important aspect of that tradition is the way in which it reveals the singer's and the storyteller's respect for and belief in language. (15) [11]

Orality and Literacy, while apparently explicating orality and making an obvious attempt to valorize it in some nostalgic way, nevertheless obscures the understanding of spoken words and their importance. While an understanding of orality is important to the study of Native literature, such knowledge cannot be properly obtained from such anthropological accounts in which orality is perceived as a vestige of primitive thinking. In other words, understandings of orality would more appropriately be obtained from people in oral cultures—assuming they are willing to share. Likewise, understandings of Native literature would more appropriately be obtained from Native people.

Critics such as Krupat, however, resolve to undermine the defenses constructed for rhetorical sovereignty and against cultural appropriation. That is, if a literary critic wishes unrestricted access to the cultural property of another, she may simply deny the existence of essential identity, trivializing any objections to appropriation. She may also, like Krupat, suggest that literature is not cultural property. The power to define determines definition, and the power to assign a definition to literature can be used to validate wholesale appropriation. Thus, in his dismissal of Robert Warrior's objection to his (Krupat's) suggestion that Native literature "'belongs' to the national literature of the United States" (Warrior, "Marginal" 30), Krupat simply reduces the argument to absurdity, suggesting that Warrior misconstrues both the suggestion he attacks and the essence of literature (i.e., as cultural property).[12] The debate, according to Krupat, hinges on Warrior's interpretation of the term *belong*, which may be used in the *American Heritage Dictionary* sense of "to be a member of a group, such as a club," as well as "to be the property of." However, Warrior is likely rejecting both senses of the term. The notion that American Indian literature can "be included" conveys some condescension. Furthermore, this type of belonging is that which precedes assimilation.

A close reading of Krupat's argument uncovers something of a colonial mentality, assuming that stylistic analyses can reveal the fingerprint of sentiment. Krupat begins by establishing a distinction between Native (material goods for all/knowledge for select individuals) and non-Native (knowledge for all/material wealth for select individuals) worldviews, and suggests that the non-Native view has been used "as an imperial excuse for overriding others' desire *not* to be 'known' or simply to keep some information." While seeming to affirm the Native position, he quickly moves on to suggest that "all verbal performances studied as 'Native American literature,' whether oral, textualized, or written, are mixed, hybrid; none are 'pure' or, strictly speaking, 'autonomous'" (*Turn* 21). He speaks particularly of literary works which are written to be published, and so are offered to everyone. This supposed impetus of production, he argues, makes it "a practice, not a thing, and as a practice, it cannot 'belong' either to American literature or to (some rhetorically constituted) Native American literature 'in its own right'" (22). This sounds not unlike "an imperial excuse."

Krupat moves swiftly from the idea of the universal ownership of Native American literature to universal ownership of oral narrative. The same principle, he suggests, applies to "those textualized oral performances of a sacred or traditionally circumscribed kind that probably never should have been transcribed, translated, and published in the first place" (22). However, in order to maintain a distinction between the unfettered use of Native literature, which he supports, and the appropriation of sacred knowledge, which he castigates, he relies on a "distinction between the *production* and the *transmission* of knowledge" (23, emphasis added). He suggests the term "friends and guardians of cultural artifacts and knowledge" for those who *transmit* sacred knowledge (22). Those who transmit knowledge with pen or computer, however, are deemed to be *producers*. In this way he is able to define himself into affinity with Native writers, thereby granting himself access to whatever knowledge and resources are available: "All those engaged in critical scholarship—intellectuals, literary critics, and so on—whatever their genetic, geographic, or cultural backgrounds, are all *producers* of knowledge. Littlefield, Jaimes, Warrior, and I, among others, select from an ever-increasing number of resource materials what we find of interest or value . . ." (23). At the same time, Indian producers of (always scare-quoted) "Native American literature" are divided from transmitters (or friends) of culture, regardless of whether they share similar aspirations in their work.

Again, Krupat's argument rests on the negation of culture and identity, which circumvents any and all claims to sovereignty. He erases culture by interrogating the purity of American Indian literature, suggesting that since its written form and publication are a Western (understood as non-Indian) practice, the resulting product is mixed, hybrid, impure (21). This type of argument, itself a species of essentialization, rests on the expectation that pure Native practices, like "real" Indians, will evince no Western appearance or characteristic. Craig Womack addresses this expectation in *Red on Red: Native American Literary Separatism*:

> When cultural contact between Native Americans and Europeans has occurred throughout history, I am assuming that it is just as likely that things European are Indianized rather than the anthropological assumption that things Indian are always swallowed up by European culture. I reject, in other words, the supremacist notion that assimilation can only go in one direction, that white culture always overpowers Indian culture, that white is inherently more powerful than red, that Indian resistance has never occurred in such a fashion that things European have been radically subverted by Indians. (12)

The separation of certain forms of discourse produced by contemporary Indians from more traditional forms is based on the assumption that Indian culture must be static and unchanging in order to be authentic. Non-traditional practices are perceived as contaminating the purity of "pure" Indian discourse. Since there is no corresponding expectation that Western discourse will remain static, no assumption that uses of electronic media and press agents somehow eliminate the possibility for "pure" American literature, such expectations for Indian discourse point to an acceptance of the myth of the vanishing Indian. The exact point at which Indian people and practices lose their purity is left unstated, so long as American Indian literature becomes a Westernized, hence universally accessible, product. At the same time, while the objections of Indian intellectuals are invalidated, the appearance of friendliness toward more "pure" Indians is maintained.

Krupat is correct in suggesting that literature is not a thing and therefore cannot, strictly speaking, be owned. However, it is interesting to note that his argument functions as a subtle re-working of the argument that Indian land could not have been stolen because Indians never, strictly speaking, owned any land. Literature is not a tangible product, but in a market economy it becomes a commodity. Careers are made and lost on its study. If the current interest in Native literature is the result of a serious attempt at cross-cultural dialogue in the hope of understanding and ameliorating oppressive social conditions, then that is a good thing. If, however, it is simply a response to current trends in academe—the turn to cultural studies, interrogations of the canon, the championing of marginalized voices, for example—then Native academics are justified in their concern and in their calls for rhetorical sovereignty. The preceding suggestion—that scholarly interest in marginalized voices may simply be a response to a trend—may seem to contradict my earlier assertion that Native literature is undervalued in the academy. However, the contradiction is only superficial and points to the crux of the problem: appearance.

Trend-based interest in marginalized literatures develops in direct proportion to the symbolic capital that accrues from the apparent effort to help the oppressed. Whether the apparent effort to help the oppressed is associated with a genuine desire to effect change or is simply the appearance of a genuine effort is irrelevant. The accumulation of symbolic profit follows the appearance of, more than any actual, effort to bring about change. The flow of capital, however, will cease abruptly if and when the subaltern is in a position to speak for him or herself. That is, in order for the flow of capital to continue, the marginalized voice must remain marginalized. The level of resistance to efforts of the subaltern to speak, therefore, corresponds roughly but appreciably to the emptiness of the appearance of effort. One can only profit from the championing of marginalized voices so long as they remain marginalized. This is the peril of the facade. Trend-based interest, laudable though it may seem, does more harm than good.

Since indigenous claims to rhetorical (and political) sovereignty run counter to received notions of history and national identity, it is not surprising that the most powerful of such scholarship would be charged with illogical argumentation. To be sure, Krupat expends much effort dismissing the challenges of Native critics through logical and semantic reductionism. He ignores serious charges entirely, while problematizing the language and logical structure of the forms in which they are expressed, and accuses his (exclusively Native) opponents of arguing rhetorically and illogically. He calls for a "distinction between philosophy ('truth telling,' logic, dialectic) [*sic*] and rhetoric" (*Turn* 6), and, although he admits that it is not possible to fully extract dialectic from rhetoric, he proceeds as if it were. He grants himself the position of dialectic ("I will do my best to argue logically and rationally") and confines his opponents to the position of rhetoric ("I try to show that some of the arguments offered by some Native American scholars have more rhetorical than logical force") (*Turn* 6–7). As mentioned, however, this dismissal of opposing arguments hinges on an *ad hoc* logical and semantic reductionism and ignores the substance of the charges. Furthermore, his insistence that Native writers adhere to the strict confines of Western argumentation functions as an attempt to enforce ideological assimilation.

Krupat himself is not unskilled as a rhetorician. In *The Turn to the Native,* he couches his arguments in frequent appeals to emotion (*pathos*). The preface contains a list of national and global concerns, demonstrating the political awareness and concern of the writer, and the attacks on Native thought are surrounded by frequent assurances of his "spirit of solidarity and support." For example, he ostensibly sympathizes with Native people when rationalizing what he perceives as the illogical nature of "some of the arguments offered by some Native American scholars" with reference to a barrage of statistics on the under-representation of American Indians in academic institutions (7). The use of such statistics, however, doubles as supporting evidence (*logos*) for his claim that "some Native American scholars" are less than logical in their writing, pointing to a supposed lack of education while ignoring the extensive training in sophisticated thought available to American Indians outside the academy. It could also be argued that this sort of dismissal of Native scholarship by influential academics such as Krupat (*ethos*) has been instrumental in producing the appalling statistics he invokes. As Elizabeth Cook-Lynn (Santee/Yankton Sioux) has pointed out:

> . . . the 'American Indian intellectual' is to many people a bizarre phrase, falling quaintly on the unaccustomed ears of those in the American mainstream. While there are images of Jewish intellectuals, European intellectuals, British scholars, African novelists, there is no image of an American Indian intellectual. There is only that primitive figure who crouches near the fire smoking a sacred pipe or, arms outstretched, calls for the gods to look down upon his pitiful being. Worse, the drunk, demoralized Chingachgook sitting alongside the road, a medallion with George Washington's face imprinted on it hanging about his neck. Or the Red Power militant of the 1960's.
>
> It is as though the American Indian has no intellectual voice with which to enter into America's important dialogues. The American Indian is not asked what he thinks we should do about Bosnia or Iraq. He is not asked to participate in Charlie Rose's interview program about books or politics or history. It is as though the American Indian does not exist except in *faux* history or corrupt myth. (111)

Not surprisingly, Cook-Lynn is a primary target of Krupat's invective, as are other powerful Native voices—Robert Warrior, Wendy Rose, M. Annette Jaimes, Ward Churchill, Terry Wilson, Daniel Littlefield, and Jimmie

Durham. Krupat does give voice to selected Native and "post-colonial" writers. In response to Robert Warrior's call for more attention to Deloria and John Joseph Mathews so as to effect intellectual sovereignty, he also admits that "[f]urther attention to Mathews and Deloria and to, perhaps, John Milton Oskison, Francis LaFlesche, Gertrude Bonnin, and a great many other formidable Native American intellectuals might, at this historical juncture, be more important than continued attention to any of a number of non-Native intellectuals" (18). What is interesting about the three "formidable Native American intellectuals" Krupat adds to Warrior's list, however, is that they have all been dead for over fifty years. The writers he attacks so vehemently, on the other hand, are very much alive and active.

In the final sentence of the same chapter, a division along racial lines becomes evident in a close reading of the language: "[His closing remarks are] an exhortation . . . to stay calm and stay committed, to distinguish between rhetoric and logic so far as possible, and to value both truth and power" (29). The sentence uses pleonastic doublets constructed around an implicit Native/non-Native binary. Recall that opposing Indian writers were deemed to be arguing with "more *rhetorical* than *logical* force" (emphasis added). By extension, the sentence suggests that Native writers have been arguing in a manner powerful (as opposed to accurate), agitated (as opposed to calm), and rhetorical (as opposed to logical). Non-Native writers are urged not to be deterred (by agitated Indian voices, one assumes) but to "stay committed" to the "logic" and "truth" of their arguments and to be ethnocritically sensitive to the rhetorical powers against them, while Native writers are urged to "stay calm." As Patricia Monture-Angus so astutely points out, such entreaties are not benign: "One of the experiences I have . . . is being called 'angry.' This labelling . . . is a form of silencing" (*Thunder* 1). Such enforced silence is commonly misrecognized as a necessary attribute of "pure" Indians. It functions (along with enforced pacifism and assimilation) to subvert the defenses of Indian academics and, more important, to permit the continuation of colonialist practices. The sentence, then, functions succinctly as a paternalistic exhortation designed to bring Native critics comfortably into union under the umbrella of assimilationist ethnocriticism as defined and directed by Krupat.

Of course, not all efforts to highlight the importance of Native literature are limited to the facade. I think here of Renée Hulan, whose *Native North America* provides a balanced collection of criticism in the field and whose own work consistently makes contact with indigenous communities[13]; of A. LaVonne Brown Ruoff, recently honored by leading Native and non-Native scholars at an MLA convention for her work in promoting

American Indian literature and encouraging American Indian scholars[14]; and of Harmut Lutz and Laura Coltelli, whose collections of interviews imply that the voices of Native writers themselves are worthy of serious attention. Helen Jaskoski's work with early American Indian writers and Julie Cruikshank's in autobiography also come to mind, among the many others. Lucy Maddox's *Removals*, yet another example, is particularly important in that it reveals the interdependence between nineteenth-century American Indian policy and nineteenth-century American literature and demonstrates ways in which assimilation and extermination, two possible solutions to the "Indian question," are worked out in the literary discourse of the nineteenth century. Widespread removals, then occurring on the American landscape, were mirrored in the literature.

Maddox also points to the need for further studies of such assimilationist and exterminationist tendencies in other areas of Western literature. Following Maddox's suggestion, a metacritical variation can be performed on the ethnocritical approach to literature. Recall that Arnold Krupat defines "ethnocriticism" as "an interdisciplinary mix of anthropology, history, and critical theory . . . needed for the study of Indian-White relations in the literature and culture of this country" (*Ethnocriticism* 4). While the need for dedicated non-Native scholars of Indian literature, those willing to use their prestigious positions and rhetorical savvy in the interests of the people whose literature they study, remains, the place to start may be with a metacritical assessment—an ethnocritical examination, that is—of the literature *about* Native literature. Given that Arnold Krupat is acknowledged as a leading scholar in the field, such that one could hardly pass through a Native studies program without at some point seriously engaging with his work, the need therefore remains for an ethnocritical "study of Indian-White relations in the [criticism] of this country." Since the existing social order as replicated in the academy benefits so very few, such a turn *for* the Native would likely be in the best interest of all people.

Chapter Two
When "I" Equals More Than "Me": Constructions of (Constructions of) Indigenous Identity

> As indigenous perspectives and knowledges find their way into the University system, they question the very foundation of traditional Western knowledge.
>
> —Viola Cordova[1]

In keeping with the object-text approach of this book, the previous chapter isolated for discussion selected texts by selected non-Native writers and critics in order to demonstrate the pervasiveness of oppressive social relations within a discourse concerning Native people and their literature. The approach is borrowed from discourse analysis which, at its best, investigates the manner in which "text produces, reproduces, and occasionally challenges the social norms and expectations of particular communities and the distribution and exercise of power among groups and individuals" (Stillar 15). Other texts could easily have been substituted for those selected. Canadian Helen Hoy's *How Should I Read These?*, for example, could have been substituted for Krupat's *The Turn to the Native* to demonstrate oppressive social relations within an ostensibly Native-friendly text. Robert Berkhofer's (American) *The White Man's Indian* could have been substituted for Goldie's Canadian text in discussions of the indigenous image. Likewise, James Fenimore Cooper's *Last of the Mohicans* could have been chosen to exemplify overt and frequently overlooked racism within non-Native literature as easily as the Canadian poetry selected for examination.

A difficulty might be raised with the approach I have taken however: viewed strictly from the perspective of Western logic, the argument might seem to be an instance of hasty generalization. That is, findings within a single text (or very few texts) may not seem capable of supporting a claim of pervasive racism in the discourse. Inductive reasoning requires that the writer supply ample instances in order to validate the generalization. Even were that the case, however, the claim would not be incontrovertible, since the evidence provided by any number of texts which epitomize oppressive social relations does not support incontrovertibly the claim that academic discourse is racist. There will always be (or usually tend to be) exceptions to the rule. In any case, my intention has not been to suggest that there are no exceptions. As mentioned, Renée Hulan's edited collection of essays conveys an astute awareness of the issues, and ranks with Jeannette Armstrong's edited collection as indispensable reading in the Canadian critical context, dominated as it is by the edited collection as genre.² A. LaVonne Ruoff Brown's work is highly respected by both EuroAmerican and Native academics, and her tireless efforts in support of Native writers, critics, and students is commendable. Similarly, as also noted, German critic Hartmut Lutz's collection of interviews with First Nations authors and Italian critic Laura Coltelli's collection of interviews with American Indian writers implicitly maintain the primacy of the writers' own voices, assertions of the non-scholarly status of the interview as genre notwithstanding. Other names come to mind: Lucy Maddox and her work on the representation of indigenous people in American literature; Edward Huffstetler, whose secondary critical interest in Native literature has produced some noteworthy material; Gwendolyn MacEwen, the Canadian poet whose work was only beginning to grapple with the troubling issues of "Kanadian" presence in Aboriginal territory when she died in her mid-forties. Many other writers and texts could be added—even Arnold Krupat's edited collection of American Indian stories, *Native American Autobiography: An Anthology*.

The point is not to set out a race-based dichotomization, nor is it to exclude writers altogether, nor even entire texts. Rather, the approach I have adopted seeks to highlight disturbing trends within key texts, and I have selected such texts precisely because they figure prominently in the scholarship. That is, the fact that this or that well known work reproduces oppressive social relations may not prove that all texts of the discourse type are oppressive; however, given that the texts are prominent ones, the fact that they function to reproduce oppression suggests very strongly that the presence of oppressive discourse is tolerated (even celebrated) in the academy of which they figure as prominent representatives. An interesting corollary to such academic tolerance and misguided celebration is presented in Elaine Dewar's *Bones: Discovering the First Americans*, her eminently readable discussion of North American anthropology debates. As Dewar points out, the Bering Strait theory, originally advanced to uphold the Judeo-Christian doctrine of monogenesis, continues to be sustained in the academy, in spite of mounting evidence of the implausibility of the theory (238–47). As Dewar's discussion also makes clear, however, scholarship that violates existing academic power structures is silenced through defamation or simple neglect (71–79).

The suggestion that the discourse of non-Native writers and critics reproduces oppressive social relations should not be surprising. What would be unbelievable is the suggestion that it does not. For the academy is a quintessentially Western institution, steeped in traditions of prestige and exclusivity. The educational ISA (ideological state apparatus) is one type, in Althusser's model, of ideological state apparatus. As an ISA, the educational apparatus reproduces the social structure and is structured according to the existing social structure. That the United Nations continues to caution Canada on its treatment of Aboriginal people suggests that oppression is alive and well in North America.[3] Since oppression persists in North America, it follows that racism will likewise be found to persist in the ISAs that produce and reproduce the social structure. The academy, as an ISA, thus functions to reproduce the means of colonization as decidedly as it does the means of production. Furthermore, to suggest that the academy is not subject to the racism that is an integral part of the social structure which it sustains and is a product of is certainly the more difficult claim to support.

The conception of language use (text) as social practice is not incompatible with the understanding of language in indigenous cultures. Social theorist Pierre Bourdieu, for example, views language use as a form of (metaphoric) capital, which is valued and exchanged in a linguistic marketplace. At each exchange, the speaker/writer is committed to a stratum on the social hierarchy, with the assigned value of an utterance (hence, of the utterer) being determined by language, dialect, delivery, body posture, and so on, in addition to the actual words used (81–89). Discourse analyst Norman Fairclough, mentioned in the previous chapter, builds on Foucault (and Bourdieu and others) and asserts that language use is always political. Language use is political insofar as it works for or against the established social order (28–42). Since an order of discourse exists which loosely corresponds to and reaffirms the social order, all uses of language are constructed by and constructing of the existing social order, but language use also has the potential to work against the existing order as suggested above (Stillar 15). Viewing literary and critical uses of language within such a framework, as politicized social practice with an assigned social value, suggests a social and linguistic reason for the marginalization of indigenous literature, which, like indigenous knowledge, has been undervalued in a market constructed for and by white literary consumers.

In the order of discourse, indigenous literatures rank far below European-based literatures, and even further below critical discourse. This book is, among other things, an attempt to re-situate and re-value indigenous literature and occasionally employs some methods and notions from discourse analysis. It is by no means a study in discourse analysis, which would have produced a markedly different book. The social instrumentality of language use as described by Bourdieu and Fairclough (and others) is, however, of particular interest, since such ideas hint at the holistic instrumentality described in indigenous notions of language. That is, though the two groups come at the situation from different angles and in different terms, they arrive at the same conclusion: for discourse analysts, as for indigenous theorists, language use has a powerful and very real effect in the actual world.

Regarding Western understandings of language, a crude split can be drawn between criticisms based on a radical severance of language from the world and those (social-based discourse analyses among them) which look at language's inherent and unavoidable instrumentality in spite of the presumed arbitrariness of the sign. Indigenous theory—that issuing from an indigenous worldview—is not rooted in a fundamental separation of name and named. Since the indigenous worldview, like indigenous languages, is process-oriented, such a separation is not conceivable. This lack of separation in the indigenous worldview may result in its frequent misrecognition as primitive; however, the culturally specific model of linear progressivity (from which notions of advancement and primitiveness issue) is, like the culturally specific separation of language and reality, not conceivable within the Aboriginal framework. Nevertheless, although they build on diverse worldviews and epistemological foundations, both socially cognizant discourse analysts and indigenous theorists arrive at a similar understanding of language's actual potency and at a similar and corresponding acceptance of social responsibility for the theorist.

My interest in discourse analysis (and other Western theories) of which I make pragmatic but limited use is based on these correspondences—in the acceptance of language's actual effect and in the acceptance of social responsibility. While I make some use of Western theories, however, I build primarily on and from indigenous theory. Any exclusion of indigenous theory, especially in the context of the criticism of indigenous literatures, is inexcusable. It could be argued in defense of such exclusion that the academy is a Western institution—as I myself suggested earlier—but even if the assumption that its being a Western entity could somehow make the exclusion of non-Western epistemologies acceptable, the academy is currently, by virtue of the burgeoning of indigenous voices, no longer strictly Western. The work of Jeannette Armstrong, Viola Cordova, Willie Ermine, Patricia Monture-Angus, Robert Warrior, Jace Weaver, Laurie Whitt, and Craig Womack, to name just a few of the growing number of indigenous theorists working as academics, suggests that the academy is becoming more indigenous every day. As such, any continued exclusion of indigenous theory in Native studies is evidence more of a racial than any academic bias.

The present chapter, then, like the entire book, builds on indigenous theory and works towards a criticism that, in accordance with the precepts of such theory, is community-based. In other words, I argue for a criticism that examines literature in terms of what it is doing for (or against) the people. Furthermore, this indigenous-centered criticism must also examine critical writing about Native literature and people, a reversal that Linda Tuhiwai Smith (Maori) terms "researching back," a necessary extension of "talking back" to the colonizer (7). Finally, since infinite connectedness is a fundamental principle of Aboriginal epistemology, such criticism, like the literature it studies, will necessarily make connections to other indigenous theories and struggles on a universal scale.

* * * *

In "Critical Mirrors: Theories of Autobiography," Charles Berryman suggests that scholarly interest (and disinterest) in autobiography has tended to reflect academic trends. Berryman points out that autobiography was not considered a suitable object of study for historians and literary critics until extreme skepticism came to dominate the academy *(74)*. Ironically, it was the skeptical destabilization of selfhood that made the self's story of itself worthy of scholarly attention. This flowering of interest in the genre as a whole may in part explain the current fascination with Native autobiography; however, autobiography has long been standard fare among critics of indigenous literatures. Non-Native study of Native autobiography has a lengthy history, beginning with the attempts of anthropologists (most notably, followers of Franz Boas) to record traces of a perceived-vanishing people by preserving and recording, among other "artifacts," their self-stories. These earlier compilations continue to engender significant interest in literary circles—despite the fact that social scientific and anthropological questions are their primary concern—but this is not surprising. Contemporary critics may spend much time (rightly) questioning the methods and the motivation behind earlier works, but current non-Native scholarship tends to be not very different from its predecessor.

Interest in autobiography, as Charles Berryman suggests, is reflective of trends in the academy. Early compilations and studies of Native autobiography generally reflect Boasian assumptions (that is, that Aboriginal people were approaching extinction), while contemporary criticism of Native autobiography mirrors more recent academic trends. Berryman points to a drift in generalist criticism of autobiography towards an autobiographical criticism, a drift which is also evident in the prevailing criticism of Native autobiography (82). Such criticism has tended to collapse into a study of itself rather than to engage in a study of the people to whom the autobiography refers or the stories they tell. However, the notion of "the vanishing Indian," which inspired the earlier vein of criticism, is an idea that itself has not vanished. This is suggested by the continued and prevailing interest in autobiographies by "traditional" Aboriginal people (the few exceptions almost invariably treating Silko, Momaday, and Vizenor), in the distinctions between "traditional" and "non-traditional" works, and in the assumed dominance of non-Native theories of self and self-writing. Contemporary criticism of Native autobiography not only reflects recent academic trends, it perpetuates the assumptions of earlier scholars. The critical constant has been a fundamental failure to acknowledge the sovereign status of the First Nations, which inevitably permits the objectification of, and proprietary orientation towards, the people and their stories.

The remainder of this chapter will examine some dominant trends and voices in the criticism of Aboriginal autobiographies in the continuing process of working toward an indigenous-centered critical approach, and finish with a demonstration of such a criticism by conducting a brief analysis of *Mankiller: A Chief and Her People*. (A more intensive study of Maria Campbell's autobiography will be conducted alongside the examination in chapter four of the question of essentialism.) I avoid any focus on "arbitrary signifiers" and "split speaking-subjects," since such a focus would detract from the text and people in question and collapse irretrievably in on itself. More important, such a focus would be based on a culture-specific (alien) philosophy of interminable individualism. My criticism of Mankiller's autobiography, then, follows Kimberly Blaeser in assuming that the theory necessary to read the indigenous text is to be found within the text (*"Native Literature"* 53–54). I will further assume the voice in the autobiography to be that of Wilma Mankiller. Michael Wallis collaborated on the writing of the book, and his important contribution is gratefully acknowledged by Mankiller, but this is essentially the story of "a chief and her people" (ix). My approach will simply examine how the voice of that chief, as evident in the text, functions in the service of her people. That is, in her autobiography, as in her life, Mankiller tirelessly works for the people. My own work will attempt to support rather than to silence that work theoretically, though it must begin by clearing away some misconceptions of some foundational criticism.

* * * *

Four book-length studies may be considered foundational to the literary consideration of Native autobiography: *For Those Who Come After: A Study of Native American Autobiography* (Krupat), *American Indian Autobiography* (Brumble), *American Indian Women: Telling Their Lives* (Bataille and Sands), and *Sending My Heart Back Across the Years: Tradition and Innovation in Native American Autobiography* (Wong). The texts seem to take a variety of approaches, but the degree of overlap suggests something of a common impetus. Arnold Krupat, for example, works toward defining "Indian autobiography" as a genre:

> The principle constituting the Indian autobiography as a genre [is] the principle of *original bicultural composite composition*. I mean thus to distinguish Indian autobiographies from autobiographies by 'civilized' or christianized Indians whose texts originate with them and contain, inevitably, a bicultural element, yet are not compositely produced. I mean as well, to distinguish Indian autobiographies from traditional Native American literature in textual form. (31, emphasis in original)

This impulse, a common one, towards generic definition results in the mapping of exclusionary lines. However, the excessive reliance on such lines ceases at an interesting point. Once the writer has discursively constructed barriers between (his definitions of) traditional and non-traditional Indian autobiography, between those whose speakers knew (or know) European languages and those who did not, his line drawing ceases, permitting the *inclusion* of the works of all Native people within the canon of American literature (136). That is, Krupat begins by arguing that "Indian autobiography" is a subset of American autobiography, because the "principle of original bicultural composite composition" places emphasis on white editorial control of the literary product. As Paul John Eakin points out in his preface to the 1989 edition of *For Those Who Come After,* "Although Krupat's ostensible subject is the Indian ... his real subject is ... white theories about the Indian" (xxi).

Krupat then moves on to argue that "Indian autobiography" must be by a non-English-speaking (or -writing) subject, that the knowledge of English would define the work out of "Indian autobiography" and into American autobiography. More correctly, the speaking-subject must be non-"civilized" and non-"christianized," which presumably implies the absence of formal education and knowledge of the English language. Therefore, "Indian autobiography" as well as any remaining works (effectively all works by all Native people) are always to be included within the American (or Canadian) canon. As noted, however, this seemingly noble goal—the widening of canonic margins to permit the inclusion of all American Indian texts—implies a simultaneous rejection of indigenous sovereignty. "Inclusion" in the American canon may seem to be a form of implicit valorization of a text. However—and this is the crux of Robert Warrior's debate with Krupat as discussed in my chapter one—such a move tacitly negates the sovereignty of the Indian nations from which the literature issues. The move is, therefore, distinctly non-valorizing and suggests the extent of the de-valuation of Native literatures as well as an inequitable distribution of power. Academic power relations function in such a way that the non-Native critic can not only assume control over the definition of Native literature but can castigate attempts to subvert dominant determinations of nationhood.

In a later (1992) discussion, "Native American Autobiography and the Synecdochic Self" in his *Ethnocriticism,* Krupat restates the earlier (above) position:

> Native American autobiography, a post-contact phenomenon in its written forms, exists in two types which I have elsewhere called the Indian autobiography and the autobiography by an Indian. The first of these is constituted as a genre of writing by its original, bicultural, composite composition, the product of a collaboration between the Native American subject of the autobiography who provides its 'content' and its Euramerican editor who ultimately provides its 'form' by fixing the text in writing. Autobiographies by Indians, however, are indeed self-written lives; there is no compositeness to their composition, although inasmuch as their subject, in order to *write* a life, must have become 'civilized' (in many cases Christianized as well), there remains the element of biculturalism. (219–20)

As in the 1985 *For Those Who Come After*—and in *The Turn to the Native* (1996)—Krupat assumes a proprietary stance with respect to Native literature by dividing the literary production of Native people into "pure" and "civilized" categories. He emphasizes white editorial control over the former and inclusion of the latter within the American canon. In either case, rhetorical sovereignty is negated. In the 1992 discussion, however, he seems to retreat from his earlier and forced distinction between Native autobiography and autobiographies by Natives, suggesting that perhaps there is something distinct about indigenous autobiography, whether or not the work has been funneled through a non-Native amanuensis: "In both sorts of texts, let me claim, we find a privileging of the synecdochic relation of part-to-whole over the metonymic relation of part-to-part" (220). He seems, in this, to support Carter Revard's assertion of the community-based construction of indigenous selfhood: " . . . the notions of cosmos, country, self, and home are inseparable" (86; qtd. in Krupat 210).[4] However, while the work ostensibly supports such a claim, it simultaneously works against itself in so many ways that one wonders if Krupat even supports his own stated position that "In both sorts of texts . . . we find a privileging of the synecdochic."

For example, he reminds the reader of the limitations of deductive reasoning: " . . . such readings tend . . . to be . . . tautological exercises in the 'discovery' of literary 'evidence' for psychological or anthropological 'truths' already established elsewhere" (210). He reminds them again of Paul de Man's radical linguistic skepticism, which renders any representation of selfhood purely figural; and he finishes his discussion with a final reminder of the final weakness of his own argument: "So far as one may generalize, however, it does *seem to be* the case that Native American autobiography is marked by the figure of synecdoche in its presentation of the self" (210–11, 231, emphasis added). In addition, the discussion in *Ethnocriticism* is based in part on Stephen A. Tyler's skeptical ethnography, for whom "A post-modern ethnography is a cooperatively evolved text consisting of fragments of discourse intended to evoke in the minds of both reader and writer an emergent fantasy of a possible world of commonsense reality, and thus to provoke an aesthetic integration that will have a therapeutic effect" (125); such ethnography "*describes* no knowledge and *produces* no action" (123). An oxymoronic emphasis on absolute relativism allows Krupat to maintain his earlier (*For Those Who Come After*) position on Aboriginal autobiographies, while stating a contradictory position. For if all is play of signification, Krupat, like de Man, need take no responsibility for nor suggest the former inaccuracy of his words. He can then profit from his acquiescence to more recent, and exclusively Western, renditions of what it is to be an Indian, while continuing to profit from his earlier (1985) promulgation.

Furthermore, Krupat's 1992 model of the self is constructed on a meta-figurative use of figurative language: three tropes of substitution (metaphor, synecdoche, metonymy) and a figure of thought (irony) are said to represent the range of possible conceptions of self. Again the discussion seems supportive of Indians, suggesting that Native American subjectivity is constructed synecdochically as opposed to the Western metonymic construction of subjectivity, and allowing for a certain distinctiveness of Native literature. However, the meta-figures also appear to be stratified according to social evolutionary theory. Only the Balinese are accorded a *metaphoric* sense of self: "If it is indeed the case, for example, that there are peoples who actually do conceive of themselves as in some very real sense interchangeable with their ancestors and their posterity (the Balinese, in Clifford Geertz's account, perhaps?), then we might expect any stories they tell about themselves to show a *metaphorical* conception of the self" (*Ethnocriticism* 212). As noted, Native American and Western writers are afforded, respectively, synecdochic and metonymic conceptions of self in Krupat's model: "Here I want to propose that while modern Western autobiography has been essentially metonymic in orientation, Native American autobiography has been and continues to be persistently synecdochic" (216). Only on occasion, however, and only in the West is the *ironic* sense of self evident: "While I am ignorant of specific instances of an *ironic* sense of self elsewhere in the world, I would suggest that some of what might be called 'modernist' senses of self in the West may be usefully categorized as ironic" (212, emphasis in original). It is not difficult to see such a model as relying somewhat on social evolutionary notions, in which the sense of self corresponds to "advancement" of the respective culture. The model also calls into question Krupat's use of the scare-quoted terms "pure" and "civilized," especially since he so frequently proceeds—except in the 1992 rendition, which he nevertheless deconstructs by reference to linguistic and ethnographic skepticism—as though the categories constructed were definitive. That is, the distinction between the "pure" and the "civilized" is sufficient for Krupat to divide Native writers according to cultural practice, whether the categories are scare-quoted or not (*Turn* 21; *For Those* 31; *Ethnocriticism* 220).

Hertha Dawn Wong is likewise interested in defining the genre; however, she disagrees with the particulars of Krupat's delineation and argues, like David H. Brumble III, for the inclusion of contemporary works and early pictorial representations of self within the generic definition being constructed. Also like Brumble, she traces an evolutionary line in American Indian autobiography. Brumble's work is primarily concerned with mapping the evolution of American Indian autobiography, which he sees as a compressed version of Western autobiographical development: "The history of

American Indian autobiography . . . parallels the history of Western autobiography in many ways. . . . The history of Western autobiography spans some 4500 years, but with Indian autobiography there is a marvelous compression of time" (5). The parallel construction allows Brumble to equate White Bull with Odysseus, Two Leggings with Achilles and Ajax, and Sam Blowsnake with Augustine (52, 56, 121). By thus constructing a "marvellous compression of time" which will "give us a glimpse of a more ancient humanity," Brumble provides non-Native scholars with a convenient model of *Western* development (117). As such, Native autobiography becomes merely the vehicle for self-interest, affording non-Native scholars the opportunity to study non-Native "progress." (A feature common to all four works, tellingly, is an emphasis on [the non-Native half of] bicultural composition.) Brumble's work also assumes a linear-progressive (evolutionary) model, which implies the inevitability and superiority of Western-style development and also implies a pre-contact stasis or social retardation on the part of indigenous societies. While Brumble discredits the social Darwinist assumptions of Herbert Spencer (150), his own work presents but a slight variation on the same theme.

Gretchen M. Bataille and Kathleen Mullen Sands, in *American Indian Women: Telling Their Lives,* are similarly interested in defining Aboriginal (women's) autobiography as a genre. As with the previously discussed texts, their interest in generic definition leads to a focus on bicultural composition. Their work, however, reveals rather strongly the proprietary nature of such a thrust. In their definition of the genre, they distinguish between "as-told-to" and ethnographic autobiographies, based on the perceived literary quality of the former and non-literary quality of the latter. This distinction is always determined, in their definition, by the quality of the non-Native editor's agency in the bicultural interaction; for, in their understanding, Native autobiographers always write ultimately for a white audience and, therefore, require the mediating presence of an editor/amanuensis (6–14). The end result is that, affirmations of partnership and collaboration notwithstanding, the focus of the reading is again on non-Native agency: "The nonsequential oral process in itself suggests that structural interpretation is an essential element of Indian autobiography. Not until the relationship of all the elements of the oral narrative are discovered can the meaning emerge. It is the job of the editor to order fragmented experience in time and in relation to narrative viewpoint and intention" (14).

The emphasis on and privileging of Western voices in this study of Aboriginal autobiography leads to a devaluing of the indigenous person in the "partnership." For example, Bataille and Sands place far more emphasis on Ruth Underhill than on Maria Chona: "Without Ruth Underhill, Chona's story probably would never have reached a wide audience, and without Underhill's particular cultural and literary sensitivities, Chona's narration would not be as effectively presented" (64). Likewise, greater interest is sensed in Nancy Lurie, David Jones, Karen Thure, and Louise Udall than in Mountain Wolf Woman, Sanapia, Anna Moore Shaw, or Helen Sekaquaptewa and their stories. Furthermore, the authors take time to distinguish between such writers as Maria Campbell and (Bobbi) Lee Maracle. Campbell's *Halfbreed* is thought to reflect an "evolution of style and theme in [Aboriginal women's] life histories" since it is considered more individualistic than earlier works: "The concern is with her [Campbell's] life, not with the larger group of Indian women who might share similar experiences" (116).

In distinguishing Campbell's autobiography from Maracle's, Bataille and Sands determine that *Halfbreed* "lacks the strident voice of *Bobbi Lee: Indian Rebel*" (116). They go on to suggest a minor role for such narratives as Maracle's in the future of the genre, "because a very small percentage of Indian women are active in Red Power movements or willing to be spokeswomen for particular ideologies. Also, autobiography is not a particularly effective mode of writing for the promulgation of political theory or action, and hence usually not adopted by writers with pragmatic goals" (136). The distinction between the two works overlooks Campbell's fervent and ongoing commitment to social action and the political motivation behind all her work (to be discussed at length in chapter four). As Gloria Bird points out, "being Indian in the United States [and Canada] is inherently political" (*"Breaking"* 28). However, Bataille and Sands seem to prefer a mediative role for Aboriginal women autobiographers:

> As Indian women have become more self-conscious about their changing roles and the effect of acculturation on their lives, their narratives have begun to reflect concern for mediating the influences of traditional Indian life and white ways, leading to themes of conflict and resolution in their narratives . . . with resolution coming through reassertion of traditional tribal identity and values. (130)

By highlighting—in a highly prescriptive manner—the individual(s) in Native women's autobiography, not only does the white editor (as co-individual in an individualistic literary product) obtain preeminence, but concern is simultaneously deflected from crucial social and political concerns.

Bataille and Sands speak of a benign and detached interest in tradition, one that mediates between depersonalized forces of assimilation and tradition. However, since Native tradition in its various forms is rooted in a deep and contextualized (politicized) concern for the welfare of the people, and since the forces of assimilation are intensely political (and personalized), any "reassertion of traditional tribal identity and values" necessarily involves political action. Both *Bobbi Lee* and *Halfbreed* (and *Mankiller: A Chief and Her People*) function to assert traditional values by constructing a political discourse. However, since Maracle's work is more overtly political, less easily reduced to the warm, non-confrontational work of cultural mediation, her autobiography is consequently silenced by epithets: "strident," "Canadian Marxist," etc. Such criticism assumes proprietorship over both the genre and the people employing it by defining the purpose and essence of Aboriginal women's writing and by defining the politics of their discourse into silence.

Perhaps most interesting in terms of defining control of the genre is the autobiographical theory of Hertha Dawn Wong. Of the four texts considered, Wong's makes the strongest moves towards post-structuralism, revealing the difficulties associated with relying on Eurocentric theories in looking at Aboriginal literatures. Almost invariably, such theoretical approaches claim to undermine the systemic privilege of prevailing criticism, but simultaneously support elitist philosophies and assumptions. In *Sending My Heart Back Across the Years*, Hertha Dawn Wong states three main objectives governing her work on Native autobiography:

> This study, then, [1] considers Native American autobiography from the context of autobiography theory, [2] delineates distinctly Native American oral and pictographic traditions of personal narrative and their interaction with Euro-American autobiographical modes, and [3] examines the relationship between nineteenth-century Native American oral modes of personal narrative and Euro-American 'female' forms of autobiography. (5–6).

It is not immediately clear how the three objectives are related or how they will work toward supporting the stated (and familiar) goal of the work: ". . . to expand the Eurocentric definitions of autobiography to include nonwritten forms of personal narrative and non-Western concepts of self and to highlight the interaction of traditional tribal modes of self-narration with Western forms of autobiography" (5). However, a careful reading of the work, especially in conjunction with the author's later essay "First-Person Plural: Subjectivity and Community in Native American Women's Autobiography," reveals a proprietary interest which makes the connection between objectives and goal perfectly clear.

It is not immediately obvious, for example, how Wong will relate nineteenth-century American Indian oral autobiography to (temporally unspecified) Euro-American women's autobiographies. In the later essay, however, she speaks more at length and more directly of her program concerning American Indian women. She begins by distinguishing (as in the earlier text) between relational and individual identities, invoking Bakhtin's preference for polyvocal over single-voiced identity and footnoting Nancy K. Miller and Paul John Eakin's insistence on the relationality of all subjectivity (169–70).[5] In other words, Wong begins by pointing out that the indigenous concept of identity is often identified as relational (that is, the person cannot be understood or imagined apart from her relations), while the European concept is often identified as individual (that is, the person is ultimately an autonomous subject). Against this distinction, Wong places Bakhtin and Miller and Eakin. Bakhtin's notion of "polyvocality" suggests that there is never an "individual" voice or identity, but that the subject is always many-voiced. Miller and Eakin contend that every subjectivity is relational, which likewise suggests that there is never an "individual" subject. The inference is—since the self, even the non-Native self, is always relational—that the distinction between Native and non-Native notions of identity (taken to be a relational/individual distinction) is not valid.

Later, in the same article Wong raises the often remarked tendency of Native women to reject "feminism," preferring to identify as *Native* (women) rather than as *women* (who happen to be Native). Janet McCloud discusses the matter most poignantly: "Many Anglo women, try, I expect in all sincerity, to tell us that our most pressing problem is male supremacy. To this, I have to say, with all due respect, *bullshit*. Our problems are what they've been for the past several hundred years: white supremacism and colonialism. And that's a supremacism and a colonialism of which white feminists are still very much a part" (qtd. in Jaimes and Halsey 332, emphasis in original). While acknowledging the pragmatic need to maintain such a priority in identity formation, Wong goes on to dismantle the premise upon which it is built: community. That is, Native women tend to privilege community over individuality in constructions of identity, a prominent feature, as will be noted, in Wilma Mankiller's autobiography. Wilma Mankiller, I will suggest, cannot tell her own story without telling the story of her people. However, Wong undermines the concept of community, as she does the concept of the individual, by pointing out that there is no single isolatable "community," that the notion of community is also, therefore, an imaginary construct (172–73). In this way, after removing the distinctiveness of the relational aspect, Wong also destabilizes the community-based aspect of

Native identity. What becomes clear is that Wong's project is (a familiar) one of dismantling the distinctiveness of Native autobiography *vis-à-vis* American autobiography. Since the burgeoning interest in general autobiography, as Charles Berryman notes, is a response to academic interest in the destabilization of the self, it follows that applying autobiographical theory (Wong's first objective) to Native works will have the further effect of dissolving Indian identity altogether.

Wong also claims to build on David Brumble's work (*Sending* 4). Her interest is puzzling given the overtly masculinist and anti-theoretical tone of Brumble's work.[6] On the other hand, Brumble's interest in the evolution of the concept of the self in American Indian autobiography is perfectly compatible with Wong's program. As mentioned, Brumble compares American Indian oral tales to ancient Greek and Egyptian tales of self and charts an evolution towards literate autobiography. The evolution myth is flawed in its conception, but applied to Indian works it invariably leads to a dominating, colonialist viewpoint. Plotting the development of Aboriginal autobiography in this manner, therefore, leads not only to an evolutionist perspective (Western texts as pinnacle of literary achievement) but also to a further dissipation of American Indian distinctiveness.

Wong's interest in this progressive linear approach (her second objective), given her seeming awareness of Aboriginal philosophical perspectives and political concerns, points again to an underlying interest in the de-particularization of Indians and Indian literature. For if Indian literature is seen to evolve towards identification with Western literature, and if the distinction Wong constructs between "traditional" Native autobiography and non-traditional/contemporary versions is accepted, then contemporary autobiographies can be dis-identified as "Indian," permitting white scholarly access to and, inevitably, control of such works. The impetus behind the third objective, then, that of relating nineteenth-century American Indian oral narratives to Euro-American female autobiography, becomes clear. Wong's three objectives (to bring autobiography theory to bear on American Indian autobiography; to trace the development of the autobiographies and their interaction [identification] with European forms; to relate nineteenth-century oral narratives to Euro-American female autobiography) point clearly to a single goal: to *include* American Indian autobiography within the American canon. Given autobiography theory's insistence on the relation of autobiography to constructions of the self, such an insistence becomes problematic, entailing the anti-sovereigntist inclusion of American Indian subjects within the American nation.

The privileging of autobiography theory (Wong's first objective) also implies a dismissal of Aboriginal theory. In "Aboriginal Epistemology," Cree artist and scholar Willie Ermine touches on this vast and complex philosophical orientation: "Aboriginal people found a wholeness that permeated inwardness and that also extended into the outer space. Their fundamental insight was that all existence was connected and that the whole enmeshed the being in its inclusiveness. In the Aboriginal mind, therefore, an immanence is present that gives meaning to existence and forms the starting point for Aboriginal epistemology" (103). To be fair, Wong does mention this orientation toward connectedness:

> Despite diverse cultures, languages, and histories, indigenous people, it is said, have a notion of self as communal or relational, while European(s)/Americans, at least since the Romantic period, envision identity as individual and autonomous. Generally, Native people see themselves as connected to an entire network of kinship relations with family, clan, community, earth, plant, and animal life, and cosmos, while Western non-Natives envision themselves as separate from such relations. ("First-Person" 169)

However, here as elsewhere, Aboriginal theory is discussed with low-modality markers.[7] Comparing usage tendencies in the parallel construction above, a disparate assessment of truth-value based on race becomes linguistically evident: "indigenous people, *it is said, have a notion* of self ... while European(s)/Americans ... *envision* identity"; "Native people *see* themselves ... while Western non-Natives *envision* themselves" (emphases added). Such stylistic markers (low versus high modality; vernacular versus Latinate verbal groupings) embedded in the language of the text, make Wong's apparent understanding of Aboriginal theory all the more troubling. She seems to understand Aboriginal ideas of language, its sacred nature and creative potential (*Sending* 19). She seems to affirm the principle of connectedness underlying all things ("First-Person" 169), and she seems to accept the Aboriginal idea of self (*Sending* 13). Nevertheless, she consistently privileges postmodern theory *vis-à-vis* Aboriginal theory in her analysis of texts which arise from that alternative worldview:

> Unpopular as Momaday's notion of names may be with postmodern scholars who find no connection between the word and the thing itself, Momaday insists that, for him (and this is true for many traditional Native American people as well), one's name and one's existence are 'indivisible' ... Similarly, Momaday's belief in 'the Indian mentality' is controversial among some academics, since it appears to

conflate cultural and racial characteristics and to encourage, particularly for nonnatives, reductive notions of Native American identity. ("First-Person" 179)

This dismissal, carefully attributed to "postmodern scholars" and "some academics," of Aboriginal theory in favor of postmodern notions presumes the naïveté and unsoundness of the former, regardless of the complexity and thoughtfulness of the theory outlined by Willie Ermine and others. However, the postmodern assumptions favored by Wong represent the end result of the rather arbitrary turn in medieval philosophy outlined in the introduction to this book. I refer to the connection between universals and particulars, which in the late medieval period went through a radical destabilization from which Western thought has yet to recover.

Universals, again, are the genera and species (the concepts) as opposed to individual things.[8] A major concern of the medieval period was the nature of these universals and their relation to individual things. To invoke again the useful oversimplification presented in the introduction, the medieval period began with realism and ended with nominalism in answer to the question of universals. Realism holds that universals are actual things, actually present in all individuals. Here, the connection to Momaday, as quoted by Wong, is evident: realism implies a fundamental connection between the name and the thing named, granting to language an extraordinary and transformative potential. Nominalism, on the other hand, is closer to the commonplace understanding. In nominalism there is no real or necessary connection between universals and individuals. The concepts are simply mental constructs that get expressed in words. Saussure takes nominalism the logical step further, suggesting that there is no necessary (only an arbitrary) connection between the concept (signified) and the word (signifier), and postmodern thinkers have toyed further still with this rejection of connectedness.

To present briefly the complex and non-linear progression from realism to nominalism, in the thirteenth century Thomas Aquinas worked out a balance between the two extremes: moderate realism. He suggested that universals do actually exist, but only as ingredients of individual things, not in and of themselves (Marías 135). He also proposed a *principle of individuation* by which the universal form shaped unformed matter into individual instances of the universal. Recall Aristotle's notion of informed matter, which Aquinas refines. This principle was later extended by John Duns Scotus to include formal (in addition to Aquinas's material) distinctions, and was carried to the nominalist extreme by William of Occam. For

Occam, the principle of individuation became purely formal, immaterial; the universals became mere names, purely symbolic mental substitutions, for the endless variety of individual things. As a result, knowledge in the Western world became symbolic, permitting phenomenal growth in mathematics and modern physics, along with the technological "advances" these symbolic fields enabled. Before long, the realist position, with its natural (as opposed to symbolic) knowledge, was deemed primitive; giving rise to the rarely stated but often implied view that Native (and medieval) thought and literature are simplistic.[9]

The Western habit of mind adopted in the late medieval period enabled the technological and scientific accomplishments that are often celebrated as evidence of progress and which subsequently gave rise to evolutionary myths. However, nominalism also cost the Western world its access to the Creator and to Creation. As Xavier Zubiri notes, from the moment of Occam's insistence on nominalism, Western humanity was thrust into an unsettling and vertiginous race towards absolute isolation: "Alone, alienated from the world and from God, the human spirit begins to feel insecure in the universe" (qtd. in Marías 138–39). Such intense isolation is realized in the extreme individualism (unsustainable [solipsistic] notions of self) and environmental destruction (unsustainable [disconnected] relations with the earth) that are concomitant parts of the Western habit of mind. For Aquinas's principle of individuation was pushed to its symbolic extreme and has yet to be balanced by a *principle of connectedness,* such as that which is a fundamental component of the Aboriginal habit of mind.

In its concern for connectedness, something similar to the American Indian understanding is evident in indigenous cultures around the world (as well as that of the Saami people of northern Europe), suggesting that the Western habit of mind is an unsustainable aberration, rather than the pinnacle of epistemological achievement. Postmodernist assumptions, as favored by Wong and others, constitute a particularly unsustainable outcome of this aberrant thought system. It would seem that Aboriginal theory offers a compelling alternative to the disconnected fragmentation of Western theory:

> One assumption [of Western epistemology] is that the universe can be understood and controlled through atomism. The intellectual tendency in Western science is the acquisition and synthesis of total human knowledge within a world-view that seeks to understand the outer space [external world] objectively. In the process, Western science, the flagship of the Western world sought answers to the greatest questions concerning our existence and our place in the universe by keeping

everything separate from ourselves. In viewing the world objectively, Western science has habitually fragmented and measured the external space in an attempt to understand it in all its complexity.... Fragmentation has become embedded in the Western worldview and is the cornerstone of Western ideology.... Those who seek to understand the reality of existence and harmony with the environment by turning inward have a different, incorporeal knowledge paradigm that might be termed Aboriginal epistemology. (Ermine 102–03)

Insofar as philosophy is an elite discourse, what I have termed the Western habit of mind may not represent Western culture as a whole. However, because philosophical discourse had treated all fields of knowledge prior to the nominalist turn, nominalism would thereafter have affected and infused all fields. Therefore, the unsustainable production and consumption of styrenics and polyethylene are as much extensions of nominalist thought (in chemical engineering and economics) as are the de-valuing of indigenous thought and culture (in literary criticism and anthropology). Furthermore, the individuation and stratification of fields of discourse is only conceivable within an individuating and symbolically driven habit of mind.

* * * *

A few years ago, *The Globe and Mail* ("Canada's National Newspaper") featured a guest-column by Cree writer Suzanne Methot. The column addressed the abundant media attention then being lavished on the movie *Grey Owl,* featuring Pierce Brosnan in the title role.[10] Grey Owl was the alternate persona of Archibald Belaney. Born in Hastings, England, in 1888, Belaney was raised by two strict and elderly aunts and often played "Red Indian" as a child. He emigrated to Canada in 1906 to live, he told his aunt, in the wilderness near the Indians. After spending some time working in a Toronto department store, he moved to northern Ontario and adopted an alternate persona. The fabricated persona, much more exciting, was one in which his Scots-American father and grandfather had been trappers, guides, and Indian fighters throughout the western part of the continent. His father left Indian fighting to join Buffalo Bill's show and married Grey Owl's invented mother, an Apache woman. Belaney claimed to have traveled with Buffalo Bill before coming to Canada, where he was formally and ceremonially adopted by the Ojibwe Nation.[11]

Although Grey Owl was an entirely fabricated identity, Belaney was probably the most widely accepted and celebrated "Native" person in Canadian history. He was accepted because he lived up to the European image of the indigenous person as discussed in the previous chapter. His identity had been obtained directly from the indigenous image of literature, and having succeeded in living up to the image, he became world-renowned as a "good Indian." Despite the fraudulent nature of his constructed identity, Grey Owl was richly rewarded, since he so meticulously matched the indigenous image as constructed in the colonial mind and perpetuated in colonial discourses. He was what Canadians (and Europeans in general) thought a Native person should be—stoical, feathered, compliant—and Grey Owl was able to peddle books of "Indian" wisdom, alongside his "Indian" identity, on hugely successful world tours. Suzanne Methot, in the above-mentioned article, objected to the extensive coverage that the Brosnan film, and by extension, Archibald Belaney, had been receiving. What should have been a national embarrassment, was being vaunted, yet again, as a national legend. The renewed attention to Grey Owl was especially bothersome in light of the scant coverage granted to *Smoke Signals*, an Aboriginal film with Aboriginal actors, which had premiered less than four months earlier.[12]

Methot's *Globe and Mail* column raised issues of indigenous identity, of colonial schizophrenia *vis-à-vis* indigenous identity, and of the systematic dismissal and exclusion of indigenous voices from the Canadian popular media—all of which bear some relation to the present discussion. However, the column was most memorable for the way it closed. After constructing a sophisticated and elegant argument, rhetorically attuned to the *Globe*'s educated and conservatively liberal audience, Methot suggested that First Nations people be consulted on the important issues of the day ("genetic engineering, the Prairie farm crisis, the civil war in Sierra Leone," etc.) because, she said, "Aboriginal thinking might just save the world." My reading of Wilma Mankiller's story accepts and builds on Methot's suggestion, arguing that *Mankiller: A Chief and Her People* manifests significant aspects of Aboriginal thinking. Furthermore, like Methot, I operate under the assumption that this mode of thought might have something to contribute to the world, assuming that the current and pervasive dismissal of Aboriginal epistemology can be overcome.

* * * *

Wilma Mankiller served as Principal Chief of the Cherokee Nation of Oklahoma from 1985 to 1995, at which time health problems prevented her seeking re-election. As Principal Chief, she was a respected leader, who initiated significant social changes in her community. Her story, *Mankiller: A Chief and Her People*, relates and performs aspects of the Aboriginal thinking that have guided her work and her life. For example, the tripartite arrangement of the text—three parts entitled "Roots," "Turmoil," and "Balance" respectively—echoes the Cherokee concern for balance. Speaking of her people's traditional ways, Mankiller writes: "We were . . . profoundly religious, believing that the world existed in a precarious balance and that only right or correct actions kept it from tumbling" (20). The same belief in the importance of balance and roots informs Mankiller's career and life, as well as her autobiography. All are part of a larger effort to restore *balance*, to work through the present *turmoil*, by a return to the people's *roots*. The effort is not strictly a personal one: if it were, the results would be negligible. However, when personal effort becomes part of a larger, unified, and collective thrust, when the individual is connected and endlessly related, then the potential for change is immeasurably great.

The aspect of Aboriginal thinking that suggests that the people must return to their *roots* in order to restore *balance* is mirrored in the textual structure. For example, Mankiller's autobiography ends with a return to roots, the place from which it began. Mankiller opens by looking at her own and her people's roots, follows these roots through the periods of greatest turmoil, and works toward the present period, which is marked by the struggle to restore balance. However, since turmoil has yet to cease, the return to roots suggested and performed must be ongoing and cyclical. The autobiography ends with a discussion of two Cherokee prophecies, both of which exhort the people to return to the old ways. The first message is from the Warrior's Nephew to the Moravians; the second is from the Cherokee prophet Charley, who emerged from the mountains with companion wolves. Both messages warn of displeasure in the spirit world over the Cherokee adoption of non-Native ways, and both speak of the necessity of returning to traditional ways (256–57). Thus, the autobiography ends with exhortations to return to the beginning: Roots. A superficial return to traditional practices, however, would result only in further imbalance. What is implied by Mankiller's text is a return to the Aboriginal thinking referred to by Suzanne Methot and Willie Ermine, a re-conceptualization of today's problems through the lens of traditional indigenous thought. Writes Mankiller: "We have indigenous solutions to our problems. Cherokee values, especially those of helping one another and of our interconnections with the land, can be used to address contemporary issues" (251). Traditional thought and values offer solutions to contemporary problems, but since connectedness and balance are important aspects of Aboriginal thinking, any return to tradition must be connected to—and in balance with—daily living. A superficial adoption of traditional practices, which neglects the orientation that gave rise to the practices, would be disconnected from life and, therefore, grossly untraditional.

Mankiller alludes here to a previously mentioned (and often noted) aspect of indigenous thought: the awareness of the connectedness of all that is, or the principle of connectedness. Cherokee/Appalachian writer Awiakta reveals her own deep sense of this state of connectedness in her description of the ancient homeland: "*The Great Smokies and their foothills, themselves, are Story—older than the Rockies, older than the Andes. Veiled in blue haze, whose source remains a mystery, the mountains were never covered by the Ice Age. Their root system of plant and forest has been continuous for millions of years. Mountain people see this ancient web of life with our eyes. We feel it beneath our feet. We know we are part of the Story* (154, emphasis in original). The same principle is sometimes acknowledged in Western scientific, especially ecological, thinking. As Awiakta points out, "*The major difference is that Native Americans consider the web sacred*" (154, emphasis in original). During the "Y2K Crisis," however, a great deal of popular and learned concern surrounded a principle of connectedness. With the threat of disjuncture in the technological web of relations, it was profoundly sensed that day-to-day existence was grounded in a pervasive state of connectedness. The awareness, however, never extended beyond technological-human interdependency. Western *lack* of connection with the earth was never glimpsed more profoundly; for the rivers were still expected to flow on January 1, 2000. Nevertheless, the fear of impending doom escalated—perhaps because the earth would have had to have been encountered in the absence of technological mediation—until the day came and the technological web remained intact. At that point, the newfound awareness of and respect for connectedness withdrew to isolated pockets of scientific and ecological understanding. The buffering effect of technology once again allowed for the principle to be forgotten or neglected. However, connectedness was and remains a familiar principle in Aboriginal thought.

In Mankiller's work, Aboriginal thought is also performed in the arrangement among chapters. Successive chapters move back and forth between the general and the particular, the past and the present, the individual and the community. The first chapter, for example, begins with a discussion of the origins of the Mankiller name, which was for her the source of much teasing as a child and later. But as Mankiller, like Momaday, writes: "Native Americans regard their names not as mere labels, but as essential parts of their personalities" (3). Thus, the Mankiller name constitutes an intrinsic aspect of her identity. At the same time, she recognizes the importance of connecting a name to all the people who have carried it in the past, especially since "Mankiller" was traditionally not a name, but an esteemed Cherokee rank bestowed only upon successful warriors. Mankiller connects the individuality of her name, which goes to the root of her personal identity, with the historical people who had to earn the name, as well as to those living and those yet to come, those who carry or will carry the name. In this way, even in this single chapter, she connects the particular with the general. She also, in this first chapter, details her family lineage, demonstrating an intense connectedness to those around her. Nevertheless, the chapter ends with a critique of her failure to include all her relations: "But I have started my story far too early. Especially in the context of a tribal people, no individual's life stands apart and alone from the rest. My own story has meaning only as long as it is a part of the overall story of my people" (14).

The second chapter begins with a rendition of the Cherokee creation story, in which the Water-beetle dives down into the original waters (15), which remains essentially the only water in existence. The same deposit of original water simply goes around and around, moving and mutating in perpetual circulation, and forming a physical and fluid connection between us and everything and eternity. In the story, the Water-beetle goes down into the original water to bring up the first tiny fistful of earth. Recall that, despite its prevalence, the big bang theory is simply an autogenous creation myth, one story among a multitude of possibilities. In the Cherokee story, the Water-beetle starts a spiral of relations and connections, while in the more commonly propagated version of Creation, a type of coincidental nothingness sets in motion an uncaused line of causation. On the one hand, a spiral is set in motion; on the other, a line. Both, however, are stories, and both theorize Creation.

The second chapter of Mankiller's autobiography begins with a Creation story, before moving on to relate Cherokee history until just prior to removal. In the third chapter, Mankiller tells stories from her childhood in Oklahoma, and in the fourth, she swings back to a discussion of the Trail of Tears. This prepares for the not unrelated discussion, in the fifth chapter, of her family's own bureaucratic removal in a government urbanization program. This textual movement, from the particularity of her own name and personal history to the generality of Creation and of Cherokee history, is a movement that continues throughout the book as Mankiller relates the particulars of her own development and the historic details of interaction between various government agencies and the Cherokee nation. This pendulum-like motion between individual story and national history is not merely a stylistic embellishment; rather, it enacts a worldview in which individual action and individual identity are inseparable from community action and community identity.

What becomes evident in reading Mankiller's autobiography is that present conditions are a direct result of a disturbance of balance in the past, and that future conditions will have been shaped by present actions or failures to act. That is, inequities and injustices between and among communities today are the result of inequities and injustices that were permitted in the past, and the same pattern of inequities will continue into a dwindling future if the balance is not restored. Each individual is charged with responsibility for balanced action, but since each individual is just a small part of the total effort required to bring about the restoration of balance, Mankiller's approach is one of humility. Whereas autobiography in the Western tradition has generally concerned a justification or promotion of the "exceptional" self, Mankiller recognizes both her indebtedness and her responsibility to a very wide circle of Cherokee people before and around her and yet to come. She also recognizes that, despite her success, she is really a tiny part of all that matters. However, given the intrinsically connected nature of things, she further recognizes that, like the Water-beetle and the tiny fistful of original dirt, she is capable of effecting great change.

It also becomes evident that Mankiller's autobiography presents a different concept of identity, fundamentally different from the prevailing concept. Hers is built upon a web-like or spiraling structure in which there are connections to all of one's relations, past, present, and future. The concept, which issues from the principle of connectedness, offers an alternative to the linear progressive model, which issues from the principle of individuation and is responsible for such misconceptions as the orality-literacy scale of linguistic evolution. Within such an understanding, Aboriginal literatures are fetishized and fossilized in a nostalgic longing after some primeval orality, because what tends to be sought is a remembrance of the colonizer's own past. This gives rise to a disdain for, or begrudging acceptance of, perceived advances in Native literature and puts the Native writer in a double bind situation. On the one hand, her work is deemed less purely Aboriginal, if it bears too many marks of non-Native culture, while on the other, her work is always tacitly deemed primitive. For in the linear progressive model, with pure orality at one end of the scale and advanced literacy at the other, the indigenous writer is forever behind, forever forced to catch up with writers of more "advanced," more "developed" cultures. The same model gives rise to myths of social evolution, in which cultures, pseudo-biologically bracketed into races, move in linear progression towards perfection. At the vanguard of the evolutionary march, in this model, are Western cultures, led bravely onward by exemplary and isolated individuals solipsistically (*solus ipse*, "alone himself") leading the race. The spiraling web model of Mankiller's autobiography, however, makes perpetual and wide-ranging connections, with attendant implications and social responsibilities. It extends outward to include all members of the Cherokee Nation, and ultimately all peoples of the world, including even those of European ancestry. As Vine Deloria, Jr. notes, "Tribal man [sic] is hardly a personal 'self' in our modern sense of the word. He does not so much live in a tribe; the tribe lives in him. He is the tribe's subjective expression" (201).

The spiraling web model should, however, be distinguished from certain anti-essentialist arguments. For example, Arnold Krupat, as discussed in the previous chapter, suggests that the use of the term "American Indian" (and, by extension, "Cherokee") is an essentialist act (*Turn* 3–5). The use of such terms, he argues, permits discussion and avoids the confusion of infinite particularity, but to go beyond this, to insist on a necessary connection of the individual with the terms *Indian* or *Cherokee*, is essentialization. (Recall the earlier discussion of nominalism. Infinite particularity results from the unrestricted and strictly symbolic operation of the principle of individuation.) The position may appear to permit a web-like connectedness, such as that performed and discussed by Wilma Mankiller, because to do away with defining (potentially separating) characteristics may appear to permit connectedness. However, this wholesale rejection of individuation is nevertheless based on individualist and individuating notions of self carried to the anti-individual and homogenizing extreme. Implosive and isolating, such notions can only be discussed with reference to an essentialist/anti-essentialist binary. Mankiller's story of self, interlaced as it must be with the stories of the concentric circles of her identity, is based on an *extra*-essentialist world view. The self is not defined as being some particular thing, because the self is not defined in the same isolated sense but is always infinitely connected to all that is. As a result, the autobiography, the story of Mankiller's self, must be subtitled *A Chief and Her People*.

A more suitable framework for reading Mankiller's story would be in terms of what Momaday has called "racial memory" or "the memory in [the] blood" (*Man Made* 13; qtd. in Martin 157). The idea, mentioned in the previous chapter and to be elaborated upon in Chapter Four, did not originate with (nor is it limited to) Momaday, but it has been vehemently critiqued by some for failing to hold up to scientific scrutiny.[13] As noted, however, such challenges not only contradict simultaneous calls for an "ethnocritical" approach to literature, they also fail to acknowledge the story-nature of Western science and philosophy, which are as steeped in story as indigenous conceptions of truth and knowledge. Blood memory, as Momaday presents it, is present in all people, whether acknowledged or not. Blood memory is story in its physical form, which implies a physical basis for the web of relations worked out in Mankiller's autobiography, a physical basis for the intrinsic connectivity and alternative ontology implied by her text. It is the physical basis of such connections that makes the imperative for selfless action, an imperative that has guided the life and career of Wilma Mankiller, all the more compelling. Mankiller's autobiography may present a distinct conception of self, one that is based on Aboriginal as opposed to Western theory, but it is a conception that may be crucial if the present imbalance in the world is to be restored to harmony. What makes Wilma Mankiller an exceptional leader and what makes her autobiography worthy of serious attention, then, is that her work and her story have never been about herself. *Mankiller: A Chief and Her People* functions as a textual extension of the indigenist politics of Wilma Mankiller. That is, what makes this autobiography important from an indigenist critical perspective is the textual inscription it performs of an immersion of self in an infinitely connected struggle for the people.

Chapter Three

Critical Warriors and "Hang-Around-the-Academy" Indians: Toward an Indigenist Criticism

> Nene-bush was going to hold a big dance. He invited everyone in the world to come to this party. But everyone did not come to the dance because they knew he was an evil fellow. Of all the creatures on the earth only the geese went to this dance.
> At the dance, Nene-bush said to the geese, "Now I am going to sing my song and you must close your eyes while you are dancing." All the geese closed their eyes and started dancing around. While they danced by, Nene-bush grabbed them by their necks and strangled them. One little goose had one eye open, however, and it shouted a warning.[1]

The decision to begin this chapter with a fragment of woodland trickster discourse seemed appropriate given that the focus here is on Native criticism and given that a prominent figure among Native critics has been Gerald Vizenor (Ojibwe). Vizenor is renowned for, among other things, having brought "trickster discourse" into the academy. His work comprises a huge body of highly respected material. Thomas King (Cherokee), for example, suggests that "Probably more than any other Native writer, Vizenor understands the trickster figure. And he writes about that trickster figure over and over and over again in a very complex and, I think, very savvy way" (qtd. in Weaver, *That the People* 142). Kimberly Blaeser (Ojibwe), in her authoritative study, points out that Vizenor has "a collection of literary works unexceeded in volume by any Native American author to date," spanning genres that include poetry, fiction, journalism, autobiography, screenplay, and literary criticism (*Vizenor* 5). Robert Warrior (Osage) writes that Vizenor's "early recognition of the social construction of language and racial identity further put him on the cutting edge of postmodern literature and theory. His agonistic invitation to enter the arena of independent thought, self-criticism, and creedal uncertainty make his work the most theoretically sophisticated and informed to date" (*Tribal* xviii). As a fellow urban, mixed-blood Ojibwe, I will add a few comments of my own in appraisal of Vizenor's contribution to Native literary criticism. For, while Kimberly Blaeser concludes that "the work of mixedblood writer Gerald Vizenor seeks and achieves a tribal connection" (*Vizenor* 199), I would suggest that his work seeks and achieves a Western academic connection and that it aggressively eschews any real-world connectedness, which is so fundamental to tribal-centered, or indigenist, writing. Instead, I would argue, Vizenerian criticism haphazardly constructs a conglomeration of European theories and adorns the melange in tribal terms for academic consumption.

In "Native Literature: Seeking a Critical Center," as quoted earlier, Blaeser calls for a tribal-centered criticism. She suggests that such criticism "seeks a critical voice and method which moves from the culturally-centered text outward toward the frontier of 'border' studies, rather than an external critical voice and method which seeks to penetrate, appropriate, colonize or conquer the cultural center, and thereby, change the stories or remake the literary meaning" (53). As noted, this idea, privileging the Native text over the non-Native methodology, is an important one, but the definition simultaneously touches upon a dilemma faced in most approaches to text from Western theoretical paradigms, even if methodology is, as it were, held in abeyance. Since post-structuralist approaches inherently preclude movement beyond the text, such criticism is never, except in theory, able to connect with community interests. With respect to the literature of the oppressed, the oversight is not inconsequential. Given Vizenor's experience as a social worker in the inner city, he is fully aware of the realities of the oppressed, and yet his writing has become increasingly theoretical and accessible to an increasingly elite audience. This highlights a difficulty with post-structuralist theories in the context of oppressed peoples: while disconnection of the signifier from the signified makes for fascinating reading, it may also make for bad politics—for *indifférance*. The reader-theorist finds herself locked in a language game that renders her, like Vizenor, unable (or unwilling) to address the issues that affect real people: "I've had people just walk into an office I opened on Franklin Avenue with nothing left in their psychic energy but that last effort to open the door. And often all you can say is, 'Too bad.' You can't solve people's lives; you can only work with humor and material" (Vizenor in Coltelli, *Winged Words* 167).

The sorts of humor and material with which Vizenor prefers to work is suggested in "Socioacupuncture: Mythic Reversals and the Striptease in

Four Scenes," in which he argues for a performance-based understanding of identity. Vizenor here builds on Roland Barthes's assertion that "Striptease—at least Parisian striptease—is based on a contradiction: Woman is desexualized at the very moment when she is stripped naked . . . as in any mystifying spectacle, the decor, the props and the stereotypes intervene to contradict the initially provocative intention and eventually bury it in insignificance" (Barthes 91). Barthes makes the point that the accoutrements and art of the striptease—and, in the case of the Striptease Club at the *Moulin Rouge*, the social ranking of the participant—paradoxically obscure and ultimately negate nudity, while the striptease simultaneously functions as an inoculation of the viewer against the flesh. The revelation that occurs in the striptease is simultaneously masked by art, spectacle, and social positioning. Vizenor inverts Barthes's striptease to discuss Indian identity: "Tribal cultures are colonized in a reversal of the striptease. Familiar tribal images are patches on the 'pretence of fear,' and there is a sense of 'delicious terror' in the structural opposition of savagism and civilization" (83). That is, for Vizenor, rather than being stripped, Native people are dressed in familiar images, such as those presented in the ever-popular Edward Curtis photographs.

Vizenor quotes John Berger: "All photographs are of the past, yet in them an instant of the past is arrested so that, unlike a lived past, it can never lead to the present" (qtd. in "Socioacupuncture" 86). In the reversal of the striptease, Native people are compelled, Vizenor argues, to identify with and present themselves as these photographic images: " . . . we were caught dead in camera time, extinct in photographs and now in search of our past and common memories we walk right back into these photographs, we become the invented images . . ." (90). As an antidote, Vizenor offers the striptease:

> The striptease is a familiar expression of theatrical independence and social titillation. In the scenes and voices here [in his essay] that delicious dance is a metaphor and in the metaphor are mythic strategies for survival.
> The striptease is the prime form of socioacupuncture, a therapeutic tease and technique that is accomplished through tribal trickeries and mythic satire, eternal contradictions that release the ritual terror in captured images. (84)

In the striptease that Vizenor theorizes for Native people, the inventors and colonizers of the indigenous image are supposed to vanish. That is, according to Vizenor, that which is construed as Indian identity is an image constructed and maintained by colonizers, and, in adopting the image, Native people partake in their own colonization. Therefore, he argues, to undo colonization, Aboriginal people need only stop performing the colonial construct.

The argument presupposes that identity is strictly performance. Like Walter Benn Michaels (see earlier, Chapter One), Vizenor would hold that a person is only Indian insofar as she performs "Indian-ness." Note here that Vizenor discards the term *Indian* altogether, routinely using it within scare-quotes, and preferring the term *postindian:* "The word Indian, and most other tribal names, are simulations in the literature of dominance. . . . The postindian warrior is the simulation of survivance in new stories" (*Manifest Manners* 10–11). Vizenor argues that identity is a performance, and the colonizer persuades Native people to perform the "traditional" image of the Edward Curtis photograph: stoical, beaded, feathered, and fringed. Since the photographs are the colonizer's images of Indians, Vizenor suggests a reversal of the reversal. Shed the image and the fact of colonization disappears: " . . . the dichotomies of past and present dissolved one last time. The inventors and colonialists vanished with the striptease, even those whose ideas he had quoted seem to vanish like petals on a pasture rose. The conference on socioacupuncture was silent" ("Socioaccupuncture" 93). What remains, then, is for "Indians" to become "postindian warriors of survivance."

The argument seems pleasing enough—if only reality could be made to conform to theory as easily as suggested. Then, simply by shedding the constructed image (by not "acting" Indian), all social problems encountered by Native people would be miraculously erased. Unfortunately, the theory comes after the fact. Even in the absence of overt cultural performance, an Indian is still an Indian, and she has only to enter a store to buy a loaf of bread, in most parts of North America, to be confronted by the inescapable fact of her identity. Whether she adorns herself in beads and braids or not, and regardless of the nature and quality of her performance, the shopkeeper will, in many cases, commence a performance against Indian identity. Furthermore, and perhaps more important, even if we accept that identity is strictly performance, it is not possible not to perform. Unlike the clothing in a Parisian striptease, identity can only be shed in the process of assuming some other identity. Nakedness is not possible, and while the Native person may aggressively eschew all cultural markers of Indian identity, the default (assumed naked) identity will most likely be a white one. In advising Native people not to "act Indian," therefore, Vizenor is implicitly advising them to "act white." Furthermore, the amount of time he spends in discrediting members of the American Indian Movement (AIM) is somewhat troubling. For in spite of their many youthful excesses, and in spite of the fact that some high profile members have moved on to Hollywood careers and the exploitation of traditional foodstuffs (Vizenor does an exceptionally careful and uncharacteristically lucid job of chronicling their faults), the movement nevertheless had an overall positive effect on the lives of Native people in North America. Specifically, it can be argued that the rise of radicalism made the assertion of Indian identity acceptable, and even desirable, for Native people in North America after many decades of coercion to "act white."

Prior to the rise of radicalism, Indian identity was decidedly not socially acceptable in North America. The murderous suppression of the Ghost Dance at Wounded Knee in 1890 coincided with a pervasive and enforced shift in the orientation of Native people towards their own cultural identity. The demise of the Ghost Dance movement was one aspect of the vast social and political upheaval occurring in Native North America at that time: during the six-year period leading up to the Wounded Knee massacre, Louis Riel was hanged; Gabriel Dumont was forced into exile; Poundmaker, Big Bear, and One Arrow (who had associated with Riel) died as a direct result of incarceration in Canadian prisons; Geronimo became a prisoner of war (he died over twenty years later, still a prisoner of war); Sitting Bull was murdered; the General Allotment (Dawes Severalty) Act was inaugurated; and the last of the great buffalo herds were exterminated by non-Native hunters.[2] Afterwards, traditional Aboriginal religious and, increasingly, cultural practices were necessarily covert, and total assimilation was deemed inevitable.

Western-style education, the "bettering" of oneself, was particularly assimilative in its orientation. First Nations people, for example, are still living with the residue of Canada's nefarious residential school policy, designed as part of a wider assimilationist strategy inaugurated by Sir John A. MacDonald, Canada's first Prime Minister, who clearly stated his intent "to do away with the tribal system and assimilate the Indian people in all respects with the inhabitants of the Dominion, as speedily as they are fit to change" (qtd. in Montgomery 13). As John Milloy notes in his incisive study of the residential (boarding) school system in Canada, the Indian Advancement Act of 1884 was one of the MacDonald government's more instrumental pieces of assimilative legislation, granting the Indian Affairs Department power over every aspect of First Nations life: "Aboriginal traditions, ritual life, social and political organization, or economic practices could be proscribed as obstacles to Christianity and civilization or could be declared by Parliament, as in the case of the potlatch and sun dance, criminal behaviour" (21).

However, as Milloy also makes clear, it was the federal government's policies in Aboriginal education that were most zealous and most devastating:

> Of all the initiatives that were undertaken in the first century of Confederation, none was more ambitious or central to the civilizing strategy of the Department, to its goal of assimilation, than the residential school system. In the vision of education developed by both church and state in the final decades of the nineteenth century, it was the residential school experience that would lead children most effectively out of their 'savage' communities into 'higher civilization' and 'full citizenship.' (21–22)

However, in spite of the systematic and pervasive effort, the residential schools—notorious for their failure to nurture, sustain, protect, or educate—failed also as tools of assimilation: "By every indicator—health, employment, income, education, housing—Aboriginal people, far from being assimilated, were still separate and second-class citizens. What unfolded . . . was a complex social, economic, and political tapestry with a single unifying thread—growing Aboriginal poverty" (9).

A. LaVonne Brown Ruoff notes that early American Indian writers and intellectuals, such as Gertrude Bonnin (Sioux), Carlos Montezuma (Yavapi), Charles Eastman (Sioux), and George Copway (Ojibwe), tended to emerge from their Western education with a firm belief in the importance of adopting Western culture. In each case, however, they ultimately rejected the feasibility of assimilation, returning later in life to their people and their traditions.[3] Nevertheless, in spite of its ultimate failure at assimilation, the Western education system has, for the most part, functioned as an overt attempt at erasing Indian identity. Interestingly, Native people have, since the imposition of Western-style education, been compelled to perform exactly the striptease advocated by Vizenor—to unlearn tradition and assume whiteness—a striptease so frequently misconstrued as the absence of cultural identity. Yet, since we are never naked of identity—which is perhaps the point of Barthes' discussion—the colonizer has never been troubled by Indians looking and acting white. The recent turmoil in Albuquerque, over Native high school students' being denied permission to wear their traditional regalia to graduation ceremonies, suggests that "looking Indian" continues to function as an overt act against colonization (Saltzstein C5–6).[4]

Furthermore, as Terry Wilson points out, the birth of American Indian Studies as a discipline was very much a result of "the Red Power movement and expressions of Indian nationalism" on university campuses in the 1960s (219). That is, without the rise of the Indian radicalism so carefully castigated by Vizenor, the market for Vizenerian discourse would not exist. At any rate, the rise of radicalism and the subsequent rise of American Indian Studies marked a turning point for American Indian students: no longer would Western-style education necessarily imply assimilation. The corresponding resuscitation of traditional cultural practices, advanced by 1960s radicals, was exactly the opposite of adhering to white expectations. AIM and other radical Indian movements, in spite of their excesses and, in large part, because of the appearance of their members, made it desirable to reclaim one's Indian identity, made it feasible again to refuse to act white. The point to note is that, since the late nineteenth century (much earlier in some areas) and until the rise of Indian radicalism, Native people have been coerced into the same rejection of tradition that Gerald Vizenor encourages them to undertake willingly.

Vizenor's work, as he himself suggests, constitutes an extended language game:

> Naanabozho, the woodland tribal trickster, is a *holotrope*, a comic holotrope, and a *sign* in a language game; a communal sign shared between listeners, readers and four points of view in third person narratives.... The trickster is a sign, a communal signification that cannot be separated or understood in isolation; the signifiers are acoustic images bound to four points of view, and the signified, or the concept the signifier locates in language and social experience, is a narrative event or a translation. The listeners and readers become the trickster, a sign, and semiotic being in discourse; the trickster is a comic holotrope in narrative voices, not a model or a tragic figuration in isolation. ("Trickster" 187–88, emphasis in original)

Here, as in much of his writing, he discusses the woodland trickster, and as Ruoff points out, Vizenor often presents himself as trickster:

> The trickster/transformer figure from Indian oral literature pervades Vizenor's recent work. Although the trickster as mixed-blood entrepreneur is one of Vizenor's favorite subjects, Vizenor also creates characters that reflect other aspects of the trickster. For example, in *Darkness in Saint Louis Bearheart*, Beneto Saint Plumero (also known as Bigfoot) possesses the enormous genitals and sexual appetite of the traditional trickster. Vizenor even portrays himself as a compassionate trickster. In both *Earthdivers* and *Wordarrows*, the author often appears as Clement Beaulieu, wise fool, truth speaker, and storyteller, or as Erdupps MacChurbbs, 'shaman sprite from the tribal world of woodland dreams and visions' (88). (61)

That is, Vizenor not only discusses the trickster figure, he performs it, presumably enabling the reader to enter into trickster discourse.

Some difficulties might be noted. First, while the trickster delivered into postmodern discourse may appear to be taken from Anishinaabe (Ojibwe) tradition, the figure differs markedly from the traditional trickster-figure in several respects. It is unlikely that the average traditional Ojibwe elder—even had she or he had the actual experience of seeing some manifestation of Nanaboozhoo skulking darkly through the bush—would recognize Vizenor's "trickster." However, Vizenor argues, "The trickster is not a presence or a real person but a semiotic sign in a language game, in a comic narrative that denies presence" ("Trickster" 204). The elders, apparently, are mistaken. Olive Dickason notes that the trickster has characteristically been perceived as very much more than a "semiotic sign in a language game": " . . . the trickster . . . could be an individual but . . . could also be an aspect of the Creator or world force" (*First Nations* 59–60). Lee Maracle suggests that the Aboriginal trickster figure that has come to dominate academic discussions of Native literature is, if anything, a juvenile manifestation of the figure (personal interview). The trickster-figure of Maracle's *Ravensong*, however, is much more complex in a holistic sense. Rather than dallying in language games, the trickster of *Ravensong* engages in "gut-wrenching" change and the "kind[s] of catastrophe we may not survive" (14, 44). Nevertheless, while the average Ojibwe elder may not recognize Vizenor's "trickster," the average literary critic would immediately recognize this figure as a minor variation on Derrida's *différance* and Bakhtin's heteroglossia. Essentially, Vizenor's entire theoretical corpus amounts to a haphazard conglomeration of the words and ideas of prominent theorists with very little added to the theoretical discussion beyond, in adopting the deconstructionist tendency to neologize, some vaguely defined terms: *survivance, manifest manners, postindian warriors, trickster discourse*, etc. Since he works in a deconstructionist vein, there is no need for definition because (conveniently) the definition is always shifting. His contribution can be summarized, therefore, as the addition of some Native terminology and some mild (but not disturbing) allusions to Native issues within a distinctly Western and elite discourse.

While the contribution is minimal, however, it does allow him to capitalize at least twice on exchanges in the linguistic marketplace. I allude here to Bourdieu's characterization of linguistic interaction as exchanges of capital within a market. As Bourdieu suggests, those with more rarified manners of speaking are able to secure a *profit of distinction* with every utterance and to obtain increased amounts of *symbolic capital*, which afford them symbolic power in the actual social order. Among manners of speaking (writing), theoretical discourse is particularly rarified, and thus, in

Bourdieu's model, it is particularly profitable on the linguistic market. For this reason, theorists obtain a profit of distinction with every utterance. The capital which accrues at every exchange and the recognition of this profit serve to reinforce the social hierarchy which makes the profit (and corresponding loss) possible. In adopting the theoretical jargon *du jour*, therefore, Vizenor secures a symbolic profit. Obscurity is frequently mistaken for complexity, and prolificacy for profundity. Since his work is opaque (because the point is there is no point, or rather, the point is always shifting), the exchange value on Vizenerian discourse is quite high. Furthermore, he simultaneously sets up a monopoly on his own meaning, since, in order to understand Vizenor, one must read more Vizenor.

At the same time, however, in introducing terms from tribal discourse, Vizenor is able to profit a second time at each exchange. In the order of discourse, which is modeled on the existing social order, theoretical discourse ranks quite high, and tribal discourse, quite low—except when exchanged as appropriated artifact. As mentioned, in speaking the language of "high" theory, Vizenor secures an initial profit: the profit of distinction. In sprinkling tribal terms and issues throughout, he appears to disrupt the social order (and the corresponding order of discourse), an order which over-values theoretical discourse and de-values tribal discourse. Since he implicitly affirms the order of discourse, however, which elevates theoretical jargon as the only legitimate language of the academy, the gesture functions as a strategy of condescension. Like the Béarnais mayor discussed by Bourdieu as exemplifying strategies of condescension, Vizenor exacts a double profit at each exchange: "By virtue of his position he is able to negate symbolically the hierarchy without disrupting it, to transgress the unwritten law and thereby exploit the hierarchy to his advantage in the very process of reaffirming it" (Thompson 19).[5]

Another of the functions of Vizenerian discourse is to introduce Native Studies into literature departments. In doing so, it destabilizes the hold of anthropologists and social scientists on the field:

> Cultural *anthropologies* are monologues with science; moreover, social science subdues imagination and the wild trickster in comic narratives. These anthropologies are at last causal methodologies and expiries, not studies of anthropos, human beings or even natural phenomena; rather, anthropologies are remains, reductions of humans and imagination to models and comparable cultural patterns—social science is institutional power, a tragic monologue in isolation. ("Trickster" 187)

Wresting control of Native Studies from anthropologists and social scientists may not seem entirely undesirable, given the troubling number of faulty constructions of "Indian-ness" and downward social gazes produced by these disciplines. However, the alternative offered by Vizenor's work is a subsequent relinquishing of control to literary theorists, rendering the study of Indians a vacuous language game played most frequently and with much zest by non-Natives. This, in itself, would not be problematic, since a Native academic's choice to engage in high theory is perfectly legitimate. As Phillip Brian Harper's important book *Framing the Margins: The Social Logic of Postmodern Culture* makes clear, "marginalized" voices have, ironically, long been at the unacknowledged center of postmodernism, since "the postmodern era's preoccupation with fragmented subjectivity represents the 'recentering' of the culture's focus on issues that have always concerned marginalized constituencies" (3–4). Furthermore, as a manner of interpreting the world, postmodernism is satisfactory, and in terms of contemporary Western epistemological models, postmodernism may be the best we have—in spite of the paucity of readable translations, which renders its usefulness dubious. "Doing" theory is always easier than translating it (making it meaningful).

However, in dealing with Native literature, I would argue that Aboriginal theory offers a more satisfying alternative, since postmodernism is characterized by fragmentation, which, in language, infers a lack of stable reference. Aboriginal theory, on the other hand, takes a more fluid, less atomistic, view of language, such that, rather than emphasizing a lack of fixable reference, the emphasis is on the unavoidability of reference (connection). Just as "the major trope of Native American literature . . . is the interconnectedness of all things," the primary emphasis in Aboriginal theory—based as it is on the Aboriginal worldview—is the ultimate and inescapable "interconnectedness of all things" (Bird, "Decolonization" 4). To look at language in terms of unavoidable connectedness, rather than in terms of hypothetical and endless play of signification, would represent a reversal of truly mythic proportions. Furthermore, the approach could then be channelled back through the theorists to the mainstream, where it could serve to reconnect a dying culture to its roots, to the earth, and to its people, as some ecocritics and others are beginning to realize.[6] As Harper notes with respect to postmodernism's being prefigured in marginalized cultures, a mythic reversal of theory is likewise prefigured in marginalized literatures.

* * * *

In "Land Speaking," Jeannette Armstrong suggests, "To speak is to create more than words, more than sounds *retelling* the world; it is to realize the potential for the *transformation* of the world. To the Okanagan, speaking is a sacred act in that words contain spirit, a power waiting to become activated and become physical" (183). The assumption of the transformative potential of language in traditional Amerindian literatures and stories is widely acknowledged by critics, and, on this point, I agree.[7] What is troubling, and what must be repeatedly negated, is the assumption that so often accompanies the notion: the idea that Indians will someday "evolve" to the point at which they no longer hold such supposed "primitive" assumptions about language. Walter J. Ong's work is admittedly dated, but it does seem that to engage in readings of indigenous literature through mainstream understandings of orality without tending towards a similar kind of deterministic social evolutionary assumption remains unlikely.[8] While Ong's ideas have had a significant influence on Vizenor, the application of such ideas to Native literature, as suggested in Chapter One, is problematic not only because of the resulting and inevitable condescension, but also because the practice misses the point of the literature entirely.[9]

As noted above, American Indian Studies and, by extension, the study of contemporary Native literature only entered the Western academy during the 1960s era of militancy on university campuses. At that time, the proliferation of interest in "Other" literatures began to include indigenous texts. Additional works by Native authors (though remarkably few) have since been added to the scholarly repertoire, and the variety of approaches to the literature has been finessed and augmented over the years. One thing has not changed, however: the dominant approach to Native literature is still the "Dominant" approach. As mentioned in the introduction, repeated calls for indigenous-centered readings have gone unheeded (assertions of "ethnocriticism" notwithstanding), and suggestions that the literature might best be served by Indian control have been dismissed as radical, naïve, and even racist. The argument has often been made that contemporary Indian writers for the most part are working in English, and their works are largely published by white-run university presses to be studied largely by white audiences in mainstream schools. Since this is the case, the argument goes, the writers must therefore be writing for white audiences. Thus, it is not at all unreasonable to have non-Native scholars dominate the study of Native literature.

For the moment, I will suppose the suggestion to be true, and I will ignore the countless statements to the contrary issued by many of the writers themselves.[10] For in some respects, it is true: EuroAmericans and Euro-Canadians are being addressed by Native literature. Applying the suggestion to Lee Maracle's previously mentioned *Ravensong* should, therefore, be a straightforward and palatable critical exercise. *Ravensong* is very much a sociology text masquerading as fiction. Of course, since sociology texts are something of a fiction masquerading as textual elaborations of objective fact, *Ravensong* is not peculiar in this regard. In the novel, Maracle inverts "dominant" expectations by suggesting that dysfunction and poverty in Native communities are not reasons for a downward sociological gaze (in other words, dysfunction and poverty are not reasons for pity) among non-Natives. Rather, since the ultimate source of the problems in Native communities is the EuroAmerican social structure foisted upon them, the novel casts these as reasons for Native people to address the root of the problems in EuroAmerican society.

The protagonist of the novel is Stacey, a high school senior in the 1950s who is the shining star and bright hope of her Salish community. She hopes to become a schoolteacher and her community is excited, for it means they will no longer be forced to send their children to "white town" for schooling. In the end, however, they find that the government will not allow them to open their own school on the reserve. During much of the story, Stacey is depicted crossing a bridge each day on her way to the existing school across the river. The bridge is a symbol, an arc representing the strength of mediation; however, as in the novel, mediation can be extremely painful. The bridge connects two isolated worlds, two completely distinct societies that Stacey moves between. As she passes back and forth, she notes the distinctions between them, performing a kind of sociological analysis of the two communities which sometimes leaves non-Native readers uncomfortable. Recall my tentative assumption here: that such novels are written for non-Native readers.

At one point, Raven, another character in the novel, formulates an idea. She is disgusted with the people of the Native community because they want nothing to do with those in "white town." Repeated negative experiences have left the community with the desire simply to be left alone. Exasperated, Raven relates her concerns to her companions (Cedar, Wind, Crow, and others): "'There isn't much time. These people [those in white town] are heading for the kind of disaster they may not survive.' ... Everyone cudgelled themselves with the dilemma of getting the people out of the houses to immerse themselves in the transformation of the world of the others" (14, 44). Raven decides to force the people of the Native community out of their isolation in order that they might find some way to circumvent the impending disaster in "white town." She forces them into action by means of a sickness that enters the community—a flu from another part of the world, which causes death of unthinkable proportions in their community. At the height of the epidemic, the community has scarcely enough members left to bury the dead and nurse the sick. Since Stacey's is a traditional community, the loss is catastrophic. It involves not merely a mournful loss of loved ones. Since, in the traditional worldview, everyone is inextricably connected with everyone and everything else, the loss of a single individual incapacitates the entire community. Each individual is vitally important to the proper functioning of the whole, and the loss of multiple individuals magnifies the catastrophe exponentially. In order to survive the disaster at all, and because the 1950s Canadian government will not send white medical personnel into a Native village, Stacey's community sends envoys to the hospital to steal some IV equipment. The knowledge of intravenous hydration is a European-based knowledge, which only enters the community as a result of Raven's catastrophe. Significantly, it is through the combination of knowledge systems that the community ultimately survives. As Old Dominic, the community healer, suggests, "The world needs a combined wisdom, not just one knowledge or another, but all knowledge should be joined. Human oneness, that's our way" (67).

Raven's overarching purpose in driving the people out into the larger world-community, though, concerns social illness, not physical. Social illness, in the form of suicide, abuse, and male-domination, simultaneously begins entering this 1950s Native community, and, like physical diseases, social ills are always more devastating when mixed with poverty. The point of the novel is that these illnesses are not parts of an "Indian problem." The devastating social ills, like the physical, were not present until they arrived with Europeans. In this way, *Ravensong* inverts mainstream expectations. The novel does not concern non-Native people's learning to "understand" Native people, nor their finding ways of "helping" Indians "catch up" with the mainstream. It is, rather, the other way around. The worldview which views Native people as needing help or wanting to catch up is, as mentioned in the introduction, also the worldview that has given rise to the HAARP program, nuclear arsenals, global warming, and "Third-" and "Fourth-Worlds."[11] Increasingly, the inherent instability of this worldview is being recognized. Since the search for solutions to the instability must involve examining other ways of viewing the world, other ways of imagining a difference, Aboriginal literature has much to offer as part of the emerging vision of a different world. Texts such as *Ravensong* are able to function as a bridge between isolated communities, allowing non-Native readers to enter, for a moment, into a traditional Aboriginal worldview. In the necessary effort to get indigenous knowledge flowing into the veins of EuroAmerican culture—to get an epistemological IV drip going—indigenous literatures offer a powerful vehicle for transfusion. In such a reading, and to the extent that Native literature is written for a non-Native audience, critics should not seek for ways to help Native people catch up, nor for ways to have their literature "belong" within colonial canons. Rather they might seek for ways to help mainstream culture survive the illness that now threatens the survival of all peoples of the world. Furthermore, given that Aboriginal theory is extremely complex—frequent portrayals of its juvenile status notwithstanding—advanced thinkers of the interpretive caliber of literary theorists would be required to take Aboriginal theory and translate it for the dominant culture.

* * * *

The similarity, if any, between the trickster discourse of *Ravensong* and that described by Gerald Vizenor is obviously superficial. Instead of engaging in the gut-wrenching and serious change worked through by the trickster-transformer of *Ravensong*, Vizenor's self-styled trickster discourse does little more than operate an extended language game. Furthermore (aside from the fact that he exacts a double profit through a strategy of condescension) and perhaps more seriously, Vizenor's use of the trickster figure allows him to sidestep the effects of his theory: to evade critique and to evade responsibility. For example, he tellingly stops short of the point at which his performance theory could effect change in the academy, an ideological state apparatus of which he is a beneficiary: "'College degrees are degrees in words, with special awards for sentence structure, uniforms in the word wars, which is not much better than being elected to the plastic flower growers association hall of fame, but we must not pluck the carrier pigeons with the documents too soon because the academics might vanish'" ("Socioaccupuncture" 93). Here, he alludes to the fact that academic credentials are as much performances of social status as Indian identity; however, just at the point at which his ideas could break free of their textual confinement and effect real change in the world (theoretically), he desists: "'because the academics might vanish.' Silence."

The performance-based nature of academic identity may be considered germane to discussions of the Vizenerian corpus, since Vizenor's formal education is limited to a bachelor's degree obtained, first, by sitting in (acting as a student) at New York University and becoming, through "a fudge of enrollment, . . . a full-time student." From that point he transferred to the University of Minnesota, where he majored in Child Development and Asian Area Studies, according to A. Robert Lee's extensive biography (*xvii*). His areas of specialization, according to Kimberly Blaeser, were child development and psychology (*Vizenor* 6). Jace Weaver suggests that Vizenor also spent a semester studying law at William Mitchell College (*That the People* 138). Vizenor later returned to the University of Minnesota to do graduate work in Library Studies and Asian Studies but left because his thesis proposal was rejected. However, in spite of the fact that he apparently attained only a bachelor's degree, Vizenor has long been living as (performing the identity of) a PhD. He has held several illustrious teaching positions, including a senior professorship in literature at UC Santa Cruz (1987), Provost of Kresge College (1989–90), David Burr Chair of Letters at University of Oklahoma, Norman (1991–92), and his most recent position, since 1993, as professor of Ethnic Studies at Berkeley. This in itself is exceptionally strong support for Vizenor's suggestion that identity is strictly performance-based, especially given the tendency for Native academics to be consistently and repeatedly denied tenure. Cook-Lynn attributes this tendency to eliminate indigenous faculty to a more widespread rejection of Native voices and the implicit disavowal of established versions of colonial history they represent: "It is in the faculty that the power of ideas resides, of course, reason enough to rid the academy of unacceptable ideas and their dangerous faculty repositories" ("How Scholarship" 88–89). While some scholars, whose academic credentials are impeccable but whose ideas are potentially dangerous to the existing social order as replicated in the academy, are denied tenure, Gerald Vizenor, whose formal education comprises a series of broken and stitched together degrees but whose ideas never leave the confines of the page, performs the identity of an illustrious professor.

Nevertheless, Tlingit elder and poet Nora Dauenhauer has stated that "we have our own PhDs," implying quite correctly that formal academic credentials, in and of themselves, account for very little in the traditional Native community (personal interview). Education, formal or otherwise, is highly prized, but only insofar as it contributes to the well-being of the community. That is, Vizenor's lack of accreditation is irrelevant from a community-centered view. What is of concern is what he does for the Native community, from whose terminology he profits so handsomely. As noted earlier, however, "often all [he] can say is, 'Too bad,'" concerning the difficulties faced by Native people; for, theoretically, "[he] can only work with humor and material" (Coltelli, *Winged Words* 167). As a language-locked Native theorist, Vizenor is not alone, and post-structuralist theories are certainly not without importance. The difficulty lies, rather, with Vizenor's relentless and ruthless attacks on the attempts of others to move beyond the text and effect actual change. For example, in a review of Linda

Hogan's *Mean Spirit,* a novel concerning the oil-boom in Osage territory in the early part of the twentieth century, Vizenor points to some minor difficulties in the writing (a New Critical reading, incidentally) and temporal inaccuracies: " . . . established time of the stories is obscured by historical misinterpretation" (168). Elsewhere, however, Vizenor subverts such obsessive interest in historical accuracy: "Histories read the past, or the past in the historical present; criticism reads the narrative; and the trickster reads neither" (*Narrative Chance* 11). The point he misses in the review, beyond his own lapse into the "hypotragic monologue" of "manifest manners," is that Linda Hogan's novel deals with actual issues confronting actual Indians. As Sarah Carney points out, he ignores what Hogan is doing for Native people: "Stemming from his own work, which he describes as an 'agonistic tradition of crossblood journalism' (169), [Vizenor] approaches Hogan's novel with an eye for detail, but markedly, without any intense concern over the socio-political issues that lie buried beneath the narrative's fictionalized front."

As already noted, Vizenor is similarly ruthless in his attacks on members of AIM, with an especially obsessive interest in discrediting Dennis Banks, another Minnesota Chippewa (Ojibwe):

> The kitschymen are the simulations of the media, the men with no real power of their own. Their speeches are not heard as leaders were heard in the past, and the associations of their resistance are an enterprise, not a real tribal discourse. . . . The American Indian Movement, a union of urban crossbloods, for the most part, was established in the late sixties. The radical leaders were nominated by the enterprise of resistance and discovered by the media; the simulations, at the time, became the absence of leadership in the sense that a simulation is the absence of the real. Some of these new chiefs had been in prison and had never been better paid for their resistance. . . . The American Indian Movement, two decades after the occupation of Wounded Knee, is more kitsch and tired simulation than menace or moral tribal visions. (*Manifest* 151–54)

Here, he continues an attack he has waged on AIM leaders since his 1970s newspaper articles, reading their identity and actions through Baudrillard and against his own proclivity toward the neologic.[12] Blaeser suggests that the term "kitschyman" may be a play on *chi-mookomaan* ("long knife," implying "white man") (*Vizenor* 61), but the term probably plays more strongly on "bogeyman" and "gitche manitou." Regardless, Vizenor is less than flattering in his assessment and sees the identity of AIM leaders, as discussed above, as adhering to and performing a dead, colonial image.

The attack is curious, partly because, as noted, American Indian Studies only came into existence on account of the activities of the activists, and partly because, if AIM members are performing the hollow identity of the "Indian activist," then Vizenor is likewise performing the hollow identity of the "Indian academic," adorning his discourse in "Indian" terms and profiting from the simulation. It may be countered that identity is only ever a performance and that any attack against the performance of academic identity is no more sustainable than the attack against Indian identity. However, the endless evasion of responsibility, even if in endless *jouissance*, carries with it a decided danger. In Vizenor's novel *Darkness in St. Louis Bearheart*, for example, a female character is depicted having sex with two boxer dogs (185). Obviously, this and other misogynist aspects of the novel have sparked considerable censure. In an interview with Laura Coltelli, however, Vizenor attributes any objections to the scene to a failure to understand his theory and his worldview:

> Well, first of all let me point out that I lean a bit more toward the margin, toward the deconstruction approach to discovering the play in a word.... All right. I answer [the objections] in two ways: first of all, you misread it, if you're offended. So it's the way you read it—that's your problem. Reread it, you might find the following things: one, I've told you stories before, other characters have told you stories in the novel about creation possibilities that all life has some relationship—it's a worldview. There have been marriages between animals and humans.... I believe it can be experienced and I did it on the page. My second statement, to somebody who finds fault with that, is you'd better reread it and then tell me what's wrong with a human being loving an animal. What's wrong with that is Judeo-Christian, not tribal. That doesn't mean that tribal people are sleeping with animals, I don't mean that, but in the story there isn't anything wrong with it. I thought it was a very sensuous act of love. I was turned on by it myself. (175–76)

In addition to the sudden and uncharacteristic attribution of essence to "tribal people," Vizenor also asserts the primacy of "trickster discourse" in order to evade responsibility for his discursive action. The assertion of the "trickster"-nature (dissemination) of language, in other words, allows him to engage in overt racism and misogyny. He reminds the theoretically-minded that the sign has no referent, that he can only possibly be playing with language because language only ever is a game. At the same time, his sudden assertion of tribal identity silences even the most justified of non-Native critique.

Since, as Nora Dauenhauer points out, education is valued in the Aboriginal worldview only insofar as it contributes to the well-being of the community, the more appropriate approach to Native literature would be that which Jace Weaver terms "communitism." The term is a fusion of "community" and "activism" and implies that a community-based approach necessarily includes activism:

> Literature is communitist to the extent that it has a proactive commitment to Native community, including what I term the 'wider community' of Creation itself. In communities that have too often been fractured and rendered dysfunctional by the effects of more than 500 years of colonialism, to promote communitist values means to participate in the healing of the grief and sense of exile felt by Native communities and the pained individuals in them. (*That the People* xiii)

The same is true of approaches to literature by and about Natives. Criticism is "communitist to the extent that it has a proactive commitment to Native community." The value of the criticism—as with the literature—is determined by the discursive action for (or against) the people, and readings from a communitist, or indigenist, position evaluate the text on those terms. Such approaches also read from and look for a Native worldview, seeking and establishing connections to "the 'wider community' of Creation." Although Weaver and Robert Warrior (possibly following Vizenor) dismiss the idea of a unitary indigenous worldview, other commentators, while rejecting colonialist notions of pan-tribalism, have argued for a striking similarity of worldview among Native people.[13] I think here of Viola F. Cordova (Mescalero Apache), Willie Ermine (Cree), Dennis MacPherson (Ojibwe), and Leroy Little Bear (Blood), among others. As noted in the introduction, it is also possible to discern a similar worldview among tribal peoples around the globe, as well as in medieval Europe. Recall my note in the introduction that the apparently rigid Aboriginal/Western binary I was constructing was but a temporary epistemological template and that I would work towards dismantling the binary. Ultimately, an indigenist framework must include all peoples. At any rate, a similar worldview, as also mentioned in the introduction, has always been evident among the Saami of Europe. It is perhaps also evident among deep ecologists, systems theorists, and other non-Native people, and the number can be expected to increase as the inherent instability of the prevailing worldview becomes more evident.

Gregory Cajete (Tewa Pueblo) suggests that similarities in educational philosophies may likewise be perceived as widespread:

> The goals of wholeness, self-knowledge, and wisdom are held in common by all the traditional educational philosophies around the world. Indeed, even through medieval times, all forms of European education were tied to some spiritual training. Education was considered important in inducing or otherwise facilitating harmony between a person and the world. The goal was to produce a person with a well-integrated relationship between thought and action. This idealized outcome was anticipated as following naturally from the right education. (*Look* 209)

The indigenist position seeks, and seeks to reproduce, such a "well-integrated balance between thought and action." To the extent that examinations of Native literature and texts about Native literature, as well as texts that construct an indigenous image and texts about that construction, are efforts to examine how the text functions for or against the community (that is, to the extent that an indigenist approach is adopted), the dismissal of writers or even of entire texts on the basis of meaningless credentialism or racialism is eliminated. From an indigenist position, then, Vizenor's "crossbloodedness" is irrelevant, as is his lack of formal academic credentials. From an indigenist position, Vizenerian discourse is examined in terms of its function in relation to the community. What becomes of concern, as mentioned, is how the Vizenerian corpus functions against the community: how it thwarts attempts, such as those of Linda Hogan and radical Indians, to effect change; how it aggressively dismantles Indian identity and promotes a perceived absence of identity, which functions to uphold colonialist, rather than community, interests.

Perhaps most serious, Vizenerian discourse, especially given its academic prominence, functions to legitimize and propagate a self-interested, as opposed to community-interested, approach to Native literature among subsequent indigenous scholars:

> If we are intimidated, our young scholars will find themselves doing the slave work of the universities, not the intellectual work of their tribes. They will think that hiring policies, salaries, tenure and promotion problems are the issues of the day. They will ask, *How can I advance my career?*, not *Is what I am doing important to the tribes?* There is reason enough to believe that they are, even now, congregating as faculties at these universities for selfish reasons. (Cook-Lynn, "Radical Conscience" 12)

Several leading and community-oriented indigenous theorists, including Jace Weaver, Robert Warrior, and Kimberly Blaeser (whose work on Vizenor is probably more important than Vizenor's own), seem to make the assumption that in order to follow in the intellectual tradition of Native academics one must follow Vizenor's misguided lead. For, while Vizenor's work is adorned with the sound of politics, while it capitalizes on an apparent radicalism through its use of tribal terminology, the language is nevertheless neutralized by an adherence to deconstruction, which permits him to capitalize a second time as a designer of intellectual *haute couture*. Since he never risks offending the cultural capitalists, however, his words have no power to effect change. Since his work willfully misconstrues and misuses both post-structuralist and Aboriginal theories while simultaneously profiting from an ostensible adherence to both, Vizenor's work is decidedly not in the indigenous intellectual tradition.

* * * *

>Nene-bush stayed there a few days to try and obtain the affection of the geese. Finally he asked them if he could go south with them when the time came. One goose replied, "How are you going to go? You haven't any wings and it is too far to walk." "It is impossible," another goose said. Then one of the geese had a bright idea. The goose said two of them could get a long stick and hold it in their beaks. Nene-bush could hang onto the centre of the stick by his teeth. Nene-bush thought it was a good idea so consequently they flew away early the next morning. Along the way everything went as it was planned. Nene-bush hung down from the pole as they winged southward. Then they went over a village and the people saw the strange sight in the air. "Oh! Look at those geese carrying the Ojibway Indian." The people were hollering and shouting and the flock of geese honked with excitement. Nene-bush became excited also and he shouted at the top of his voice. As soon as he opened his mouth he came down through the sky and landed in the middle of the village. Everyone ran over to him to see what had happened. Nene-bush lay on the ground, he was almost dead. Then the people called a wise old man to the scene. The old man knew right away what had happened; he knew it was Nene-bush. "This man did not know enough to keep his mouth shut," he told the people.[14]

* * * *

In *Tribal Secrets*, Robert Warrior (Osage) works toward establishing what he terms intellectual sovereignty: "I contend that it is now critical for American Indian intellectuals committed to sovereignty to realize that we too must struggle for sovereignty, *intellectual sovereignty,* and allow the definition and articulation of what that means to emerge as we critically reflect on that struggle" (97–98). One would think that intellectual sovereignty would render any slavish adherence to dominant discourse and theory, such as that practiced by Vizenor, obsolete. However, whether *Tribal Secrets* makes such bold and sovereigntist manoeuvres remains unclear. Warrior outlines an intellectual history and reads Native intellectual production in terms of that history. In doing so, he makes some significant points. First, he suggests that Native criticism should open itself to internal criticism: "American Indian critical discourse . . . continues to evidence an avoidance of internal criticism, opting instead for a general pose of criticizing non-Indian scholarship in specific and U.S. society in general . . . The tendency to find in the work of other American Indian writers something worthy either of unmitigated praise or of unbridled criticism stands in the way of sincere disagreement and engagement" (*Tribal* xviii). Just as criticism of the many and varied oppressive colonial strategies should not be reduced to racialism, so too should criticism of indigenous texts and theory not be reduced to mindless flattery (or dismissal) simply on the basis of the author's Indian identity. Gloria Bird (Spokane) argues similarly against an unquestioning acceptance of a text based on the writer's Indian status and has critiqued the internalization of stereotypes in the work of such well-known writers as Louise Erdrich (Ojibwe) and Sherman Alexie (Spokane/Coeur d'Alene). Like Warrior, Bird suggests that a writer's Indian identity does not guarantee an anti-colonial message: "We can read Native American texts in terms of post-colonialism and while I find [Helen Tiffin's] ideas of counter-discourse compelling and potentially generative as a focus for future Native American writers, I am not convinced that what Native Americans write will automatically be classified as counter-discursive" ("Searching" 40).

Another important contribution made by Warrior's *Tribal Secrets* from an indigenist (or communitist) perspective is its sovereigntist arguments for the privileging of Native sources in the criticism of Native literature:

> A guiding principle of my work, from its inception several years ago, has been to produce a book that explores the extent to which, after more than two centuries of impressive literary and critical production, critical interpretation of those writings can proceed primarily from Indian sources. . . . I have tried to respect the demand that Native writers be taken seriously as critics as well as producers of literature and culture. . . . The critical issues I raise in what is still, for the most part, uncharted territory all revolve around my analysis of the ways American Indian intellectuals write about and speak to each other about the role of intellectual work in the social, political, economic, cultural, and spiritual struggle for an American Indian future. (*xvi*)

Again, Gloria Bird concurs: "What is Native literature? The answer to [this] question . . . is one that I hope Native writers and Native academics will someday reach a consensus upon. (And here I must interject that, yes, I am saying that specifically *Native* writers and *Native* academics need to take control of the dialogue, to define their literary traditions in the same manner that other nationalist literary movements have done)" ("Breaking the Silence" 28).

Warrior's work also makes the suggestion that Native intellectuals dispense with identity and authenticity questions, since these tend to issue from essentialist and colonialist positions:

> [B]oth American Indian and Native Americanist discourses continue to be preoccupied with parochial questions of identity and authenticity. Essentialist categories still reign insofar as more of the focus of scholarship has been to reduce, constrain, and contain American Indian literature and thought and to establish why something or someone is 'Indian' than engage the myriad critical issues crucial to an Indian future. (*xix*)

While he does critique radical scholarship, Warrior's critique is not a wholesale dismissal, as is Vizenor's, but is based primarily on the perceived essentialism of the writers:

> At their best, these streams of criticism have offered a strong counternarrative to received academic and popular understandings of American Indian people and cultures. Appeals to essentialized worldviews, though, always risk an ossifying of American Indian existence. Such a commitment to essentialized indigenous worldviews and consciousness, over the course of the decade, became a pervasive and almost requisite feature of American Indian critical writing. (*xvii*)

Warrior sees the present period in indigenous intellectual history as being self-reflexively concerned with the act of criticism, but finds fault with its frequent concern with unifying the various strands and voices in Native intellectualism, which, he contends, is not really possible. He connects this errant strand in criticism to the earlier radical period: "Such calls for unity come most often from 'hard-line' scholars who continue to draw inspiration from the activism of the 1970s" (43). Warrior's anti-essentialism is rooted in the justifiable concern that essentialism risks ossifying the fluctuation of traditions that connect past and present (79); he argues instead for a non-ossified approach to traditional spirituality (84).

While Warrior's daring and important moves set a high standard for Native intellectualism, several difficulties might also be raised. As Diana

Fuss notes, absolute anti-essentialism is not possible; constructionist arguments invariably spawn new, albeit more subtle, forms of essentialism (4).[15] Warrior is correct in noting that Vizenor is stridently anti-essentialist: "The strongest and most controversial critic of essentialism has been Gerald Vizenor" (*xviii*). However, his arguments for an Indian intellectualism could also be construed as a (displaced) form of essentialism: if there is no "Indian," there can be no "Indian intellectualism." Perhaps, as will be developed shortly, Warrior's (unspecified) definition of Indian intellectualism is not static and, therefore, evades the charge. Nevertheless, as Gloria Bird suggests, the entire anti-essentialist discussion is frequently a reactionary one: "In academia, if one argues for any type of distinction, or uses any means to determine who is Indian, the argument is often dismissed as 'essentialist,' a convenient term that is used to undermine native people's unique legal and political position to determine for themselves who are their members" (Harjo and Bird 27). Thus, if one must choose between essentialist and constructionist positions, a tentative acceptance of essence would allow her to align her efforts with those dismissed as "radical," who are working to improve social conditions in the community. Warrior notes that the importance of American Indian intellectual work is in its ability to engage in "the social, political, economic, cultural, and spiritual struggle for an American Indian future" (*xvi*). However, in defaulting to the anti-essentialist position, he permits convenient dismissals of attempts at asserting sovereignty over intellectual and cultural production to go unchallenged. More important, the whole discussion is based in Western epistemology, which tends to conceive of identity only in terms of the essentialist/constructionist binary.

The second major problem with Warrior's approach is that in constructing an American Indian intellectual history, he begins following the demise of the Ghost Dance, neglecting altogether the possibility of a pre-European intellectual tradition. As Willie Ermine points out, however, Aboriginal people were engaged in "alternative expeditions and discoveries in subjective inner space" when Europeans first arrived on this continent. The "insights into existence" uncovered through such explorations, Ermine argues, came precariously close to being abandoned and have yet to be fully elaborated (101–02). The point is, as Ermine's discussion makes clear, that American Indian intellectual history is as old as the people themselves, radically predating the demise of the Ghost Dance with which Warrior begins his intellectual history.

As suggested earlier, the demise of the Ghost Dance marked the point at which indigenous education began to be centered in the boarding school system, a system which was heavily assimilative in its orientation. Early "successes" from the boarding school period include those intellectuals (Eastman, Bonnin, Montezuma, and others) named in the first of Warrior's intellectual periods, 1890–1916. As he points out, though they tended to retreat from their acquired assimilationist orientation later in life, much of their early intellectual work involved the overt promotion of assimilation (5–14). Such anti-Indian sentiments were typical (unavoidable) among students emerging from the boarding schools, as the early-nineteenth-century letters of Catherine Brown (Cherokee) make evident:

> My mother said, if I remained here, she did not expect to see me again in this world. Indeed, she wished she had never sent me to this school, and that I had never received religious instruction. I told her, if she was a Christian she would not feel so. She would be willing to give me, and all she had, up to Christ. I told her I did not wish to stay on account of my own pleasure; but that I wished to get more instruction, so that it might be for her good, as well as for mine. (Anderson 45)

Beginning an intellectual history with the boarding school period therefore risks the assumption, intended or not, that intellectual production is only possible as a by-product of Western education, and the framework Warrior constructs implies the same sort of assimilative thrust for which he critiques the scholars of this period.

A third problem with *Tribal Secrets* is the adoption of a process-centered approach. More correctly, since Aboriginal epistemology can correctly be described as process-oriented, the problem is with the *type* of process-centered approach adopted. Unfortunately, Warrior offers no precise definition of "process": "I have consciously employed a large set of terms without defining them in detail. Categories such as sovereignty, self-determination, tribal, and process appear without much detailed specification of how I am using them" (*xxi*). Nevertheless, it is fairly obvious that he is using "process" in the sense developed by process philosopher-theologians, especially Alfred North Whitehead and Charles Hartshorne. As Whitehead notes, the philosophy implies the theology: "whatever suggests a cosmology, suggests a religion" (141). Having received advanced degrees from prestigious theological institutes, Robert Warrior would certainly have a working familiarity with process philosophy, which can be crudely defined as a form of meta-pantheistic existentialism. Following the encyclopaedic genius of Whitehead (1861–1947), process accounts for all major developments, including mathematics and physics, in Western thought. The fundamental principle of process philosophy is the idea that existence is not static, but is rather a series of molecular occasions of experience: "Process thought by definition affirms that process is fundamental. It does not assert that *everything* is in process; for that would mean that even the fact that things are in process is subject to change. There are unchanging principles of process and abstract forms. But to be *actual* is to be a process, not a full-fledged actuality" (Cobb and Griffin 14).

Existence, then, can be likened to drops of water that fall from a leaky faucet: the drops form and fall away in an ongoing series of entrances into and exits from existence. Process is that which occurs among and within the drops of existence. A separation between the drops is necessary to account for individuation: "If the process constituting our world were a single smooth flow, the boundaries of events would have to be placed upon them by perception or thought, and there would be no real individuals" (Cobb and Griffin 14–15). (Recall the discussion, in the previous chapter, of the Thomist principle of individuation.) For process philosophy, however, while individuation is accounted for, the individual is subordinate to the interdependent. Relations are accorded primacy. In this sense, process thought is in agreement with ecological understandings. It also apparently shares some affinity with Aboriginal thought, which likewise emphasizes process and relatedness. As noted earlier, "the major trope of Native American literature [and thought] is the interconnectedness of all things" (Bird, "Decolonization" 4). This process-oriented nature of indigenous thought is exemplified in the languages, which tend to be dominated by verb-structures, such that existence is something that happens, in a fluid sense, rather than something that statically occurs:

> Anishnaabemowin [the Ojibwe language], unlike English, is a language of action, motion, life. The world it describes lives, moves, does. This is fundamental to the way of thought, as all language is for each group of people raised to speak it from the first. For Native Anishinaabemowin-speakers, the world—conceived and expressed in a child's first language—is *alive* before any kind of conceptualizing, religion, or explanations of the world are formed. By contrast to the active, living cosmos that is expressed (and conceived) in Anishinaabemowin, the cosmos of English (and other Indo-European languages) is a static, moveless framework of objectified scenery and objects within it—nouns, pronouns. A few of these objects are agents, actors, movers, but the big picture that comes with the infant's first language is a sort of stage these few animate objects move around within. (Geise)[16]

In spite of the seemingly monumental similarities, process philosophy presents something distinctly different from indigenous thought. For example, in order to account for the assumed fact of the big bang, process theology comes to be grounded in nothing, or, more correctly, it is grounded in the very fact of process.[17] The big bang and the subsequent existence in time of the universe constitute a universal event, a cosmic drop of existence, which may or may not be part of a larger series of universal drops.[18] Process philosophy does offer an elegant and intellectually satisfying cosmology, although it tends towards a deification of the intellect; however, the emphasis on process is as a type of linear evolution, into which interdependence is read and from which a linear system is constructed. Process philosophy suggests a series of linear beginnings and endings, in which process provides the basis for relations: "There can be no denial of the reality of time nor can there be any doctrine of its circularity" (Cobb and Griffin 16). For Aboriginal theory, conversely, fundamental relatedness (community) provides the basis for the process, while the system constructed is circular (more correctly, spiral), allowing process to be related even to itself.

While process philosophy coincides with indigenous theory in several respects, therefore, the two are ultimately incompatible. Most notably, the emphasis on progressive linearity, which provides a rationale for Warrior's examination of American Indian intellectual traditions as a species of evolution (historical development), is incompatible. One wonders, then, why Warrior would neglect Osage theory as a basis for criticism, choosing instead to ground his work in an obscure Western theory. One can only assume that, as with the structural implication in *Tribal Secrets* that American Indian intellectual tradition began only after the introduction of Western education, Warrior mistakenly (if unwittingly) assumes that Osage theory lacks the complexity of process thought. Of course, since Aboriginal theory emphasizes connectedness even at the epistemological level, the incorporation of Western ideas is perfectly compatible with an indigenist approach. The difficulty arises when the work begins with Western theory and any Aboriginal thought or literature incorporated afterwards is forced into conformity. This leads Warrior to dismiss radical writers (deemed essentialist) and their work, or to perceive their work as quaint and uniformed in spite of the community-centered activism in which they engage. Furthermore, since the terms of reference are not outlined at the outset, readers are never quite aware that when Warrior speaks of "intellectual sovereignty," for example, he is speaking of individuals' experiencing process to the fullest as advocated by process theology, rather than an anti-colonialist assertion of indigenous rights and dignity:

> If our struggle is anything, it is the struggle for sovereignty, and if sovereignty is anything, it is a way of life. That way of life is not a matter of defining a political ideology or having a detached discussion about the unifying structures and essences of American Indian traditions. It is a decision—a decision we make in our minds, in our hearts, and in our bodies—to be sovereign and to find out what that means in the process. (123)

Within process thought, "God is the divine Eros urging the world to new heights of enjoyment," such that one is compelled to view the history of colonization as an evolutionary step towards "new heights of enjoyment" (Cobb and Griffin 26).[19] Thus, Warrior argues for an anti-radical and anti-essentialist position: "Far from a discourse that is merely about the future of Indian sovereignty, this inclusive discussion itself becomes part of the future, a demonstration of possibilities. By withdrawing from the increasingly noisy village of discourse about Indians and embracing ourselves and each other in the fullness of our humanity, we can experience the fullness of our past, present, and future" (122). If sovereignty equals our "embracing ourselves and each other in the fullness of our humanity" instead of the recognition of an indigenous nationhood which has yet to be legally or ethically abrogated, then there can be no space for the uncomfortable antagonism of radical politics. As a result, Warrior makes only cautious and inoffensive moves against the colonizer and, like Vizenor, essentially adorns a Western theory in indigenous terminology. Nevertheless, *Tribal Secrets* does function effectively for the community in some respects. As mentioned, Warrior suggests that Native people now have sufficient theory developed to make recourse to Western theory unnecessary:

> The present [Warrior's] work is concerned primarily with American Indian creative and critical writers, and a look at the Bibliography reveals that it is dominated by references to American Indian writers. ... American Indian intellectual discourse can now ground itself in its own history the way that African-American, feminist, and other oppositional discourses have. (*xx*, 2)

Furthermore, and more important, Warrior makes continual reference to the social concerns of indigenous people and to the fact that sexual orientation, gender, class, etc., are too often overlooked in more general discussions of Native issues (122). In other words, since its social function mitigates oppression, *Tribal Secrets* is much too important a text to neglect altogether.

Since the effort to produce a meaningful criticism of Native literature has so often meant adorning Western theories in tribal terminology, an indigenist criticism would more effectively follow the lead of writers like Craig Womack. Womack suggests (like Norman Fairclough) that since discourse is inherently political, the criticism of literary discourse cannot be otherwise:

> In [*Red on Red*] I will concentrate on the idea that Native literary aesthetics must be politicized and that autonomy, self-determination, and sovereignty serve as useful literary concepts. Further, I wish to suggest that literature has something to add to the arena of Native political struggle. The attempt, then, will be to break down oppositions between the world of literature and the very real struggles of American Indian communities, arguing for both an intrinsic and extrinsic relationship between the two. I will seek a literary criticism that emphasizes Native resistance movements against colonialism, confronts racism, discusses sovereignty and Native nationalism, seeks connections between literature and liberation struggles, and, finally, roots literature in land and culture. This criticism emphasizes unique Native worldviews, and political realities, searches for differences as often as similarities, and attempts to find Native literature's place in Indian country, rather than Native literature's place in the canon. (11)

When a criticism works to disrupt oppressive social relations, attempts are frequently made to diminish its potency by labeling the writer radical. However, given the conditions under which Native people continue to live, and given the ongoing colonialist assumptions of the academy, it might fairly be asked whether it is reasonable to expect an indigenous critic not to be radical: "There is certainly a history of research of indigenous peoples which continues to make indigenous students who encounter this history very angry" (Tuhiwai Smith 16). Furthermore, as this book suggests, all criticism is inherently political to the extent that it works for or against the existing social order. The perceived apolitical criticism is simply so perfectly in accord with the prevailing social order (an oppressive one in many respects) that it appears to function in absence of the political. With this in mind, Craig Womack refuses to abandon "essentialism" or to enter into the prevailing postmodern (*laissez faire*) skepticism over history and identity: "It is way too premature for Native scholars to deconstruct history [and identity] when we haven't yet constructed it" (3). Instead, he maintains that "a queer [and, by extension, an Indian] frame of reference causes one to see the world differently than a straight [or non-Native] one" (300). Womack proceeds as if Diana Fuss's "risk of essence" and Gayatri Spivak's "strategic essentialism" were worth the cost. More correctly, his position *vis-à-vis* essentialism would be similar to that outlined by Linda Tuhiwai Smith (Maori):

> The concept of essentialism is also discussed in different ways within the indigenous world. It is accepted as a term which is related to humanism and is seen therefore in the same way as the idea of authenticity. In this use of the word, claiming essential characteristics is as much strategic as anything else, because it has been about claiming human rights and indigenous rights. But the essence of a person is also discussed in relation to indigenous concepts of spirituality. (74)

Since Womack's *Red on Red* is one of the most powerful indigenist criticisms to date, it is also, as evident from Arnold Krupat's recent review of the book, disturbingly political.[20]

Anti-essentialist arguments against indigenous researchers, as also the silencing epithets "angry" and "radical," work to subvert efforts at eliminating oppression and ultimately to abrogate sovereignty claims. Thus, critics like Craig Womack and Gloria Bird consistently disregard the complaints of *laissez faire* criticism and focus their efforts instead on a community-centered criticism, one that inevitably enters into a concern for social and environmental matters. Recall that community includes "the 'wider community' of Creation itself" (Weaver, *That the People* xiii). Bird's discussion and performance of Native autobiography in "Breaking the Silence: Writing as Witness," for example, moves seamlessly from a recounting of Spokane and family traditions, into a discussion of the colonial construction of the indigenous image, and further into a discussion of the impact of uranium mining on her community: "I've come to the conclusion that the politics and social concerns that surround Native representation and existence are of primary importance to me as a writer and need to be addressed" (48). The concerns of an indigenist criticism, therefore, are far-ranging and move also into a global concern for indigenous peoples.

Robert Warrior suggests that such a move is undesirable because of the (assumed) tendency to ossify Indian existence:

> In Fourth World formulations exemplified in the work of Ward Churchill (Creek/Cherokee Métis) and M. Annette Jaimes (Juaneño/Yaqui), the radical and polemical call to understand American Indian culture (including literature) as a part of a global consciousness shared by all indigenous people in all periods of history [is] the central category.... Appeals to essentialized worldviews, though, always risk an ossifying of American Indian existence. Such a commitment to essentialized indigenous worldviews and consciousness, over the course of the decade, became a pervasive and almost requisite feature of American Indian critical writing. (*xvii*)

The commitment to "Fourth World formulations," however, is not limited to American Indian critical writing. Maori researcher Linda Tuhiwai Smith, for example, consistently makes connections with global indigenous theorists and researchers (132–33, 156–57). For her, the community-centered basis of Aboriginal epistemology (its orientation towards connectedness) implies such networking with other peoples and fields of endeavor. Moreover, Tuhiwai Smith asserts a politically instrumental form of intellectual sovereignty for indigenous peoples. She dismisses the efforts of indigenous researchers whose work is anti-indigenous and bases her answer to the question of the involvement of non-indigenous researchers in the indigenist project in terms of the impact such involvement will have on the indigenous community (184–85).

While answers to the question of non-indigenous involvement may vary, non-Native researchers nevertheless have *de facto* control over Native studies—in some cases, as with the land, they claim to have discovered it—by virtue of the fact that they occupy an inordinate number of positions (particularly tenured ones) in Native Studies departments. Tuhiwai Smith, however, proceeds as if intellectual sovereignty were a reality—making it, *ipso facto*, a reality—and as if academic control were an irrelevant matter in the larger, global struggle for indigenous sovereignty. She outlines some of the advances in indigenous legal rights made by international coalitions of indigenous peoples and points to further possibilities (Tuhiwai Smith 107–18). Note, however, that Andrew Jackson's willful disregard for U.S. Supreme Court rulings concerning the sovereignty of the Cherokees in Georgia and, more recently, Jean Chrétien's disregard for a Canadian Supreme Court decision concerning Native fisheries in New Brunswick suggest that colonial adherence to colonial law can only be expected insofar as the law sanctions colonialist imperatives.[21] Furthermore, the entire foundation of international law concerning indigenous peoples is in violation of itself. The doctrine of discovery, which must be postulated in order to support colonialist claims to usurped land, is medieval and racist in origin and violates contemporary human rights laws; but the doctrine continues to be the primary basis for the denial of indigenous rights. Treaties which uphold the international legitimacy of territorial claims asserted by colonizer states imply the sovereign status of indigenous nations, since treaties can only be forged between sovereign nations. Protection of colonial sovereignty, however, rests on a denial of sovereignty to indigenous people, a denial that can only be sustained by denying their humanity (in contravention of contemporary human rights law) and by simultaneously subverting colonial claims to territory which are legitimized through treaties with (implicitly sovereign) indigenous nations (Venne 8–10).

Since the Western legal system is so riddled with contradiction and so easily ignored where Native peoples are concerned, the legal system in and of itself cannot be expected to rectify injustices. Patricia Monture-Angus points out that the legal system has most frequently functioned as an instrument of injustice concerning indigenous peoples: "A decade or so ago, I believed that law was a (perhaps *the*) solution to the Aboriginal struggle for political freedom. Since then I have learned that there are many examples of law's complicity in the oppression of Aboriginal Peoples. Canadian laws established residential schools, outlawed ceremonies, denied women their birthright, and outlawed our forms of government" (*Journeying* 30). Furthermore, an indigenist criticism, and the indigenous research agenda of which it is a part, must consistently, and in accordance with indigenous theory, establish connections with other disciplines and with other indigenous peoples. As Tuhiwai Smith suggests, an indigenous research agenda will also involve a process of "reporting back" and "sharing knowledge" as means of "disseminating knowledge and of ensuring that research reaches the people who have helped make it" (15). As suggested earlier, however, reporting back should be a reciprocal process. That is, non-Native interest in Native culture, rather than assuming a voyeuristic and colonizing posture, should proceed from an interest in connecting non-Native peoples through indigenous cultures to a harmonized struggle for global survival. In answer to the question of non-indigenous involvement in the indigenous research agenda, then, non-Native people are, by virtue of their existence on this earth, already involved. Since the global indigenist project involves re-situating the earth's peoples *vis-à-vis* each other and their relationship with the earth, no peoples can be excluded from the movement.

Whispering in Shadows, the 2000 novel by Jeannette Armstrong (Okanagan), is an indigenist text that illustrates the importance of a global conscience and consciousness. The text immerses and implicates the reader in the present global crisis, in the economic and environmental devastation of the earth, which affects all people but affects indigenous communities particularly so. The reader of *Whispering in Shadows* must supply the connective tissue between the fragments of descriptive fact, dialogue, epistle, theory, etc., that comprise the story. The reader is thereby drawn into a realistic depiction of contemporary existence: a situation in which, no matter where we live, we have no choice but to eat, drink, and breathe poison. The reader is simultaneously, through this method, implicated in the devastation: "A deep and silent rage settles inside. A rage for all that she is somehow complicit in, simply by being" (184). The reader's inevitable complicity, however, implies a corresponding responsibility for action. Since the text establishes connections among indigenous peoples and global environmental and economic issues, and since it works to ameliorate conditions affecting the community, it thereby functions as indigenist art.

The protagonist of the novel is Penny, an undergraduate student at the University of British Columbia and, eventually, an avante garde visual artist. The Okanagan people offer copper and tobacco with their prayers, and in many respects Penny's life and her story are prayer and offering. Native people tend to be particularly affected by environmental catastrophes, in large part because of the tendency to locate uranium strip-mines and nuclear disposal facilities in close proximity to reserves and reservations.[22] As a result, Penny, like so many Native people (like so many people everywhere), gets cancer, another term for environmental poisoning. She dies after having spent her life struggling against the global insanity that is killing all of us—the poor may die first, but eventually everyone dies. The fragmented, self-oriented worldview that made its appearance on this continent just over five hundred years ago has now engulfed the world, and *Whispering in Shadows* paints a ruthlessly detailed picture of the results. The plot is relentlessly (but realistically) gloomy, immersing the reader in near-total hopelessness, but a tiny flame motif emerges as a vestige of hope in the novel. In one instance, Penny goes to Mexico, where she witnesses the devastation wrought by NAFTA among the Mayan people of the Chiapas region. While visiting one of the communities, she attends a traditional prayer service conducted by Mayan priests. Candles are lit in a small room and the priests begin chanting and praying. At one point, Penny notices that a light bulb overhead has begun swinging in a circle on its chain. She is transfixed by the inexplicable movement until her companion, a translator, motions her to concentrate instead on a tiny flame. Later, after the prayer service, one of the priests speaks to her through two translators, Mayan-Spanish and Spanish-English. The priest says quietly, "There is always light if we keep the flame in focus" (182).

Whispering in Shadows is much like that flame in the darkness. The novel functions as a tiny whisper among the deepening shadows that are engulfing our world. There is hope that its message will be heard, but there is a difficulty, a significant one: the dominant society has a long history of ignoring the ideas and concerns of Native people. To give just two examples, complaints over racist sports mascots have been ignored as have complaints over the non-Native colonization of Native literatures. Since these relatively minor issues have been persistently ignored there would seem to be little hope that indigenous concerns regarding the destruction of the earth and its peoples will be acknowledged. As readers and as human beings, we might simply give up hope and wait for death, but like the flame of *Whispering in Shadows,* a tiny hope remains: the colonizer may listen to calls for concern, if people of prestige—people like EuroAmerican and EuroCanadian professors of Native literature—were to relay the message. With this in mind, just as I would argue that Native literature is (in some respects) written for a non-Native audience, I would also argue that the non-indigenous critic is (in some respects) vitally important to an indigenist criticism.

Chapter Four
The Essential Métis: Being *Halfbreed*

> They came for our land, for what grew or could be grown on it, for the resources, and for our clean air and pure water. They stole these things from us ... and now ... they've come for the very last of our possessions; now they want our pride, our history, our spiritual traditions. They want to re-write and re-make these things to claim them for themselves.
>
> —Margo Thunderbird[1]

I begin this chapter with Margo Thunderbird's words because they allude to a tendency toward contradiction inherent in the colonial mentality. As Thunderbird implies, the appropriation of Native homelands, resources, and so forth, was justified (when it was justified) by denying the validity of Native culture. However, now that the appropriation appears to be nearing completion, now that untold billions of dollars have been acquired at the expense of Native people and their lands, these same cultures, previously invalidated, have themselves become valuable commodities susceptible to pillaging. In the context of the present chapter, Thunderbird's words are also important because they have proven so dangerously subject to extension. As Laurie Anne Whitt makes clear in "Cultural Imperialism and the Marketing of Native America," the oppressive strategies and faulty logic that enabled the appropriation and commodification of land, culture, and knowledge systems have more recently been deployed to permit the theft of indigenous cell lines, this time in the name of the Human Genome Diversity Project (HGDP) (156–57).[2]

Australian Aboriginal John Liddle concurs: "If the Vampire Project [the HGDP] goes ahead and patents are put on genetic material from Aboriginal people, this would be legalized theft. Over the last 200 years, non-Aboriginal people have taken our land, language, culture and health—even our children. Now they want to take the genetic material which makes us

Aboriginal people as well" (qtd. in Whitt 157). While scientists of the HGDP are busy collecting DNA samples from the blood of the earth's Aboriginal people, busy digging up that "wealth of information buried in their genes"(Roberts 1617), cultural and literary theorists are just as busy on another front, denying through complex argument that there is anything fundamentally Aboriginal at all. Such theorists, some of them mentioned in earlier chapters, maintain that "the Indian" is purely a social and cultural construct, that there is no thing, at least nothing physical or constitutive, that makes an Indian an Indian. The tendency toward contradiction in the colonial mentality is, it seems, also realized in conflicting pursuits among various fields of scholarship concerning Aboriginal people.

Arguments over what it is to be Indian have serious implications, extending well beyond the realm of the literary and theoretical. With respect to the Métis, for example, externally imposed determinations of identity have historically been used to exclude them from the benefits of both Native *and* Canadian life, and, at a more fundamental level, to deny the validity of Métis nationhood and culture altogether. Using a "logic of domination," which Whitt describes as "a structure of fallacious reasoning that seeks to justify subordination," Canada has consistently excluded Métis people by identifying them as either white or Indian, depending on which identification functioned best to exclude in the particular instance (159). On the academic front, however, several works on Maria Campbell's *Halfbreed* have focussed on the "liminality" or "hybridity" of the writer. Jodi Lundgren, for example, speaks of the autobiography in terms of syncreticity: "Hybrid by definition, Metis identity is *predicated* upon . . . cultural syncreticity. . . . Discourses of race divide people by suggesting that their differences are genetically entrenched. Cultural syncretism, conversely, emphasizes hybridity, and the Metis identity has always been syncretic. . . . Thus, Campbell's text is a site of cultural syncretism" (63, 66, 74). Agnes Grant suggests that Campbell is "preoccupied with telling *non-Natives* what it is like to be a Halfbreed" [sic] (126). Despite "indicat[ions in the autobiography] that Métis are not hopelessly caught between two cultures," Grant concludes that "Until [Campbell] wrote the book, 'halfbreed' was nothing but a common derogatory term; now it means a person living between two cultures" (126–28). Such arguments may appeal to an academic audience, but they simultaneously negate the Métis as a people by assigning them to a constructed between-ness.

While anti-essentialist critics may claim to counter such arguments, working against racially determined exclusions, they do so by denying the physical nature of identity (essence) altogether.[3] In either case, Métis people are denied a place in critical theory as they have been in history. Instead, they are confined to the space that is nowhere, placing them (historically and theoretically) at the crux of the contradiction unmasked by Margo Thunderchild's statement (above). That is, when advantageous, Métis "blood quantum" has been used against them in one direction; when advantageous, it has been used against them in exactly the opposite. Like their Indian relations, Métis experience with colonialist Canada has been much like playing with a child who changes the rules as he goes along, or she, always to his or her own benefit. This chapter on Maria Campbell's *Halfbreed*, then, while it begins with an extended discussion of essentialism prior to examining more specific features of the text, will seek ultimately to stop playing this colonizer's game. The chapter will argue that *Halfbreed* functions not only as an assertion of Métis identity, but that, in the Métis tradition, it *stories* survival in a most powerful and Métis way.[4]

* * * *

One of the bases for argument in this chapter is the First Nationhood of the Métis people. Such a statement immediately calls forth preliminary qualifications and explanation, especially in a Canadian context. For in Canada, "First Nation" is a sovereignty-affirming self-designation among Indians. "Indian," in turn, is a legal term for the people explicitly defined by the Indian Act, 1876, which states, "The term 'Indian' means *First*. Any male person of Indian blood reputed to belong to a particular band; *Secondly*. Any child of such person; *Thirdly*. Any woman who is or was lawfully married to such person." Beyond the overtly patriarchal nature of its definition, the Indian Act distinctly and purposefully excludes the Métis. It also excludes the Inuit.[5] Earlier manifestations of the Indian Act, however, were not as restrictive. For example, the 1850 Act for the Better Protection of the Lands and Property of the Indians included "All persons intermarried with any such Indians," as well as those "whose parents on either side were or are Indians." The subsequent 1859 Civilization of Indian Tribes Act of the Province of Canada suggested that "the term 'Indian' means only Indians or persons of Indian blood or intermarried with Indians, acknowledged as members of Indian Tribes or Bands residing upon lands. . . ." Intimations of Métis exclusion were already evident, but with the transfer of British imperial authority to Canada at Confederation (1867), the settler nation sought more overtly "to narrowly limit its responsibilities and costs," a trend in policy which has continued to this day (McNab, *Circles* 31).[6]

According to section 91 (24) of the Constitution Act, 1867, the Canadian government is responsible for "Indians and the lands reserved for Indians." Since the legal definition of "Indian" would, at the time, have been drawn from the 1859 Act, that responsibility should have included Métis people. Nevertheless, the new federal government acted without delay to radically reduce its constitutionally prescribed responsibility. The Métis—and women, as Winona Stevenson points out—were immediately targeted (67). Shortly after Confederation, an amendment to the existing Indian Act introduced new patriarchal limitations and an especially insidious form of racism: "Indian women marrying other than an Indian shall cease to be an Indian within the meaning of this Act, nor shall the children issue of such marriage be considered Indians." The definition was further tightened in 1876 by the Indian Act, which remains the primary document governing legal determinations of Indian identity in Canada. Although Métis (and Inuit) people were included in the Canada Act, 1982, and in Bill C-31, An Act to Amend the Indian Act, of 1985, no provision has yet been made to secure land rights and claims, nor is there a process to this day to address such title (McNab, *Circles* 33). The apparently liberal wording of contemporary acts and amendments has proven little more than liberal wording.[7]

Despite Canada's consistent efforts to exclude the Métis whenever possible, however, the historical record suggests that they were considered close relations by Indians. As Stevenson notes, early attempts by French authorities to assimilate the First Nations through intermarriage produced a new Aboriginal nation rather than a new French one:

> By the turn of the 16th century the 'Frenchification' [of Indians] program was announced a dismal failure. In far too many instances mixed families did not produce a sedentary farming population. French men preferred fur trading over farming and Aboriginal lifestyles over French, and Aboriginal women rejected the confining yoke that settlement life imposed. Colonial authorities were baffled by the resistance to settlement life and at their apparent 'blindness' towards the benefits of 'civilization.' (52)[8]

Lieutenant Governor Alexander Morris likewise discovered, during the negotiations of Treaty Three (1873), that Métis people in the Northwest Angle were considered relatives of Indians in the region. Mawedopenais, Chief of Fort Frances and principal negotiator for the Aboriginal signatories, made specific requests that his Métis relations be included in the treaty (Morris 50–51, 68–69).[9] Morris at first declined, insisting that the Métis must choose whether they would be Indian or white, that there would be no specific provisions for persons of mixed ancestry. However, negotiations had proven especially difficult for the Crown: "Recalling the negotiations, Morris said that the government had made two previous attempts before the successful third round; even so, it had taken 14 days of hard bargaining" (Dickason, *Canada's* 316). In closing the treaty negotiations, therefore, Mawedopenais was able to obtain the concession, as he displayed both his shrewdness as a diplomat and his flair for the dramatic. With a skillful blend of understatement and sarcasm, he presented a counterfeit silver medal, one of several which had been given to the Red River chiefs during negotiations there:

> I will now show you a medal that was given to those who made a treaty at Red River by the Commissioner. *He* said it was silver, but *I* do not think it is. I should be ashamed to carry it on my breast over my heart. I think it would disgrace the Queen, my mother, to wear her image on so base a metal as this. (Here the Chief held up the medal and struck it with the back of his knife. The result was anything but the 'true ring,' and made every man ashamed of the petty meanness that had been practised.) Let the medals you give us be of silver—medals that shall be worthy of the high position our Mother the Queen occupies. (Morris 74)

Morris expressed his dismay at the deception practiced by government officials, and Mawedopenais chose that moment to remind him of the assistance he had received from the Métis in securing a particularly difficult and strategic treaty. Morris agreed to pursue the matter, and, in this exceptional case, two Métis reserves (Rainy Lake Nos. 16A and 16D) were established by an 1875 adhesion to Treaty Three.[10] Indian negotiators habitually asked that their Métis relatives be included in treaties; however, with the exception of Treaty Three, the inclusions were either denied at the outset or later rendered ineffective: " . . . during the bargaining for Treaties Four and Six, the Indians requested that their 'cousins' be included. At first this was accepted . . . ; however, as a consequence of the Red River troubles, Ottawa changed its mind and amended the Indian Act in 1880, excluding 'half-breeds' from both the provisions of the Act as well as from treaties" (Dickason, *Canada's* 254).[11]

Note that the area covered by Treaty Three (also known as the Northwest Angle Treaty) was part of Rupert's Land, as were what are now the entire provinces of Manitoba and Saskatchewan. Furthermore, a portion of Treaty Three lands are in modern-day Manitoba. When Rupert's Land (ten times the land-base of what had then been "Canada") was sold by the Hudson's Bay Company to Canada in 1870, it became known as the

Northwest Territories. Once Treaty Three was secured, Canada assigned the "surrendered" lands to Manitoba. The move was vehemently contested by Ontario, most notably in the first Aboriginal rights case in Canada, *St. Catherine's Milling v. The Queen*. In other words, the Métis of Treaty Three should not be considered "Ontario" Métis, if a distinction is to be made, since the land relinquished was, at the time, part of the Northwest Territories, as was Maria Campbell's home (Dickason, *Canada's* 315–16; *Halfbreed* 9). That Mawedopenais had possession of a medal from Red River suggests that interaction between peoples of the two areas was frequent. Furthermore, as Jacqueline Peterson notes, " . . . there were several regional populations which converged at Red River after 1815 to become métis [and one of these] occurred during the eighteenth century a thousand miles to the east in the Great Lakes Region" (38). What is important to note for the present discussion, however, is that, from earliest times and throughout the treaty-making period, Indian and Métis people lived and acted as relatives.

Nevertheless, as Frantz Fanon points out, an inevitable consequence of colonization is the emergence of horizontal violence among a people:

> While the settler or the policeman has the right the live long day to strike the native, to insult him and to make him crawl to them, you will see the native reaching for his knife at the slightest hostile or aggressive glance cast on him by another native; for the last resort of the native is to defend his personality vis-à-vis his brother. . . . Thus collective autodestruction in a very concrete form is one of the ways in which the native's muscular tension is set free. All these patterns of conduct are those of the death reflex when faced with danger, a suicidal behavior which proves to the settler (whose existence and domination is by them all the more justified) that these men are not reasonable human beings. (54)

Fanon deals with the psychology of "collective autodestruction" with great subtlety, but the sociology is probably not so complex. Starvation precedes division, just as division precedes conquest. In other words, since colonization turns inward in the face of diminished resources, economic oppression is a precondition to colonization. Starvation proved a useful expedient in ensuring the signing of treaties and the removal of children into residential schools, and today economic deprivation continues to promote collective inertia among Aboriginal people.[12]

The Aboriginal Healing Foundation, for example, is an ostensibly generous allotment of funds recently set aside by the Canadian government for the purpose of buying a solution to massive social problems created via the residential school system.[13] Such healing, of course, cannot be purchased—

the wounds are immeasurably deep and pervasive—and the more likely outcome of the "Healing Fund" will be a deepening of divisions within the Native community. Predictably, funds are to be administered, after a complex and competitive application procedure, by government-appointed overseers. This allows the Canadian government to assume the role of benefactor, while its paternalism toward (and infantilizing of) the Native community, an orientation which fostered the establishment of residential schools in the first place, continues. More important, the federal government is able to obstruct unity among Native people as it has always done. Maria Campbell records a similar experience in the 1960s:

> Community Development, the organization that government had created to keep white radicals busy, suddenly became very threatened. Their objective had been to phase themselves out when Native people no longer needed them. Native people didn't need them anymore and said so. Suddenly their priority became survival. There were thousand-dollar-a-month jobs at stake if these Natives meant business. The Native leaders, whom Community Development had handpicked—and underestimated—would not be dictated to any more. Government, seeing the handwriting on the wall, phased out Community Development and gave us money. Not very much, just enough to divide us again. (*Halfbreed* 156)

Discord also occurred following the creation of Indian reserves, the membership of which was determined according to a restrictive and imposed definition of "Indian." Métis people often took up residence at the outskirts of the newly prescribed community. However, as food and provisions became scarce, animosity often developed between them and their relations. In some cases, a reserve community would ask the Department of Indian Affairs to remove their Métis relatives in order to alleviate shortages (McNab, "Metis" 72). As Campbell points out in *Halfbreed*, the division that accompanies deprivation also plagued radical movements of the 1960s among Native people: "The proposal for a federation was rejected by the Treaty Indians. They felt that the militant stand that would be taken by such an organization would jeopardize their Treaty rights. 'The Halfbreeds,' they said, 'have nothing to lose, so they can afford to be militant'" (155). Since economic isolation and dwindling resources continue to plague Native communities, it is not surprising that the exclusion of Métis people continues to be evident in some places.

Historical and legal realities notwithstanding, I wish to make the claim that the Métis are a First Nations people. My intent here is not to erase the distinction between Métis and Indians any more than I intend to erase the distinction between Cree and Ojibwe, or Haida and Tlingit people. To be sure, while Indians historically saw the Métis as relatives, they also saw them, as they did themselves, as a distinct people. Campbell makes the distinction clear:

> Then there were our Indian relatives on the nearby reserves. There was never much love lost between Indians and Halfbreeds. They were completely different from us—quiet when we were noisy, dignified even at dances and get-togethers. Indians were very passive—they would get angry at things done to them but would never fight back, whereas Halfbreeds were quick-tempered—quick to fight, but quick to forgive and forget. . . . However, their old people, our "Mushooms" (grandfathers) and "Kokums" (grandmothers) were good. They were prejudiced, but because we were kin they came to visit and our people treated them with respect. (26–27)

The national pride imbued with intertribal rivalry that characterizes LeAnne Howe's *Shell Shaker* and Richard Wagamese's *Keeper'N Me* is also evident here.[14] However, the idea that relatedness and distinctiveness can coexistent, a conception that characterizes Aboriginal discussions of self and community, is also evident. Cherokees (and people of other corn-based cultures) understand the notion in terms of the Corn-Mother: "The Creator's wisdom of unity in diversity—from the many, one—is evident in the ear of corn, where each kernel remains individual, yet plays its part in the whole" (Awiakta 243). As Gregory Cajete notes, the understanding is widespread among Native peoples:

> American Indians are a homogeneous, yet heterogeneous, people. Though this statement sounds paradoxical, it is valid from a mythological perspective. Indigenous people of the Americas share elementary ideas and cultural values whose symbolic meanings and archetypes are similarly interpreted from tribe to tribe. In spite of anthropological and archeological statements that American Indians are as different from one another culturally as Germans and Chinese, Indian people from the tip of South America to Alaska recognize their innate relatedness. As a whole, Indian people share guiding thoughts, elemental ideas, symbols, and metaphors that cannot be denied. (*Look* 137–38)

Distinctions that isolate into discrete categories—rigid, impermeable, and confining—are a habit of mind not characteristic of Aboriginal thought. The apparent inverse of such a habit, erasing the distinctions altogether, is simply an extension of the same tendency. Carried to its extreme, impermeable categorization leads to an infinite mass of indistinguishable categories, each divided ultimately out of distinction. At any rate, my intent is not to erase the distinctions between Métis and Indians, but rather to attribute to the Métis a firstness of nationhood, to speak of them in contradistinction to the Settler Nations—Canada, America, Mexico, and the like—which have consistently rejected any relationship with the First Nations.[15] By First Nation, then, I refer to the Métis connection to the land, to that which makes them Aboriginal people and grants them a firstness of nationhood which they share with the Inuit and with indigenous peoples outside Canada, where the term "First Nation" has most currency. As noted above, the defining of indigenous peoples has always held great importance for the Canadian government. The answer has determined the cost of its constitutionally framed responsibility, the size of the population for which they (in theory) hold Crown lands in trust, and the numbers with which they must (again, in theory) honor treaties. For this reason the Canadian government has used the question of indigeneity and its own carefully formulated (hence, legally binding in its own courts) answer to limit the extent of that responsibility. The definition formulated has, throughout the short history of Canada, been constructed so as to exclude as many people as possible.

Among cultural theorists, the defining of Native people has taken a different though no less dangerous path through tiresome discussions of essence. Essence is defined as "the invariable and fixed properties which define the 'whatness' of a given entity"; as "that which is most irreducible, unchanging, and therefore constitutive of a given person or thing" (Fuss *xi*, 2). Since, essence cannot be isolated and measured, there are believers and non-believers in its existence. Those who believe in essence are called (by others) essentialists; believers in the non-existence of essence are called anti-essentialists, or social constructionists. An essentialist would hold that there is an irreducible something that makes an Indian an Indian, that while there may be accidental differences among Indians—variations in height, weight, sex, tribal affiliation, etc.—there is nevertheless an irreducible something that defines (or, more correctly, constitutes) what it is to be Indian. Momaday's "memory in the blood" would be such a position, inferring that essence resides as memory in blood. Opponents to such a view reject claims to essence outright, maintaining that all categories, including *Indian*, are socially constructed. In other words, what makes an Indian an Indian is simply a set of cultural practices, socially determined to be Indian.

The discussion has huge implications. To accept essentialism, constructionists claim, is both naïve and dangerous. Naïve, because one rarely comes to the constructionist position without some level of graduate school training; dangerous, because historical atrocities can be attributed to essentialist assumptions. Nazis justified their genocidal practices by claiming an essential inferiority of Jews; Americans enslaved Africans, again, claiming an essential inferiority of the enslaved. The attempts at exterminating indigenous peoples of the Americas and the wholesale theft of their homelands has likewise been justified by positing their essential inferiority *vis-à-vis* all things European. In each case, the atrocity, it is said, was predicated on essentialist assumptions and would not have occurred, presumably, had the perpetrators been social constructionists. Social constructionists argue that it is this belief in the fundamental nature (race) of various peoples that is at the root of racism. The antidote to such oppression, they argue, is to deny essence altogether, because, it is suggested, racism cannot exist without essentialism. The essentialist position is for this reason extremely unpopular among academics. Nevertheless, as suggested in Chapter Three, it is a position often assumed by Native scholars. Apparently, from beyond the colonizer's gaze, the matter is not so simple. Assurances from academics that eliminating essentialism will necessarily eliminate racism are not very convincing, because the theory comes after—it does not create—the fact. Furthermore, as Jace Weaver points out, the liberation promised by such theories never moves beyond academic (or even disciplinary) walls: "[Post-colonialism's] error, like that of postmodernism, is that it mistakes having deconstructed something theoretically for having displaced it politically" (14–15).

There is, however, a more insidious side to the social constructionist position, especially with respect to Indians. For abandoning essence means abandoning any and all claims to the little that remains after the ravages of colonialism. The constructionist position inherently undermines any claim to sovereignty, since, within this framework, arguments for sovereignty cannot be made without recourse to an essentialist position. That is, in order to argue that Indians have sovereignty over land, resource, or culture (including literature), one must maintain that there is something more tangible than an idea socially construed that makes an Indian an Indian. Since abandoning essence, then, entails abandoning claims to sovereignty, it is not hard to see why Indian scholars have, when pressed to choose, favored essentialism. It is also not hard to see that if social constructionist arguments did somehow manage to move beyond academic walls, they would more quickly eradicate Indian claims to sovereignty than eradicate racism. For this reason, the fact that non-Native theorists have continued to promote anti-essentialism among Indians—for their own good, as it were—becomes slightly suspect. Jace Weaver is more forthright in his assessment of the theoretical climate: "[I]t is no coincidence that just as the peoples of the Two-Thirds World begin to find their voices and assert their own agency and subjectivity, postmodernism proclaims the end of subjectivity" (14).

Expositors of racism have not overlooked the connection between sovereignty and essence, even when the discourse is more populist than academic. Mel Smith (author of *Our Home or Native Land?*) and Tom Flanagan (author of *First Nations? Second Thoughts*), for example, have argued (to popular acclaim) that Canadian Aboriginal policy is flawed because it privileges a certain group and is therefore racist.[16] These writers contend that "we are all equal," and that to continue to provide treaty-guaranteed benefits to Native people is racist, not to mention fiscally irresponsible. Patricia Monture-Angus makes it clear that "equality" for such "thinkers" only ever becomes an issue when their heavily privileged position is threatened in some way: "Canadian definitions of legal equality which rely on the rule of law often guarantee only rights of sameness. This thinking, when extended to the political realm, casts Aboriginal difference as a form of special rights. The argument is then constructed that no one deserves special treatment and rights. This reasoning must be understood for what it is—the colonial mentality" (*Journeying* 32). As Monture-Angus demonstrates, the position is both historically short-sighted and legally and logically flawed. Nevertheless, this idea of equality is one of the governing principles of the Canadian (Reform) Alliance Party, a group with questionable links to racist organizations, which served as the official opposition in Canadian Parliament. More to the point, however, this brand of equality requires the assumption that there is no tangible (essential) link between contemporary Native people and their ancestors, an assumption not unlike that of social constructionists.

Nevertheless, it is important to note that difficulties also arise with the essentialist position. While essentialism may in some respects protect claims to sovereignty, it is also responsible for externally imposed pan-Indianism.[17] The idea that all Indians are the same, that there is some certain thing that all Indians are, and that the failure to live up to that something makes one somehow less Indian, is a form of essentialist thinking that denies the multifarious ways of being and the distinct nationalities that have always existed among indigenous people. This manner of thinking gives rise to the popular notion that "real" Indians are only ever nineteenth-century Plains people, beaded and ponied. Never allowed from this perspective is any post-nineteenth-century adaptation, and always overlooked, as Maria Campbell points out in an interview with Hartmut Lutz and Konrad Gross, is that beads and ponies were European imports as much as English language and automobiles: "I also believe that culture constantly changes. It doesn't stay in one place. We didn't have horses, then the horse came, and became a part of our tradition. So much so, that we have horse spirits and horse dances. We didn't have beads. The beads came, they're now a part of our culture" (46). Also overlooked is that if a pan-Indian practice does exist, it probably involves this tendency to adapt to and relate with a shifting environment—physical, cultural, political, spiritual. Since this form of essentialism (that all Indians are x and not y) is vehemently argued against by Indian scholars, unquestioned essentialism is not acceptable either.

Diana Fuss, to whom the present discussion owes some debt, has worked out a compromise to the problem. As mentioned in the Chapter Three, she suggests that it is not possible *not* to be essentialist. Constructionism simply makes the essentialism more difficult to locate; it "operates as a more sophisticated form of essentialism" (*xii*). Fuss contends quite convincingly that we can only then speak of *essentialisms,* and the better question is not whether a text is essentialist or not, but rather, if it is essentialist, how and why is that the case (*xi-xii*). This seems a compelling position. We would then deem the essentialism among Native people to be politically motivated (hence, justified), and arguments for indigenous control of the literature, essentialist, but likewise well motivated. The difficulty is that even with such a compromise we are caught playing the colonizer's game, subject to his rules. According to the terms of the compromise, arguments for sovereignty are only condescendingly accepted. That is, arguments for sovereignty may be accepted, but they are taken as naïve by the constructionist, who "truly" understands the sophisticated terms and irresolute nature of the debate. Sovereignty under the compromise is only granted (by someone else) as a matter of convenience or conscience rather than as a matter of fundamental principle.

Such discussions have direct bearing on the Métis. As mentioned, theories of "mixed-bloodedness" have frequently discussed Métis people in terms of hybridity. Robert Young points out that hybridity comes in several varieties. For our purposes, it is only necessary to mention three. First, the classical nineteenth-century (when the term "hybrid" was coined) racial theory variety emphasized "the prior existence of pure, fixed and separate antecedents" (25). The essentialism in this version is easy to locate: the focus is on the purity and separateness of Indian and white people. A second variety, the *amalgamation* thesis, focuses more on the hybrid offspring of "full-blooded" parents, claiming that "all humans can interbreed prolifically and in an unlimited way; sometimes accompanied by the 'melting-pot' notion that the mixing of people produces a new mixed race, with merged but distinct new physical and moral characteristics" (18). The third variety, a negative reading of the amalgamation thesis, claims that miscegenation creates "a mongrel group that makes up a 'raceless chaos,' merely a corruption of the originals, degenerate and degraded, threatening to subvert the vigour and virtue of the pure races with which they come into contact" (18). Interestingly, it is this third variety which has proven most attractive to contemporary theorists. Following Bakhtin, who moved the discussion into the realm of language (more correctly, the realm of the utterance), Derrida, de Man, Bhabha, and others have emphasized the ironic unmasking of essentialism contained in this most detestable reading (the third version) of hybridity. For, if hybridity creates an infinite instability of forms, a "raceless chaos," such that the stable (the racially pure) becomes indistinguishable from the unstable (the "mixed blood"), then the categorization of form (racism) becomes infinitely impossible (20–24).

This version has been developed to a level of great complexity by certain Black cultural theorists. It has also been advanced by "mixed-blood" Ojibwe theorist Gerald Vizenor, who focusses on the "loosen[ing of] . . . seams in the shrouds of identities" which Aboriginal hybrids enact ("Crows Written" 101). In the same vein, Stuart Hall claims: " . . . colonisation so refigured the terrain that, ever since, the very idea of a world of separate identities, of isolated or separable and self-sufficient cultures and economies, has been obliged to yield to a variety of paradigms designed to capture these different but related forms of relationship, interconnection and discontinuity" (258). However, as Young points out, even when the emphasis is on the moments of ironic reversal, hybridity of any variety necessarily rests on—as in nineteenth-century racial theory—an assumption of "the prior existence of pure, fixed and separate antecedents." Discordant logic and lofty declarations of anti-racism notwithstanding, the essentialism in contemporary hybridity theory is simply (as Fuss also contends) displaced and made more difficult to locate: "Today it is common to claim that in such matters we have moved from biologism and scientism to the safety of culturalism, that we have created distance and surety by the very act of the critique of essentialism and the demonstration of its impossibility: but that shift has not been so absolute, for the racial was always cultural, the essential never unequivocal" (Young 27). The extreme denial of distinctions offered by hybridity theory, therefore, is simply an extension of the same habit of mind that so rigidly constructed the distinctions in the first place. Furthermore, as Jace Weaver insists (noted earlier), the experience of Native existence is somehow grounded regardless of theoretical postulations to the contrary:

"And certain genuine consequences flow from those accidents of birth and culture" ("I-Hermeneutics" 14).

Speaking at the "Women in View" festival in Vancouver, Maria Campbell discussed her own experience of being: "Sometimes it seems I've spent my whole life dealing with racism. As an aboriginal woman in Canada it's part of our daily life" ("Strategies" 7). Campbell here points to something that the whole discussion of essentialism misses entirely. Her experience of racism was (is) not mitigated because she is Métis, or a "hybrid" person, or not "fully" an Indian in essence; but neither is it mitigated because the "social construction" of her identity combines aspects of both Native and non-Native culture. Racists do not ask a person's blood quantum and adjust their hatred accordingly; neither is the experience less devastating if one recognizes (in a constructionist vein) that it is merely the deferred sign of her being that is being oppressed and dispossessed. Essentialism is not the source of racism, and the suggestion that stamping out essentialism will somehow stamp out racism must finally be understood as ludicrous. Rather, it is the fundamental failure of the Settler Nations to acknowledge (the sovereignty and firstness of) the First Nations that is the source of racism in this hemisphere. This failure to acknowledge is also responsible for a failure to acknowledge Aboriginal thought systems and the obvious answers they might provide.

So-called "ethnocritical" approaches to Native literature, for example, while they seem to acknowledge indigenous thought, nevertheless imply an outright rejection of alternative epistemologies. The first step towards any acceptance of indigenous thought in approaches to indigenous literature would have to be a recognition and acceptance of the "ethno-" status—that is, the socio-cultural situatedness—of Western literary criticism. As Joe Kincheloe and Ladislaus Semali point out (with specific but generalizable reference to scientific knowledge), Western knowledge is "a local knowledge system that denies its locality, seeking to produce not local but translocal knowledge" (28). They further suggest that "the denigration of indigenous knowledge cannot be separated from the oppression of indigenous peoples" (29). Western knowledge, like all knowledge systems, is situated in a specific social context, the product of a certain culture. However, contemporary socio-political realities are such that indigenous knowledge systems are subjugated and Western knowledge is in a position to mis-recognize (and cause to be mis-recognized) its own situatedness as universal.

Speaking of the tendency in various fields of Western knowledge to undertake "ethno-" studies, Kincheloe and Semali suggest that in such cases the Western knowledge system is taken as the non-ethnic default against which all other systems of knowledge are perceived as culturally bound. The indigenous source for the ethno-knowledge (in this case, ethno-criticism) is valued only insofar as it can add, in some way, to the default Western view and to the existing Western knowledge base (21). That is, certain forms of dominant criticism explore and map indigenous literature and aesthetics for that which can be added to Western criticism and established understandings of literature, rather than looking for intrinsic merit (even vital contemporary importance) in indigenous literature and approaches to literature. To give an example, it would be possible, in an ethnocritical spirit, to force an Aboriginal theory of being into the Western paradigm, to cast some aspect of indigenous knowledge into the essentialist/constructionist debate. We could integrate the Aboriginal principle of balance into the discussion, saying that either essentialism must be balanced so as to avoid racism or constructionism must be balanced so as not to become anti-sovereigntist. However, as Semali and Kincheloe make clear, if anything is socially constructed, it is the idea that the only way of looking at identity or any other issue is through a Western paradigm. Since the whole argument (essentialism vs. constructionism) is only relevant within a Western paradigm, and since indigenous theory comes equipped with its own convincing and workable model for discussions of Indian identity, attempts to look at Indian identity through a Western lens are superfluous at the outset. The need for Aboriginal theory is nowhere more obvious than in discussions of Native identity; for what is needed is an indigenous theory of being—a theory implied by indigenous theories of language.

* * * *

Western understandings of being and language, as discussed in Chapter Two, simultaneously emphasize and isolate the individual—from the community, the land, and the Creator. In Aboriginal thought, on the other hand, language is understood as sacred, alive, and inherently connective. As suggested in the previous chapter, the process-centered nature of indigenous thought is implied in the verbal orientation of indigenous languages, which "unlike English, [are] language[s] of action, motion, life. The world [they] describe . . . lives, moves, does. This is fundamental to the way of thought, as all language is for each group of people raised to speak it from the first" (Geise).[18] Jeanette Armstrong points out in "Land Speaking" that indigenous languages spring from the earth:

> As I understand it from my Okanagan ancestors, language was given to us by the land we live within. . . . It is said in Okanagan that the land

constantly speaks. It is constantly communicating. Not to learn its language is to die. . . . The language spoken by the land, which is interpreted by the Okanagan into words, carries parts of its ongoing reality. The land as language surrounds us completely, just like the physical reality of it surrounds us. Within that vast speaking, both externally and internally, we as human beings are an inextricable part—though a minute part—of the land language.

In this sense, all indigenous peoples' languages are generated by a precise geography and arise from it. Over time and many generations of their people, it is their distinctive interaction with a precise geography which forms the way indigenous language is shaped and subsequently how the world is viewed, approached, and expressed verbally by its speakers. (175–79)

Armstrong, here, discusses something far more complex than that which in English is termed *language*. Among the insights shared, Armstrong speaks of living *within* the land. If the land is sacred, in that life only ever springs from it, then everything that lives must be sacred to some extent, since everything that lives is connected to the land; and the principle of connectedness, which binds all that is, is sacredness itself. It follows, then, that to live within the land is an experience of the sacred. It is an experience of the relentless connectedness of our existence in the vastness which surrounds, permeates, and constitutes us. Willie Ermine calls this experience *mamatowisowin*: " . . . the capacity to connect to the life force that makes anything and everything possible" (110).[19] That primal life force, which Armstrong identifies as "Land Speaking," is called in Cree *muntou* (or *manitou*). Ermine describes *muntou* as an immanence: "Aboriginal people found a wholeness that permeated inwardness and that also extended into the outer space. Their fundamental insight was that all existence was connected and that the whole enmeshed the being in its inclusiveness. . . . It is a mysterious force that connects the totality of existence—the forms, energies, or concepts that constitute the outer and inner worlds" (103). Armstrong suggests that in speaking her ancestral language she enters (inextricably, though minutely) into the vast and eternal Land Speaking. She is physically rooted in the land, in that everything of which she is physically made ultimately comes from, returns to, and cannot exist without it; and through her language, the speaking of her language, she *experiences* her rootedness in the Land and its Speaking. As such, both her physical being and her speaking existence are rooted in the earth; both are impossible to conceive without the prior existence of Land Speaking.

The discussion encounters difficulties when rendered in English. First, *being* and *existence* are somewhat synonymous in English and trip over each other in attempts to tease them apart. That is probably as it should be, since it is not possible to have entity without existence, or vice versa. However, English can *conceive* of existence and being in isolation. Jeanette Armstrong discusses this difficulty with reference to the word *dog* in English and the Okanagan word *kekwep*. She describes the Okanagan word for dog as "an experience," an occurrence of being, whereas in English the word evokes a disembodied and decontextualized concept. This verbal-rootedness of the Okanagan is, as mentioned above, evident in most Aboriginal languages. A dog concept in English is conceivable in isolation from any actual existence. As Armstrong notes: "It must be a frightful experience to be a dog in English" (190). Likewise, the separation I have forced (above) between spoken and physical realities is artificial and only conceivable within certain realities. Ermine's suggestion that "a mysterious force . . . connects the totality of existence—the forms, energies, or concepts that constitute the outer and inner worlds" infers a reality in which the principle of connectedness infuses *even* the spoken and conceptual realms and binds them to the physical. Therefore, to discuss the physical and spoken as if they were separable is a distinctly Western manner of speaking, and the suggestion I am working towards, that language has the capacity to root the being within the land, is a banal claim from within an Aboriginal framework.

Again, Land Speaking is Armstrong's term for the wholeness that connects and infuses all that is, "the life force that makes anything and everything possible" (Ermine 110). Our own being-speaking is a (minute) part of that vastness, and since it emanates from and has the capacity to root us within the land, language is sacred. As Armstrong points out, language (which comes from the earth) shapes the way the world is viewed, approached, and expressed. It is that through which we understand, communicate, and interact with the sacred wholeness that encompasses and constitutes us. However, present-day "standard" English will immerse its speakers in a certain reality, a reality radically different from that of indigenous languages and one that tends toward a conceptual disembodiment and decontextualization. Willie Ermine also comments on the diverse realities which get realized in incompatible epistemological systems (worldviews). He urges further exploration of Aboriginal languages and cultures for the fundamentally important understandings inherent in their lexicons and practices (104). Based on his fieldwork with the Hopi Indians of New Mexico, Benjamin Whorf also notes the existence of "separate realities" springing from a particular people's language (215–18).

Given the existence of such radically "separate realities," and in order to prevent a colonial reality from impinging on the indigenous, the Aboriginal writer in English must constantly search for "new ways to circumvent [its] invasive imperialism upon [her] tongue" (Armstrong, "Land Speaking" 194). That is to say, the Aboriginal writer must find some way of speaking an Indian reality through English (192). Maria Campbell calls this re-invention of English "putting the Mother back," the Mother being the land. In her interview with Hartmut Lutz and Conrad Gross, Campbell recalls the words of an Elder to whom she had complained that the English language was manipulating her. His response was straightforward: "[W]hy you have trouble with the English language, it's because the language has no Mother. This language lost its Mother a long time ago, and what you have to do is, put the Mother back in the language" (51). Since the experience of rootedness in the earth comes through language, the difficulty is more than a strictly stylistic or semantic one. Our speaking determines our conception of and our connection to the Land. It determines, moreover, whether the profundity and pervasiveness of that connection will even be conceivable. The language poetry quoted in the introduction, for example, while an extreme manifestation, exemplifies the widespread fracture between and among words, concepts, and reality which began in the medieval period. From such a viewpoint, connection to the land is inconceivable.

Campbell and Armstrong both cite Rez English as an infusion of Aboriginal reality through English.[20] Such infusions enable existence to be rooted within the Land Speaking. However, "Standard" English, like the Settler Nations from which it emanates, is spoken in isolation from the greater Land Speaking. Since their languages have yet to become part of the Land Speaking, the Settler Nations have also yet to become rooted within the land. A Settler language (or Nation) can only become part of the Land Speaking by connecting to and relating with the speaking and being of the First Nations; for the First Nations and their speaking are (and have always been) part of the Land. The Settler Nations, conversely, have conceived of their existence in isolation from the Land Speaking—as if that were possible—just as their linguists have conceived of language in isolation from the speaking of it. A language, however, cannot exist in isolation from the speaking (writing) or hearing (reading) of it—its being only *is* in its existing. Neither can a people exist in isolation from the Land Speaking that surrounds and constitutes them. Nevertheless, it is possible to conceive of language in isolation from its speaking, and it is likewise possible to conceive of human existence and nationhood in isolation from the Land Speaking. This is what makes a Settler Nation possible, and is also why I have said that America (like Canada) is only an idea. The Settler Nations are ideas without roots, conceptions of nationhood in isolation, which is a dangerous way to live. As Armstrong

The Essential Métis   127

notes: "Not to learn [the land's] language is to die" ("Land Speaking" 176). Given that the constructionist position holds consciousness to be structured by language, the position may not seem incompatible with the present discussion. Note, however, that from the constructionist view, language is purely symbolic and, therefore, ultimately incapable of connection to the land. This is not to say that particular "constuctionist" theories are entirely unimportant. Rather, any use of such theories—as inferred by the previous chapter—must be from within an indigenist framework since constructionism is incapable of connection to the land in and of itself. Such an infusion of Western theory with an Aboriginal worldview is not unlike developments in Rez English.

The Métis Nation, according to this view, is a First Nation. The Métis have always lived in relation to—very close to, respectful of, and connected with—the Land and its People. Métis languages (whether Rez English, Rez French, Michif, Cree, Ojibwe, or otherwise) have always functioned to bind the speaker to the Land Speaking. Michif, incidentally, is neither a pidgin nor a Creole, but, as Olive Dickason points out, a rare example of a truly mixed language: "Its Cree and French components are correctly used, which means that those who created it must have been fully bilingual. Michif has been called the 'nec plus ultra' of contact languages" (*Canada's* 146). John C. Crawford also notes its exceptional nature among the world's languages:

> Michif is . . . significant in itself for three reasons: it is an important part of the development of language in the métis tradition; in its nature and by implication in its development it is unusual if not unique among the world's languages; and in the range of métis linguistic phenomena it is near the Indian end of a continuum ranging from the most clearly Indian to simply French. (231)

Michif, like its speakers, is inherently connected to the land that gives it being. The important point is that, whatever the Métis language, it is an Aboriginal one because it is a speaking of language within the Land Speaking. Furthermore, Métis existence is an experience of Aboriginal being (connectedness) within the land. In other words, the Métis are a First Nations people.

It is possible, however, to be Métis and not live within the land. It is possible for a Native person of any "blood quantum" to live in isolation from the land and community, in other words, to "act white."[21] This is what assimilationist policies and practices have been designed to achieve. It is also possible for a Native person to "*act* Native"—to flaunt his or her Indian identity, acquire all the cultural trappings, learn the language, practice "traditional" spirituality, and so forth—in such a way that it is strictly for personal gain. This marketing of Indian identity has led Elizabeth Cook-Lynn and others to condemn urban mixed-bloods, among whom the practice seems especially prevalent ("American Indian Intellectualism" 124–26). That the practice is so self-absorbed and detached from community interests immediately suggests that the actor is not *living as* a Native person, whatever the blood quantum or birthplace and no matter how convincing the performance. Living as a Native person has consequences, as Jace Weaver notes, which extend infinitely beyond the self ("I-Hermeneutics" 14). Living as a Native person involves living within the Land, relating to the sacred wholeness that encompasses all that is, of which the self is but a minute part. Explorations of indigenous tradition within this framework are community-interested, as opposed to self-interested. That is, the language is restored so that the inherent understandings of living within the Land can be recovered and enhanced, and traditional spiritual practices are renewed for the healing and education of the community, not for the power, prestige, or profit of the individual. Similarly, from within a community-interested framework, explorations of *non*-Native practices seek to infuse the particular practice with an Aboriginal worldview, in order that it may be adapted to the needs of the community. This is something at which the Métis have historically been adept, and Maria Campbell's *Halfbreed* is one such fusion.

* * * *

In the introduction to her autobiography, Maria Campbell writes of searching for the happiness, peace, and beauty she had known as a child. She speaks of returning to her childhood home in an attempt to recover that sense of belonging but, finding the place grown over and sadly changed, she was forced to the realization that "if [she] was to know peace [she] would have to search within [her]self" (7–8).[22] This realization may have engendered the autobiographical urge that produced a national bestseller, but when Campbell began writing she was thinking only in terms of her survival. She was without food or money and was, as she notes in an interview with Hartmut Lutz and Konrad Gross, on the verge of being made homeless (56). She considered a return to prostitution because she had no other option, but realized that such a move would inevitably lead back to drug use. In order to survive the moment, Campbell needed to speak with someone, but she found herself without even the luxury of a person to listen. It was from this sense of absolute hopelessness and frustration that the over two thousand pages of original manuscript emerged (Lutz 42). Campbell had no way of knowing, however, that in plunging into the depths of her being and recording what she found, she would emerge with seeds of survival for her people. It was very much an unintended result that her work became part of the movement into literature of a timeless impulse to story survival.

Campbell has called *Halfbreed* a first song. More correctly, she has called the movement in storytelling, of which *Halfbreed* is part, "our first song." She used the term in responding to criticisms that, in depicting the disquieting aspects of her earlier years, the book perpetuates existing stereotypes of Native people: " . . . when you are oppressed, and when you are trying to be born again, when you are trying to reclaim, you have to go through all of the pain. That's the first thing that comes out, and we have to deal with that. That's our first song" ("Strategies" 9). I would like to speak of the text in those terms, as first song, and to elaborate on the significance of such a claim. For while *Halfbreed* is an autobiography, which, as noted in Chapter Two, is conventionally deemed a distinctly Western story form, it is also part of something much greater. It functions as a grand and early voice in an unfolding chorus (sometimes called Aboriginal literature) which is telling—and discovering as it tells—the story of what happened in this hemisphere over the past five hundred years and why. *Halfbreed*'s status as a bestseller makes it especially important as a part of this movement, not *because* it was a bestseller but because it announced to Native people the possibility for the dissemination of story to a much wider community. Interest in Native literature in the Canadian publishing industry, however, was very short-lived, as Greg Young-Ing notes: "Despite all it has to offer, Aboriginal literature continues to be discriminated against in the Canadian publishing industry. Larger Canadian publishing houses will publish a novel by a recognized author like W.P. Kinsella, which mocks life on the Hobema Reserve, before they will publish books by Aboriginal authors" (184).

The burgeoning interest in Aboriginal literature in Canada, which began in the late-sixties, had tapered off by the mid-seventies. At that time, the novelty value of Aboriginal writing subsided and a colonial publishing industry turned its attention back to the sound of its own voice. This in large part accounts for the fact that, despite having authored a bestseller, Campbell's subsequent works have only been published by small presses. The re-issue of *Halfbreed* itself was picked up in paperback by Goodread Biographies, rather than the more prestigious McClelland and Stewart, publisher of the original. McClelland and Stewart authors include Margaret Atwood, Robertson Davies, Guy Vanderhaeghe, Alice Munro,

Michael Ondaatje, and Jack Hodgins. The entry of Aboriginal names to the list, however, has been infrequent and brief. As Young-Ing correctly observes, Native writers can rely only on Aboriginal publishers to accurately and consistently communicate their ideas in their own voice (185–87). Regardless, the movement in Native storytelling, of which *Halfbreed* was an early part, is not one that seeks to carve a niche for Native people in the mainstream publishing industry. Rather, it is a community-interested song of survival.

Campbell, for instance, has never identified herself as a writer *per se*, but as a storyteller, which she defines as a community worker, a healer and facilitator, who happens to use writing as one of her tools (Lutz 41–42). Neither has Campbell ever written out of a desire to be a writer of fine literature: "When I say I don't write to create anything, I really mean that. I wish sometimes that I had the luxury of just staying home and creating beautiful things" ("Strategies" 7–8). Instead, it was first her need to survive, and then her longing to connect her own struggle to that of the community, that drove her to autobiography. In this, she has been preeminently successful, which makes Agnes Grant's observation, that "The ultimate irony is that [Campbell's] book has never been taken seriously as literature," entirely beside the point (128). The goal of this movement in storytelling has never been to be "taken seriously as literature" by the arbiters of greatness (although that would have been nice). Its goal has been utterly more serious. It has been to connect with the greater struggle for survival, a struggle that is beginning to encompass all the peoples of the earth, including those who so flippantly discount Native literature.

The traditional function of storytelling is multifarious, encompassing education, ecology, healing, entertainment, history, sociology, and so much more, always in the interests of community survival and cohesion. *Halfbreed* enacts that ancient storytelling function within a new framework, that of autobiographical literature. This allows the text to function as a Métis text in two senses: it is written by a writer who happens to be Métis, and, what is far more important, it fuses a non-Native practice with an Aboriginal worldview. It enacts the fusion so completely that it is possible to say that Campbell is experiencing what Ermine calls *mamatowisowin*. That is, she is tapping into the force of connectedness discussed earlier: *muntou* or Land Speaking. To borrow from Ermine yet again: "*Mamatowisowin* is a capacity to tap the creative force of the inner space by the use of all the faculties that constitute our being—it is to exercise inwardness.... It is through dreams that the gifted in our Aboriginal communities 'create' experience for the benefit of the community through the capacity inherent in *mamatowisowin*" (104–08). In conversation with Lutz, Campbell recalls how she dreamed the voices of Grandmothers advising her to listen, that she would be cared for if she did, and that she would work with writers, painters, and singers (53). Not long afterwards, she wrote her autobiography; and within weeks and quite by "accident," the book was picked up by McClelland and Stewart. The dream had been accurate in its prediction of Campbell's creation of an "experience for the benefit of the community."

Just as *Halfbreed* is a Métis text in two senses, so too is it an educational text in two ways. It is an education in story, in the traditional sense, but it is also a story of education, the story of how the school as institution works to determine who we are and what we will become. Campbell's first experience with formal education was in a residential school. Much has and remains to be said about the residential school system, which in Canada was enforced by a coalition of church and state. The alliance was so "successful" that very few Native people in Canada remain untouched by this forcible confinement of generations of children.[23] Although the Canadian government has been very strict and exclusive in its definition of Indians for legal and treaty purposes, it was not nearly as careful when it came to residential school attendance. Nicholas Flood Davin's 1879 *Report on Industrial Schools for Indians and Half-Breeds*, which became the justification and policy statement for residential school incarceration, defines indigeneity quite broadly, suggesting that the exclusion of Métis people in contemporary acts and amendments was more a matter of convenience than conviction.[24] A much more expansive definition of "Indian" was employed when it came to mandating residential school attendance. However, Maria Campbell notes that the children of her community were not permitted to attend school at all until 1951. They were excluded from residential schools because they were not "Indian," and since their parents were not deed-holding land owners and did not pay property taxes, neither were they permitted in schools for white children (Lutz 51). This recalls David McNab's statement that the "federal government's views on the Metis . . . cannot really be dignified by the term policy" ("Metis" 67).

In spite of government interference and inconsistency, the Métis have always placed a high value on education. Louis Riel had been a promising student in the formal sense and was sent to Montreal as a young man to train for the priesthood and later for the legal profession. Gabriel Dumont was not formally educated but spoke six languages. Education was likewise important to Campbell's family as recorded in *Halfbreed*, although the family was divided as to whether Maria's education should be European or traditional. Her mother and grandmother (Grannie Dubuque) wished her to be educated in the European manner, as they had been, and arranged to have her sent to a residential school when she was seven (44). Campbell says very little in the autobiography about her residential school experience, beyond stating that it was horrible, terrifying, and that the town school was "Heaven compared to the Residential School" (46). Her reticence says a great deal, especially given that the town school experience she describes is anything but pleasant.

Cheechum, Campbell's great-grandmother, and her father are very much opposed to a residential school education, but since her mother and Grannie Dubuque had both grown up in convents, they had ingested the idea that Western education is superior. The dispute here runs deeper than a preference for a particular mode of schooling; for the effects of the residential school system are disturbingly manifested in Campbell's mother and Grannie Dubuque. Her mother, for example, reads Shakespeare, Dickens, and Longfellow to her children from a collection of books she had received from her own father (Pierre Dubuque), a Frenchman from Iowa. Although the stories ignite Maria's imagination and become excellent fodder for childhood play-acting, they also suggest her mother's veneration of European culture and education over Aboriginal. Pierre Dubuque had wanted his daughter (Maria's mother) to marry "a gentleman" and was quite disappointed to find she had married a Métis man (17–18). The preference Campbell's mother gives to European story and the extravagance she reserves for Grannie Dubuque's visits suggest that at some level she considers her father's disappointment warranted (43–44).

Grannie Dubuque, for her part, visits infrequently during Campbell's childhood, but when she comes she brings with her boxes of goodies, toys, linens, and fine fashion for her daughter's family. Her style and bearing exude European cultural refinement: "She wore nice silk dresses trimmed with white lace and a white lacey handkerchief tucked into her belt. She also wore a small hat with a veil, gloves, and shoes with heels while carrying a real handbag. She was the only woman I remember in my childhood who used face powder and perfume" (43). Although Maria is awestruck by the finery and displays characteristic reticence with respect to the visits— traditional storytellers generally do not demean their listeners by overtly making all the connections and extrapolations for them—the picture she presents is something of a caricature of Western refinement. Grannie Dubuque obtains her "wealth" working as a domestic servant, and the gifts she brings are castoffs from her affluent employers. In effect, Maria's mother and Grannie Dubuque are two "success stories" from the residential school system. Residential schools were not designed to produce great scholars and activists, but domestic servants, farmhands, and unskilled industrial laborers. They were simultaneously designed to instill a reverence for European refinements. Not having endured a formal education, Cheechum and Campbell's father do not share this reverence. In their desire to preserve family peace and to avoid offending the women, however, they can do nothing more than intimate indignation when Grannie Dubuque announces her plans for Maria's education: "It sounded exciting, but looking at Dad's shocked face, Mom's happy one, and Cheechum's stony expression—a sure sign of anger—I was confused. Dad went out after dinner and did not return until the next day. Meanwhile Momma and Grannie planned my wardrobe" (44).

Throughout the autobiography, Campbell shows the most profound respect for her Cheechum, her ways and beliefs. Nevertheless, it is Grannie Dubuque and her preference for the trappings of Western culture that Campbell follows as she becomes a woman. She longs to make a "better" life for herself and her siblings:

> Take for example the driving ambition and dream of a little girl telling her Cheechum, 'Someday my brothers and sisters will each have a toothbrush and they'll brush their teeth every day and we'll have a bowl of fruit on the table all the time and, Cheechum, they'll be able to do anything they want and go anywhere, and every day we'll have a glass of milk and cookies and talk about what they want to do. There will be no more mud shacks and they'll walk with their heads high and not be afraid.' The little girl's Cheechum would look at her and see the toothbrushes, fruit and all those other symbols of white ideals of success and say sadly, 'You'll have them, my girl, you'll have them.' (116)

What Cheechum realizes—what it takes Maria a long time to understand—is that she has confused the life that Métis people have historically striven to achieve with the "better" life that colonial Canada has historically thrust upon them in one way or another. Campbell does acquire the trappings she desires, but her dream "lead[s] to the disintegration of [her] soul" and to the almost complete loss of her life and her children (116). Before too long, Campbell finds herself, not unlike her Grannie Dubuque, a caricature of Western refinement:

> I moved into Lil's house in North Vancouver and she took me to a fashionable dress shop where I was fitted with clothes I never thought I'd wear, and to a beauty parlour where my hair was cut and styled. When I was finally pushed in front of a mirror, I hardly recognized the woman staring back at me. She looked cold and unreal, rich and expensive. 'Dear God,' I thought, 'this is how I've always wanted to look, but do the women who look like this ever feel like I do inside?' (116)

The passage describes Maria's entrance into the street trade, her entrance into one of the very few niches readily available to Native women in Canadian society. Cheechum understands all along that a residential school "education" will breed a desire for such finer things, and she knows that the desire will lead to degradation, but as she tells her great-granddaughter much later, "'Each of us has to find himself in his own way and no one can do it for us. If we try to do more we only take away the very thing that makes us a living soul'" (150).

Campbell spends a relatively brief period of time in the residential school, and yet, although Cheechum is a frequent and influential visitor in the family home, she nevertheless develops a deep reverence for Western culture and material wealth. This is not surprising given that Campbell begins attending a town school at age nine. The town school occupies the place of the residential school, instilling in her a sense of her own worthlessness. As noted in Chapter Two, Louis Althusser's notion of the ISA (Ideological State Apparatus)—the education system being a most powerful example—explains the maintenance of existing power relations. Althusser suggests that subjects are "interpellated," or called into being, as either ruling class or proletariat. To extend the model to a Canadian colonial context, we would say that the educational apparatus also calls subjects into being as either landed settler (Canadian) or displaced indigene. That is, the Native person (especially the Métis person) is positioned through the education system as a non-entity in Canadian society. The primary function of schools is not to teach children "the basics," a relatively simple task, but to teach them who they will be in society. In the case of Native people, the education system teaches children that they *are not*. Residential schools were indispensable, then, in displacing the First Nations; and while the town school may represent a welcome departure from the absolute social devastation of the residential school, it is nevertheless modeled on the same principles and functions in much the same way. That is, the school teaches Aboriginal children that they do not belong, that they are not, and that the only way they can *be* is to "act white." Campbell's experience makes this clear, and, unfortunately, she is a quick learner.

The school, of course, does not act alone. Campbell records the indispensable part played by the church in teaching dispossession. Without the school, however, especially the residential school, the church would be powerless. Canadian society is likewise instrumental in reinforcing and enforcing the lessons of the school. The "kind" families who deliver their castoffs to Métis homes at Christmas are one such example (28). These families recall "the kind Canadians" of Margaret Atwood's novel *Bodily*

Harm. In the novel, Canadians make "generous" donations of canned ham, but fail to recognize their own implication in the poverty of the Caribbean recipients of their "kindness." Such donations salve the conscience, eliminate the need (or possibility) for awareness, and simultaneously reinforce a social hierarchy that positions the islanders, like the Métis in *Halfbreed*, as less than their "benefactors." Cultural representations also contribute to the social positioning of the Métis. Campbell recalls a popular film depicting Louis Riel and Gabriel Dumont as buffoons and the Northwest Rebellion as a comedy. Such a depiction would be a manifestation of the Métis image, counterpart to the indigenous image discussed in Chapter One.[25] Cheechum storms out of the performance in indignation. Most audience members, however, including Métis audience members, laugh uproariously at the portrayal (97). The fact that both Native and non-Native people would find a racist and historically inaccurate depiction entertaining suggests that, as much as the educational apparatus instills inferiority in Aboriginal children, it also instills superiority in non-Aboriginal children.

In spite of having attended several non-Native institutions, the only education Campbell receives, beyond the destructively negative socialization of the school, is transmitted informally in her community. The only way the school can succeed in its socialization is by removing children from this otherwise most influential teacher, the community. This is the motivation behind the residential school system and its successors, compulsory town school attendance and the foster care system. Nevertheless, and although the lessons of the school wreak disastrous consequences in her life, Campbell also receives a traditional education: "As far back as I can remember Daddy taught me to set traps, shoot a rifle, and fight like a boy. Mom did her best to turn me into a lady, showing me how to cook, sew and knit, while Cheechum, my best friend and confidante, tried to teach me all she knew about living" (19). Her true teachers are those who care most deeply about her, in contrast to the unsavory "teachers" at the town school: "We had many different teachers during those years; some got the girls pregnant and had to leave; others were alcoholic; and because our school attracted everybody else's rejects, we had a constant stream of teachers" (48).

Teaching in the traditional manner, such as that which Maria receives in her community, is deeply integrated:

> Holistic learning and education has been an integral part of traditional Native American education and socialization until relatively recent times. Teaching and learning was a natural outcome of living in close communion with the natural world. . . . Experiential learning is the most basic and the most holistic type of human learning, and is a part,

in one form or another of every Native American context and mechanism of learning. (Cajete, *Igniting* 53–55)

As Gregory Cajete notes, such learning also includes dreaming, storytelling, rituals and ceremonies, and formal mentoring relationships (53–60). Regardless of the aspect of education considered, traditional learning is highly contextualized. The integrated nature of traditional education affects its description in Campbell's text. Just as her actual (traditional) education is fused into every aspect of her life, not allotted discrete slots of time after the Western fashion, the discussion of Campbell's community-based education is woven into and occurs throughout the narrative:

> Our parents spent a great deal of time with us, and not just our parents but the other parents in our settlement. They taught us to dance and to make music on the guitars and fiddles. They played cards with us, they would take us on long walks and teach us how to use the different herbs, roots and barks. We were taught to weave baskets from the red willow, and while we did these things together we were told the stories of our people—who they were, where they came from and what they had done. Many were legends handed down from father to son. Many of them had a lesson but mostly they were fun stories about funny people. (20)

The education offered by Cheechum is especially invaluable and is dispersed throughout the text. For example, when Maria comes home from school angry and in tears, ashamed that she does not have the same fine foods and possessions as the white children, she tells her parents that she hates them and "'all of you no-good Halfbreeds.'" Cheechum puts Maria's response into a historical context. She retells Métis history and explains how the struggle was ultimately lost because some began fighting against their own people:

> "They fought each other just as you are fighting your mother and father today. The white man saw that that was a more powerful weapon than anything else with which to beat the Halfbreeds, and he used it and still does today. Already they are using it on you. They try to make you hate your people." She stood up then and said, "I will beat you each time I hear you talk as you did. If you don't like what you have, then stop fighting your parents and do something about it yourself." (47)

At the time, Maria hears the words but fails to understand the lesson. On other occasions, Cheechum tries to relate the teaching through a blanket metaphor: "My Cheechum used to tell me that when the government gives you something, they take all that you have in return—your pride, your dignity, all the things that make you a living soul. When they are sure they have everything, they give you a blanket to cover your shame" (137).

Just as Maria must unravel the full significance of the metaphor, so too is the reader allowed to come to her own gradual comprehension. A useful comparison to the "blanket" which accompanies oppression is the anecdote Campbell relates of her family's mule (46). The blanket is like the grass tied to the end of a stick and used to stop the mule from resisting. The mule never reaches the grass, but it is distracted from its resistance. The blanket which the government offers functions in a similar way, and it can take many forms: alcohol or drug abuse, material wealth, the social prestige of a business or academic career, and so on. The blanket is anything that distracts the person from the reality of social oppression. Cheechum "used to say that all our people wore blankets, each in his own way. She said that other people wore them too, not just Halfbreeds and Indians" (137). The blanket prevents a person from seeing what she has become and, thus, from understanding the process of her colonization. Self-examination may be incredibly painful, rendering the blanket difficult to discard, especially when the person has nothing else; however, acknowledgement is the only way to "stop fighting your [people] and do something about it yourself." As Cheechum points out, "'The blanket only destroys, it doesn't give warmth'" (150). In *Halfbreed*, Campbell describes not only her slow and unwitting acquisition of a blanket of her own, but also her path to acknowledging its existence and discovering the means of throwing it away. She exposes the disturbing periods of her life, "go[es] through all of the pain," and emerges a person who can begin to struggle for freedom in the Métis tradition. At the same time, she stories the road to recovery for others who may likewise find themselves wearing blankets.

While a Western post-structuralist reading of Maria Campbell's *Halfbreed* might concern itself with an imposed and flickering racial hybridity, the prevailing struggle in the text is not between some constructed aspect of the author's white and Indian "racial composition." Rather, it is between the forces of assimilation—manifested so impeccably in the education system—and the forces of resistance. The struggle, and Maria's confusion, is between the destructive blanket that Grannie Dubuque unwittingly urges her toward and the Métis freedom that Cheechum has always lived. (Since Grannie Dubuque is a "full-blood" and Cheechum is a Métis woman and the niece of Gabriel Dumont, the outcome is, therefore, not one determined by "blood quantum.") Cheechum provides the information and encouragement her great-granddaughter needs to make a salutary choice. However, in her quest for the "better" life of Grannie Dubuque, Campbell acquiesces to the social conditioning of the school and requires many years and much pain to truly comprehend Cheechum's teaching:

> I began to understand what Cheechum had been trying to say to me, and to see how I had misinterpreted what she had taught me. She had never meant that I should go out into the world in search of fortune, but rather that I go out and discover for myself the need for leadership and change: if our way of life were to improve I would have to find other people like myself, and together try to find an alternative. (143)

Although *Halfbreed* was originally published over thirty years ago, its importance as an education in story has yet to be fully acknowledged. The description of Campbell's indigenous education—especially its historical, philosophical, spiritual, and sociological elements—is fully integrated into the text. *Halfbreed* functions both as a story of education and as an education in story. That is, the reader is able to experience aspects of an Aboriginal education.[26] As is characteristic of Métis storytelling, a vast amount remains to be learned by listening again; for in facing the unattractive truth of her personal and social reality, Campbell not only discovers what she has become, she discovers (and discovers for us) the reasons why. To recall Cajete's assessment of indigenous pedagogical theory: "Holistic learning and education [is] an integral part of traditional Native American education and socialization" (*Igniting* 53). The lessons learned, in this model, are "a natural outcome of living in close communion with the natural world" (53). If one is subjected to crushing poverty and pervasive social rejection—if forced to live, as Maria, in close communion with a racist Settler Nation—the natural outcome will be sociological and psychological devastation, such as that recalled in *Halfbreed*. It is not possible, in other words, to avoid learning holistically—for better or worse—from the natural and social environment in which one is immersed. Campbell's autobiography, chronicles a descent into socially determined despair. In the Métis tradition, however, the text also stories (as it is a story of) survival. That is, *Halfbreed* uncovers in story the mechanisms of oppression, and thereby discovers, also in story, the means of survival. The text becomes a literary re-kindling of the time-honoured Métis struggle for Aboriginal freedom. In reading and re-reading this first song, we begin to realize that Cheechum's words may be prophetic: "'. . . some day, my girl, it will be different'" (15).

Chapter Five
Spirals, Maps, and Poetry: Re-Reading Joy Harjo

> American Indians believe it is the breath that represents the most tangible expression of the spirit in all living things. Language is an expression of the spirit because it contains the power to move people and to express human thought and feeling. It is also the breath, along with water and thought, that connects all living things in direct relationship. The interrelationship of water, thought (wind), and breath personifies the elemental relationship emanating from 'that place that the Indians talk about,' that place of the Center where all things are created.
>
> —Gregory Cajete[1]

Throughout this book, I have discussed and suggested the implications of indigenous theory in an effort to argue for and engage in an indigenist criticism. I have referred, on several occasions, to Kimberly Blaeser's call for a "tribal-centered criticism . . . [one which] seeks a critical voice and method which moves from the culturally-centered text outward toward the frontier of 'border' studies, rather than an external critical voice and method which seeks to penetrate, appropriate, colonize or conquer the cultural center, and thereby, change the stories or remake the literary meaning" ("Native Literature" 53). I have argued that an indigenist criticism would be tribal-centered and would conduct its analyses in the manner suggested by Blaeser: "from the culturally-centered text outward." I have also noted, on several occasions, Gloria Bird's suggestion that "the master trope of Native American literature [is] the interconnectedness of all things—of people to land, of stories to people, of people to people" ("Decolonization" 4). This frequency in the literature of connectedness as trope, topos, and structuring principle is understandable, given the status of interrelatedness as the *sine qua non* of indigenous theory. As Willie Ermine notes (also quoted *passim*): "Aboriginal people found a wholeness that permeated inwardness and that also extended into the outer space. Their fundamental insight was that all existence was connected and that the whole enmeshed the being in its inclusiveness. . . . It is a mysterious force that connects the totality of existence—the forms, energies, or concepts that constitute the outer and inner worlds" (103). If this principle of connectedness, as Ermine suggests, infuses even "the forms, the energies, or concepts that constitute the . . . inner world," it follows that the literature (as also the criticism) produced from within such a worldview will be infused with connectedness. Consequently, as Jace Weaver points out, the concerns of an indigenist literature and criticism will be community-centered in a comprehensive sense: "Literature is communitist to the extent that it has a proactive commitment to Native community, including what I term the 'wider community' of Creation itself. In communities that have too often been fractured and rendered dysfunctional by the effects of more than 500 years of colonialism, to promote communitist values means to participate in the healing of the grief and sense of exile felt by Native communities and the pained individuals in them" (*That the People* xiii).

I have also suggested, particularly in the previous chapter, that indigenous theory is exemplified in and through indigenous languages. Such languages are, as Gregory Cajete indicates (above), living and infuse the being. I have noted, again in the previous chapter, Maria Campbell's concept of "putting the Mother back" and Armstrong's notion of "listen[ing] to sounds that words make in English and try[ing] to find the sounds that will move the image making, whether in poetry or prose, closer to the Okanagan reality" (Campbell, Interview 51; Armstrong, "Land Speaking" 192). That is, rather than simply adorning a Western theoretical base with indigenous terminology, the indigenist writer/critic/theorist will infuse a Western (or any) form with an indigenous worldview. In looking at the work of an indigenist (tribal-centered) poet, therefore, we should find that the language, even in English, expresses and is infused with indigenous theory—since poets, if I may be permitted the generalization, know the power of language innately. Note again, that to be an indigenist poet is to live and to create in an indigenist manner. That is, following the language-based theory of being developed in the previous chapter, indigenist poetry is that which participates in the endlessly connected struggle for human survival. In this chapter, then, I examine the poetry of Joy Harjo in an attempt to uncover the indigenous theory embedded within. I continue to argue for, while conducting, an indigenist criticism in my examination of the work of this well received Creek poet, and make the corresponding suggestion (ever so gently) that mainstream readings have, for the most part, underestimated the indigenist significance of Harjo's poetry. I wish to make the point that, just as the movement of trickster discourse into the academy—should that ever occur—will necessarily, if unceremoniously, transform the institution, so too will an examination of indigenous literature from an indigenist perspective necessitate not only an alternative criticism, but a radical shift in modes of thinking and being in the world.

Harjo's poetry lends itself to mainstream readings, as a quick perusal of the MLA Bibliography will reveal.[2] However, it is the distinctly indigenous poetics evident in the work—that in which the beauty, the excellence, the extraordinary, originate beyond the individual—that renders her work significant from an indigenist perspective. Harjo's poetry functions in the manner of a common crow, humbly picking up the scraps that already litter the external world and working through language to enact the inherent connections:

> My house is the red earth: it could be the center of the world. I've heard New York, Paris, or Tokyo called the center of the world, but I say it is magnificently humble. You could drive by and miss it. Radio waves can obscure it. Words cannot construct it, for there are some sounds left to sacred wordless form. For instance, that fool crow, picking through trash near the corral, understands the center of the world as greasy scraps of fat. Just ask him. He doesn't have to say that the earth has turned scarlet through fierce belief, after centuries of heartbreak and laughter
> —he perches on the blue bowl of the sky, and laughs.
>
> If you look with the mind of the swirling earth near Shiprock you become the land, beautiful. And understand how three crows at the edge of the highway, laughing, become three crows at the edge of the world, laughing. (*Secrets* 2–4)

The language and imagery here may be striking, but that which is exemplary and worthy of comment from an indigenist perspective are the connections and leaps being executed, between the inextricably connected things of the external world, between contrasting places, perspectives, and temporal loci, and between the infinite and the mind of the viewer. The shifting images and perspectives evident in this prose poem, that is, suggest an absorbing interest in indigenous metaphysics—a fascination with the infinite multiplicity of possible perspectives and the endlessness of connections—and an attempt to enact, in verse, an Aboriginal worldview. A crow in a trash heap, the turbulence of a major city, the vastness of the earth evident in a Stephen Strom photo: each has its own uniqueness and vitality that emerge as the viewer occupies the perspective of each.[3] Each also is inextricably linked with the other—a fundamental principle of indigenous thought. The beauty of a Harjo poem from an indigenist perspective, therefore, is in the multiple ways in which its own inherent connectedness is fused with the inherent connectedness of all that is. Furthermore, the simultaneous shifting in perspectives that Harjo's poem takes the reader through produces a "magnificently humble" awareness of the impossibility of ever grasping the totality of such immensity and of the inconsequential nature of one's own perspective in light of that totality. The viewer is likewise met with an awareness of the impossibility of ever putting all of Creation and its infinitely connected complexity into words: "for there are some sounds left to sacred wordless form."

The fascination evident in Harjo's poetry is not a preoccupation with some discretely contained genius which exists within the poet's own mind; it is rather a fascination with the genius of Creation, the unfathomable relatedness of everything. To linger in the uniquely individual, no matter how critically acclaimed the individuality, produces a solipsistic instability. Interior fixation also precludes a recognition of the connectedness of all things and of one's own humbling but necessary place in that infinite relatedness. For not only is everything ultimately unique, but all things (including the mind of the observer) are ultimately connected and integral. Commenting on the photographic art of Stephen Strom, her non-Native collaborator in *Secrets from the Center of the World*, Harjo notes in the preface that his "photographs are not separate from the land, or larger than it. Rather they gracefully and respectfully exist inside it. Breathe with it. The world is not static but inside a field that vibrates. The whole earth vibrates. Stephen Strom knows this, sees this, and successfully helps us to remember" (n.p.). Harjo's poetry likewise exists within and breathes with the land, and her poetry likewise helps us to remember the vibrancy of the world and our place within it.

* * * *

In *The American Poetry Wax Museum*, Jed Rasula examines the question of the *politics in* and the *politics of* poetry—that is, the distinction between politics as subject matter and the politics of disrupting conventional constraints of form, reference, metrics, and so on (363–413). The question is a pivotal one: whether the purpose of poetry is to *do* politics at all; and, if so, whether there is a better, or more effective, manner of doing poetic politics.

Don Byrd suggests that poetry is simply "entertainment for the most demanding audience, those who require greater complexity, which is to say, those who have more surplus attention to absorb" (175). I would argue that such a poetics of cerebral aestheticism produces implicit, if unwitting, support for and of existing power structures. I would also argue that the poetics of dissent, that which issued from the anti-establishment movements of the 1960s with its coincident awareness of the political potential of the arts, is that which currently produces the most innovative and socially relevant work, and I would suggest that Joy Harjo's poetry can be seen to occupy a unique position in relation to such work.

Three strands of American protest poetry may be identified: the protest lyric, performance poetry, and language poetry. Such a division is arbitrary and is intended only to organize the present discussion. Much overlap is evident among my three categories, which is not surprising given that the poets arose from (somewhat) similar social milieus and share many of the same objectives. Furthermore, just as the anti-establishment movement was not a specifically American phenomenon but was a worldwide awakening, so too do the source and practice of the poetics of dissent extend beyond the boundaries of "America." In addition, "American poetry" is admittedly as much a mental construct as "America" itself. Nevertheless, by "protest lyric," I refer to the use of conventional form to convey explicitly political subject matter—an example of Rasula's *politics in poetry*. Denise Levertov's anti-war poems, Adrienne Rich's feminist and lesbian work, and Amiri Baraka's African-American poetry of dissent are examples. (The permeable nature of my categories becomes immediately apparent: Baraka is also a notable performance poet.) In each case, the poet attempts to raise consciousness by weaving an informed discussion of social concerns into well-crafted verse. Such poetry tends to be highly accessible to a wide audience. However, the ease with which it is approached is also its greatest weakness; it is as easy to dismiss as it is to approach. In an entertainment-saturated culture, in which readers rapidly become consumers, conditioned to the expectation of regular entertainment "fixes," such poetry can easily be construed as yet another medium of personal enjoyment. The occasional "feeling" of repugnance or of outrage is simply added to the emotional salad of the literary gourmand, quickly consumed and forgotten.

Performance poetry, with its immediacy and intensity, attempts to circumvent such circumvention of social action. Locating itself in the moment, in time and in space, the performance event thrusts itself upon the "reader," resisting consumption. The movement has quasi-theoretical roots in (what was) a new understanding of primary oral culture. Jerome Rothenberg's translations of Native songs and poetries in *Shaking the Pumpkin* (1972) uncovered the possibility for a new intensity in poetry. (In the interests of brevity, I will ignore, for the moment, the overtly appropriative nature of much of Rothenberg's work.)[4] With a renewed understanding of the power of the spoken word appropriated from indigenous cultures, poets began to explore the transformative nature of performance. The performed event lifts poetry from the facile, obedient page and moves it into the realm of action. This "lifting" breaks the boundary of the printed page and simultaneously breaks the boundaries of form and genre. Poetry bursts into the previously closed realms of drama, music, song, dance, visual art, and becomes charged with their formal and generic energies. Since performance poetry is not tied to mainstream institutions, such as universities and publishing houses, the borders excluding "minorities" are also simultaneously broken. Thus, the socio-cultural identities of the performance poets are as rich as the socio-cultural contexts from which they arise. Poets of the performance movement include Amiri Baraka, Jayne Cortez, Ed Sanders, John Giorno, and Alan Ginsberg. One potential difficulty facing performance as a site of struggle, however, is the rapidity with which it can be commodified. As Paul Hoover notes, "While performance art began as a way to decommodify the art object, its inherent theatricality quickly reinvests it with commodity value" (*xxxix*). This swift repackaging undermines its potential for dissent; the greater the influence of performance poetry (the wider the audience), the greater the potential for (or certainty of) commodification.

Armed with a daunting body of theory, language poetry consciously precludes commodification. For language poets, the very materiality of language is recognized as a site of political struggle. Traditional lyric verse—that which accepts and reproduces conventional formal constraints—is seen as implicit support of existing power structures, since language, it is argued, does not exist in a political vacuum. The existing hierarchy is inscribed in dominant usages and forms, with the corresponding and arbitrary rules of correctness and value. Language poets work against such stratified arbitrariness through a conscious rejection of correctness and value. As noted in the introduction, however, a potential problem with language poetry is that in problematizing the language, the work becomes accessible only to an exclusive body of elite readers and constructs precisely the sort of hegemonic reader-writer relationship attacked by the language poets.[5]

Joy Harjo's work fuses these three strands of political poetry. Her performances, most notably with the band Poetic Justice, weave music and informal commentary into poetry readings; her verse contains the overt politics and approachability of the political lyric writers; and her work is infused with a highly developed (though alternative, since indigenous) theory of language and existence. For the most part, while Harjo's poetry has received a considerable amount of critical attention, very little has concerned itself with the theoretical subtlety of the work. Arguably, Harjo's poetry, like that of other sanctioned Native poets, has been condoned by the academy because it bears enough similarity to mainstream writing, while retaining sufficient marks of Aboriginality to identify the work as marginal and, thereby, to affirm the established writers. The inclusion implicitly validates a canon that is full of poets who affirm the self-determined mainstream. However, Harjo's work suggests an Aboriginal worldview, an aspect that has been largely overlooked. Her poetry is steeped in the web-like connectedness of the indigenous model and conveys a spiraling motion in which the movement perpetually returns to something new. In other words, Harjo's poetry enacts indigenous theory in verbal art:

> To pray you open your whole self
> To sky, to earth, to sun, to moon
> To one whole voice that is you.
> And know there is more
> That you can't see, can't hear,
> Can't know except in moments
> Steadily growing, and in languages
> That aren't always sound but other
> Circles of motion.
> . . . .
> Breathe in, knowing we are made of
> All this, and breathe, knowing
> We are truly blessed because we
> Were born, and die soon within a
> True circle of motion,
> Like eagle rounding out the morning
> Inside us. (*Mad Love*, "Eagle Poem," lines 1-9, 17-23)

The piece depicts that which is inside, inside all of us, opening outward to the external, and simultaneously embracing, drawing within, all that is outside in a circularity of motion that never begins and never ends. The breath that comes spontaneously in brings with it an element of all that is external. Recall Cajete's suggestion that "it is the breath that represents the most tangible expression of the spirit in all living things . . . [since it is] the breath, along with water and thought, that connects all living things in direct relationship (*Look* 42). The theory is exemplified by "Eagle Poem," which reinforces existing connections among the particular and the universal, the physical and the spiritual, as well as past, present, and future.

While I may seem to vacillate at times between demanding the inclusion of Native literature and critiquing such inclusion, my argument is nevertheless a unified one. In chapter one, I argued against efforts to include Native works within the canon of American literature. Warrior and others have made the same argument ("Marginal" 30). I argued against "inclusion" in this sense due to the implied negation of sovereignty. That is, to divide literature according to national affiliation and then to include indigenous works within the American (or Canadian) canon is to imply that indigenous nations are subordinate entities to the American (or Canadian, Mexican, etc.) nation. If the argument is irrelevant, one would expect little opposition to be raised against attempts to read indigenous literatures as separate from colonial literatures. Much opposition has, of course, been raised, as chapter one makes clear. This is not to say that indigenous texts should be ignored altogether, and, given that finance theory and the profit motive increasingly determine university decisions, even at the departmental level, it is unlikely that more (if any) specialized Native literature courses will be offered. Therefore, the difficulty is not with including the texts within a course on American or Canadian (or any other) literature. The difficulty arises when they are included *as* American (Canadian, etc.) texts. This would be a colonizing gesture, even if one takes pains to destabilize the defining lines in the process. I have argued throughout against colonization through literature (adding to the canon), as I have against self-absorptive readings (which defuse the communitist function of the literature), and against reading strictly according to aesthetics (which usually means according to a Western aesthetics). Any aesthetic reading would need to be according to an indigenist aesthetic, which implies a distinctly different orientation, one that cannot be limited to aesthetics. In short, while I argue that indigenous literature should be studied, I also argue, like Blaeser and Hulan and Warley before me, that it should be read on its own (indigenist) terms. My justification for such a radical statement is simply that (at its best) Native literature has a vital message to convey.

With respect to Joy Harjo, while the prevalence of metaphysics in her poetry—the seamless fusion of theoretical complexity and stylistic mellifluousness—may recall Wallace Stevens' poetics, Western theoretical critics and critical theorists have nevertheless found other topics of interest. For example, one prominent scholar discusses Harjo's poetry, along with that of Chickasaw poet Linda Hogan, in terms of the cultural exclusion facing the reader/critic when approaching American Indian women's poetry. This critic suggests that the unfamiliar metaphors of the poems serve as a form of cultural mediation, a bridge between (EuroAmerican and Indian) cultural islands. She praises what she calls the "exemplary array of different metaphoric mediations among cultures" in the poetry, and suggests that the metaphors work to "establish a cognitive middle ground between cultures" (Jahner 163). That much is pleasant and, at a certain level, valid, but the writer goes on to contend that the analysis of such metaphors "involves the *critic* in still another mode of mediation . . . so that the critical narrative becomes a model and summation of the *entire* range of different negotiations, transferals, and translations" (emphasis added). From that point, the essay becomes more about the difficult, incredibly more complex, task facing the critic than about anything that Harjo and Hogan have to say. It becomes much more about "the critical narrative" than the poetic.

This type of approach, not at all uncommon, concerns itself with finding space within the literature to hear one's own voice, even as clever self-interrogations and apparently self-negating critiques are performed. The same essay functions more as a lament over the white critic's burden than as an instrument of social change, which suggests an underlying motivation behind many excursions into the margin. But perhaps the motivation doesn't matter. Perhaps the critical impulse is its own justification. I would argue (and have argued), along with many discourse analysts/theorists (Norman Fairclough and Pierre Bourdieu, for example), that language use is inherently political. To the extent that it works for or against existing social conditions (or fails to), language use is political. If language use is political, then the use of language among oppressed people is more urgently so, and the recasting of attempts at political transformation (such as Harjo's) as intersubjective "negotiations, transferals, and translations" suggests that such critical narratives may actually be covert instruments of oppression, even if unwittingly so. While intersubjectivity may be a necessary element in political transformation, it must nevertheless function *inter alios* at every juncture; that is, the intersubjective element must consistently reach far beyond the strictly critical-narrative and must resist the temptation to collapse into solipsistic interrogations.

Language use is political because of its constitutive nature. As much as language is imbued with constitutive potential, it is also imbued with transformative potential. That is, just as language constructs reality, so too might it transform reality. Constitutive potential implies a transformative potential. This quality of language may or may not be acknowledged by the mainstream, but indigenist poets proceed as if the transformative potential of language were a given—hence, the interest shown by performance poets in traditional Native verse. Harjo's "Transformations," for example, from the collection *In Mad Love and War,* is an attempt to perform transformative meaning:

> I don't know what that has to do with what I am trying to tell you except that I know you can turn a poem into something else. This poem could be a bear treading the far northern tundra, smelling the air for sweet alive meat. Or a piece of seaweed stumbling in the sea. Or a blackbird, laughing. What I mean is that hatred can be turned into something else, if you have the right words, the right meanings, buried in that tender place in your heart where the most precious animals live. (lines 8–14)

As Harjo notes in an interview with Laura Coltelli, the poem was designed to transform the hatred of a former friend into love (*Spiral* 72).

The poem "Promise" (from *The Woman Who Fell From the Sky*), which is dedicated to her granddaughter, likewise concerns transformation, a prominent theme in Harjo's work:

> I am always amazed at the skill of rain clouds who outline the weave of human density. Crickets memorize the chance event with rainsongs they have practiced for centuries. I am re-created by that language. Their predictions are always true. And as beautiful as saguaro flowers drinking rain.
> . . . .
> In two days the girl will be born and nothing will ever look the same. I knew the monsoon clouds were talking about it as they softened the speed of light.
>
> Cedar smoke in a prayer house constructed in the last century pervades my memory. Prayer lingers in the ancestral chain.
>
> You can manipulate words to turn departure into aperture, but you cannot figure the velocity of love and how it enters every equation. It's related to the calculation of the speed of light, and how light prevails. (62)

"Departure" and "aperture" are phonologically and morphologically related, but they are also semantically related, since it only requires a logical skew or semantic spiral to transform departure (*a parting from*) into aperture (*an opening into*). Likewise, the past is connected inseparably to the present, as the words of ancestral prayer linger like sacred smoke, pervading the present of the poem and blessing the birth of a child. Crickets and rain clouds also participate in the blessing. They have a language, and hence a transformative potential, of their own, although their language may be, especially in the clamor of cities, difficult to hear, let alone understand.

Since human language of the present moment is but a tiny aspect of the totality of language, a totality that includes the languages of all time and space and of all aspects of Creation, it is impossible to express the fullness of any meaning with human words. Therefore, despite Harjo's exceptional attention to aspects of other worlds—dream-worlds, afterworlds, non-human worlds, and so on—in an attempt to encompass the totality of her meaning, she must return to the complaint voiced in several of her poems over the final inadequacy of human language:

> This land is a poem of ochre and burnt sand I could never write, unless paper were the sacrament of sky, and ink the broken line of wild horses staggering the horizon several miles away. Even then, does anything written ever matter to the earth, wind, and sky? (*Secrets* 30)

Nevertheless, human words are part of the interconnected totality of language, part of the immense potential for meaning and transformation, and are capable of (hence, they carry the responsibility for) effecting transformation.

Everything is related in what Harjo calls a "spiral of tangential stories" (*Mad Love*, "Death is a Woman," line 5). Or, as she writes in the poem "Original Memory," "In the Muscogee world, one would have a circle of relatives (everyone is ultimately a relative) [*sic*] recalling similar events, to establish connection, and to convey the event lovingly into a past" (*Mad Love* 47–48). Just as every*one* is ultimately a relative, so too are every*thing* and every*where* ultimately related. Harjo's poetry suggests a humbling realization that we are a very small part of a much grander totality. Yet, it is a reality in which "love enters every equation," a reality in which "light prevails"; and, as she notes in the title to one of her poems, "The Real Revolution is Love" (*Mad Love* 24). Elsewhere, Harjo writes, "I believe love is the strongest force in this world, though it doesn't often appear to be so at the ragged end of this century. / And its appearance in places of drought from lovelessness is always startling. / Being in love can make the connections between all life apparent—whereas lovelessness emphasizes the absence of relativity" (*Woman* 30).

The realization that we are a part of a greater and spiraling connectedness may be humbling, but, as mentioned, it also points to a responsibility for and possibility of making things right in the world. This responsibility might be called political activism, but it is not politics in the narrow sense (the political as a separate activity), which may do more damage than good, but a politics that struggles in behalf of preserving balance in this totality of relatedness in which we exist. This is the type of political activist that Joy Harjo is, and this is the kind of activist she addresses. Her work functions as a call to action and a cry for revolution, but the interrelatedness of everything makes it necessary that the real revolutionary action be love. For love is *"the very gravity holding each leaf, each cell, this earthy star together"* (*Woman* 10). Love is Harjo's term for the life-force discussed in earlier chapters, otherwise known as *manitou* or the principle of connectedness, that which embraces, infuses, and constitutes all that is. If Harjo's poetry is a language of love, in this expansive sense of the word, and if love (that which binds everything together) encompasses and constitutes language (which has the potential for global transformation), then to focus on the (imagined) closed space of the literary critical world, without reaching out into the connective tissue that is existence, is to miss the point of Harjo's work entirely.

* * * *

Although, predictably, Harjo's work has matured since *The Last Song* (1975), her first chapbook, a similarity in theme and metaphysical orientation is also evident throughout all periods of her poetry. Most obvious, the diction in more recent pieces is executed with greater precision, while the shorter lines of her earlier work begin to lengthen considerably as she matures. In other words, the meaning becomes paradoxically more compressed and precise as the lines loosen up. These stylistic changes, which are considerable, can be attributed to experience. However, significant similarities, threads of thematic and theoretical connection, are also discernible between her early and later work. The opening poem of *The Last Song*, "Watching Crow, Looking South Towards the Manzano Mountains," for example, is one of many early poems in which connections to later work are evident. The title of the poem is a participial phrase modified by another participial phrase. This enacts grammatically the Aboriginal ontology discussed in chapter four—that being only *is* in its happening—and as inferred by Harjo's work in all its phases. This ontology is depicted most eloquently by the wind, as suggested also (above) by Cajete. Wind's existence is only known in its happening. Wind gives no evidence of its existence except in its doing. Furthermore, it is only in its doing *to others*—the trees, our faces, the cracks between the panes of glass—that the wind's

Spirals, Maps, and Poetry

being is known. Not surprisingly, then, wind figures prominently even in Harjo's earliest collection. Wind makes the crow's being known and vice versa:

> wind is an arch
> a curve
> on the black wing of crow (lines 9–11)

In "Isleta Woman Singing," another participial title and also from *The Last Song*, the woman of the poem is both wind and mother:

> in the other room
> my son moans in his dreams
> the wind pauses
> and breathes back the song in her throat
> she quiets until he sleeps
> she is a mother
>   too (lines 11–17)

Wind's happening may be captured in words or by some other art. For example, in "for a hopi silversmith," Harjo describes the motion of wind as depicted by a fellow craftsperson:

> he has gathered the windstrength
> from the third mesa
> into his hands
> and cast it into silver
>
> i have wanted to see
> the motion of wind
> for a long time (lines 1–7)

Here, in one of her earliest pieces, Harjo depicts the wind's happening at two removes, suggesting the theoretical complexity that will come to characterize her work. The silversmith's work is not the actual happening of the wind, and Harjo's description of the description is twice removed. Yet, if we focus on the similarities—on the inescapable connectedness on all that is, as Harjo does—we note the likeness of the silver art to wind, and also to the words of the poem. The silver connects with the happening of the wind in its movement, and the poem connects with the happening of the silver in the hands of the silversmith. The three happenings are related even while distinct. As Harjo will later come to make clear, "everyone is ultimately a relative," and, as noted, every*thing* is also ultimately a relative (*Mad Love* 47–48).

Harjo's very early works, as mentioned, are marked by the staccato shortness of the lines, while the later works are notable for their distinct drift towards prose. This loosening of the line corresponds to Harjo's development as a storytelling poet, such that the form increasingly comes to mirror the content. Even in *The Last Song*, though, the story thrust is evident. The poems of this earliest collection strain towards story, being at times morsels of narrative arranged in lyric form:

>   chicago
> and the attendant doesn't know
> that third mesa
> is a part of the center
> of the world
> and who are we
> just two indians
> at three in the morning
> trying to find a way back ("3AM," lines 8–16)

This incipient thrust towards story, as with the length of lines, increases in later works. The diction also, as mentioned, is tightened considerably as Harjo matures as a poet and develops an increasing confidence in the strength of her own voice.

As Harjo suggests in a 1990 interview with Laura Coltelli, there are developments in style and technique between *What Moon Drove Me to This?* (1979) and *She Had Some Horses* (1983), and even more between the earlier books and the then new *In Mad Love and War* (1990): "If I didn't see [changes], didn't see growth, then I wouldn't do it any more. . . . I feel like I am just now learning how to write a poem. It has taken me over ten years to get to this point of just beginning" (*Spiral* 69). The same changes Harjo notes in her earlier work are also evident in considerations of *The Woman Who Fell from the Sky* (1994) and her most recent collection *A Map to the Next World* (2000). These general trends, which mark a coexisting similarity and difference, include an increasing drift towards prose, a growing political consciousness, and a simultaneous deepening of metaphysics.

The drift towards prose is not in any way an abandonment of lyric form. If lyric is taken to refer to an emphasis on the musical in poetic form, then we might say that Harjo's lyricality only increases. Her interest in jazz manifests itself in the syncopated rhythms and counterpoint stylings of the later works, something not as clearly evident in the earlier poems; for the musicality of her words increases with maturity as the line is loosened. Furthermore, even in the most recent collection (*A Map to the Next World*),

Harjo shows herself as capable as ever of producing a powerful poem in a short-lined mainstream-contemporary form:

> Faster and faster
> she whirls in the dark, the jealous
> green dark, the make-witchcraft-
> in-the-holes dark. Faster and faster.
> *Here is a hole made by a cigarette.*
> *I couldn't stop it then,* she said,
> *and I won't stop it now.*
> Faster and faster.
> *I want that lover of sweet madness*
> *that powwow prancer*
> *I want prettier than you,*
> faster and faster.
> That car, that house,
> that child on your hip,
> a cigarette,
> faster and faster she whirls ("Whirlwind" 1–16)

While prose form tends to dominate the most recent collection, occasionally, as in this excerpt, the lines are quite short. However, the short lines are in no way confining. The diction, repetition, and line length give the poem a hard-driving rhythm that suggests the movement and destructive force of a whirlwind. Here, Harjo shows how compression in the language—condensing the inherent power of words—can be used to charge a poem with explosive potential. Although such compression is an effective means of communication, allowing for meaning to explode in the imagination of the reader, Harjo is not confined to it or by it.

In an interview with Bill Aull *et al.*, Harjo was questioned on her seeming preference for longer lines. She was asked whether she had difficulty with the fusion of the Native American poetic tradition and English poetry, whether prose poetry was somehow more flexible for such a fusion. Her reply was that the fusion was not a problem for her at all, but that it might present a problem "for someone who prefers or is more comfortable with European prosody" (*Spiral* 106). As mentioned, this tendency towards prose, a tendency towards story that gets freed with maturity, can be located even in her earliest poetry. Narrative elements are obvious in *The Last Song* (1975), which is dominated by short lines. For example, the story is told of a crow in "Watching Crow, Looking South Towards the Manzano Mountains." Crow becomes a dancing horizon, and "a warm south wind / if it stays for a while / will keep [her] dancing for thirty years"

(12–14). In "San Juan Pueblo and South Dakota are 800 Miles Away on a Map," night-life vignettes are woven into a larger and single fabric. Throughout this earliest work, the story impulse is strong. However, as her poetry progresses, the line becomes longer and finally breaks into prose. That is, the story impulse becomes increasingly reflected in the style.

Comparing *A Map to the Next World* (2000) to the earlier and more widely acknowledged *She Had Some Horses* (1983), the drift towards prose is immediately evident. *She Had Some Horses* is still dominated by shorter lines (though not as short as those of *The Last Song*). *She Had Some Horses* is possibly the most painterly, the most abstract, of Harjo's collections, as evident in the title poem.[6] Critics often puzzle over the meaning of the horses that figure so prominently in this collection and elsewhere in Harjo's work. Speaking to Joseph Bruchac, she admits, "I see [horses] as very sensitive and finely tuned spirits of the psyche. There's this strength running through them" (*Spiral* 28). However, speaking with Bill Aull *et al.*, she is more reticent:

> I don't like to explain what I do. In fact, I can become quite evasive. . . . Part of that is because I feel a sense of privacy about the act of poetry itself. I feel this especially about the horses. I have a kinship with horses that is beyond explanation. No, I'm not actively involved in raising horses, living with them, yet they are a presence beyond any corral I could construct for the keeping of horses. You ask how I conceived of the horse. . . . Maybe, the horse conceived of me. This world is an interactive world. That's all I want to say. (*Spiral* 109)

As Angels Carabi points out—and Harjo concurs—"She Had Some Horses" deals with the reconciling of polarities (*Spirals* 134). A primary concern of Harjo's work is the harmonization of dualities evident in this, her signature poem: "She had some horses she loved. / She had some horses she hated. / These were the same horses" (49–51). Overall, though, Harjo has been reluctant to comment on the meaning of the horses or of this particular poem. In other words, for her a horse just is, heavily symbolic, immensely powerful, and evocative. Horses may partake in the reconciling of opposites that constitutes much of her work, but for Harjo horses will not succinctly equal anything. At the same time, however, she has claimed that "As a poet I feel that it is my responsibility to be clear and alive in my work, to not add to the confusion" (*Spirals* 17). The claim seems to contradict the evidence, though not necessarily so. As she suggests, Harjo does not write poetry with the intention of obfuscating, of being impenetrable, opaque. In general her work is refreshingly lucid. With respect to such works as "She Had Some Horses," however, the answer to the question "what does it mean?" would be that its meaning is already provided. The meaning has already been stated as clearly as possible; for when communication moves beyond the level of expressing a thought or feeling, when it moves into another state of being—which will include elements of thought, feeling, and story, along with potent and concrete imagery—words become less precise, the "meaning" less possible to locate.

This other state of being that art opens into is sacred creative space, a place apart from the ordinary but communicable through art and other avenues of transcendence. To communicate the meaning of sacred creative space and the gleanings of excursions into such space requires an extra-ordinary language, such as the language that is art or prayer. This extra-ordinary language, then, becomes an avenue into and framework for that other state of being. However, since the language is by definition not ordinary, its meaning may apparently elude. Furthermore, the language of the ordinary is ultimately inadequate to convey such extra-ordinary meaning. As Harjo writes in "Bird," a poem in honor of legendary jazz saxophonist Charlie Parker: "All poets / understand the final uselessness of words. We are chords to / other chords to other chords, if we're lucky, to melody" (7–9).

Harjo has often commented on her frustration with the inadequacy of the English language, and of written language in general, to communicate the meaning to which she aspires (*Spiral* 99–100). Nevertheless, in spite of the difficulties associated with writing, and in spite of the impossibility of fully articulating its meaning, when we read such extra-ordinary poems (or view such paintings, listen to such music, as the case may be) the meaning, which is actually heightened, since beyond the ordinary, eventually (potentially) makes its meaning at a supra-conscious level. A connection is made with the reader/viewer/listener, who in turn potentially enters into the universal connectedness opened up by the art. The experience is described by Willie Ermine: "*Mamatowisowin* is a capacity to tap the creative force of the inner space by the use of all the faculties that constitutes our being—it is to exercise inwardness. . . . the gifted in our Aboriginal communities 'create' experience for the benefit of the community through the capacity inherent in *mamatowisowin*" (104–08). In short, the horses just are—like the bold brush strokes of an abstract painting, in which the colors and form speak, even while an exact interpretation of the strokes is impossible. As with all such work, pausing to absorb the sounds, colours, and so on, has the potential to draw the reader/viewer into another space.

> BILL MOYERS: *You said this morning that you discovered your language came from some other place and that it was different from the language being spoken around you as you were growing up. What was that place?*
>
> JOY HARJO: I guess you would call it that mythic place—that river ultimately—that is within all of us which is not tapped as often with the general public as it used to be in cultures which had living oral traditions and very vital heroes and heroines. In our time it's tapped by the artists—you could hear it today in the performances as people pulled on that incredibly rich source. (*Spiral* 36)

* * * *

Another example of such transcendence through art (though in a different, more story-based, sense) is "The Woman Hanging from the Thirteenth Floor Window" from *She Had Some Horses*. Harjo has often commented on the number of people who claim to know the woman of the poem:

> Many people have come up to me after a poetry reading and asked me about this woman who was hanging from the thirteenth floor window, because they were sure they knew her, or one of her cousins, her sister, or they had read about her story in the newspaper where they lived, be it New York or Lincoln, Nebraska, or Albuquerque. It was familiar to them, haunted them after hearing the poem because it evoked some possible memory.
>
> I know there is a woman; perhaps many women are this woman. And you know her, or thought you did, or will. Because it's a story that has happened; perhaps it's happening now. (*Spiral* 19)

In my own reading, I was reminded of a woman from my childhood in a working class district of Toronto. The woman of Harjo's poem is real and the event described is very real. In my reading, the woman of my childhood, like so many others, enters into the poem. As readers, we also enter the poem. We enter as the people around her, watching her, doing nothing or anything, as the people she has known, and sometimes we *are* her.[7] She and we come into the poem, not for the sake of therapy or gratuitous shock, nor strictly for memorial purposes. Such events must be remembered—as Harjo points out, "to acknowledge these lives, in print, is a radical thing" (*Spirals* 80)—and the poem does have aesthetic merit:

> She thinks of Carlos, of Margaret, of Jimmy.
> She thinks of her father, and of her mother.
> She thinks of all the women she has been, of all
> the men. She thinks of the color of her skin, and

> of Chicago streets, and of waterfalls and pines.
> She thinks of moonlight nights, and of cool spring storms.
> Her mind chatters like neon and northside bars.
> She thinks of the 4 A.M. lonelinesses that have folded
> her up like death, discordant, without logical and
> beautiful conclusion. Her teeth break off at the edges.
> She would speak. (49–59)

Here, the litany-like repetition and vibrant imagery produce an hypnotic immediacy that is characteristic of Harjo's work. Nevertheless, the overarching value of the poem is not aesthetic, nor is it to memorialize a woman (who is more an amalgam of persons than any particular one). Rather the poem opens up a creative space into which all the women she has been and all the people who have and will know (about) her may enter. The creative space is a place for the meeting of many, and, as Harjo suggests in the title to another poem (from *In Mad Love and War*), "We Must Call a Meeting." We must call a meeting to imagine a world in which women no longer lead lives of such desperation and to imagine the path to such a world. For this among other reasons, transcendent art such as Joy Harjo's poetry remains vital in contemporary culture.

The poem "We Must Call a Meeting" captures in a single piece the major themes and movements of Harjo's work. The poem is in some ways a collection of fragments, but it does not remain such. The tangled images include some powerful Aboriginal symbols—arrows, lightning, pottery, feathers. The piece is characteristically melodic, but the images are not synthesized into a coherent message of triumph. Instead they work to create a relentlessly dissonant mood of destruction. The state of endless obstruction and failure they describe approaches despair:

> I am fragile, a piece of pottery smoked from fire
>
>   made of dung,
>
> the design drawn from nightmares. I am an arrow, painted
>
>   with lightning
>
> to seek the way to the name of the enemy,
>
>   but the arrow has now created
>
> its own language. (1–7)

The rhythm and diction here are pleasingly melodic, but each of the images nevertheless paints a picture of futility. The speaker is "a piece of pottery," solid and earthy. However, in this case the pottery is fragile, a shard made in a dung fire—dung being the fuel of the poorest of the poor—whose design comes from nightmares. The speaker is also an arrow, a symbol of indigenous potency, but has lost her language, speaks now "a language of lizards and storms" (8), which makes "the way to the name of the enemy" much more difficult. In many ways, the images are like indigenous societies in the Americas. Social conditions seem hopeless, much is lost, and every attempt at regeneration is thwarted. The greatest loss is the language, something about which Harjo comments more fully in an interview:

> My frustration with the language, particularly the English language, stems from anger with the colonization process in which the English language was a vicious tool. The colonizers knew what they were doing when they tried to destroy tribal languages, and which, infuriatingly, they were successful at in many instances. Language is culture, a resonant life form itself that acts on the people and the people on it. The worldview, values, relationships of all kinds—everything, in fact, is addressed in and through a language. (*Spirals* 99)

As second-language speakers frequently note, a language carries with it a distinct mode of thinking and perceiving. For example, heavily inflected languages cannot but engender a different mode of understanding from that of uninflected languages, such as present-day English. Such languages, as classical Latin, can and frequently do place the verb at the end of the sentence. Predication is often reserved until the closing word and may be preceded by prepositional phrases, relative clauses, heavily modified subjects and objects, and so on. As a result, speakers of such languages have the potential to float images and relations in the air for some time before the predicator finally arises to snap the sentence into meaning. This would produce a significantly different way of thinking and relating in the world from that produced by present-day English, which has become almost completely dependent on word order. Latin, however, is one of the forebears of present-day English. The differences would be immeasurably greater with respect to indigenous languages, and the worldview they encapsulate must be likewise different. The human potential that was destroyed, therefore, by the deliberate attempts of the colonizers to eradicate such languages is untold.[8]

Harjo's "We Must Call a Meeting" immerses the reader in such ravaged potential. The pottery is fragile, the arrows are ineffective, the speaker

Spirals, Maps, and Poetry

tries to fly with prayers but gets "caught in the cross fire of signals" and her "spirit drops back down to earth" (lines 24–25). Every image of indigenous power in the poem is circumvented, mirroring the results of attempts by Native people through the centuries to resist invasion, or retain homeland, or protect resources, or re-assert sovereignty. In virtually every instance, and despite the varied and ingenious strategies employed, the result has been further devastation until the people have been all but consumed by despair. Nevertheless, the poem ends by raising the possibility that the people might come together and, against terrible odds, find a way to resurrect hope:

> I am lost; I am looking for you
>
> who can help me walk this thin line between the breathing
>
> and the dead.
>
> You are the curled serpent in the pottery of nightmares.
>
> You are the dreaming animal who paces back and forth in my head.
>
> We must call a meeting.
>
> Give me back my language and build a house
>
> Inside it.
>
> A house of madness.
>
> A house for the dead who are not dead.
>
> And the spiral of the sky above it.
>
> And the sun
>
> and the moon.
>
> And the stars to guide us called promise. (26–39)

The "you" of the poem may, and probably does, refer to other Native people, who are living the devastation and loss of vision depicted.[9] The very fact of Indian survival over the past five centuries has been against terrible odds, and "We Must Call a Meeting," like all of Harjo's work, anticipates revitalization. Yet, the colonizer, who is told to "Give me back my language," is also being addressed in this poem. Indigenous languages have been lost, and what remains is necessarily changed, but the current global predicament renders the turn to a radically different perspective, such as that from which Aboriginal languages issue, crucial. The devastation that has embroiled Native people in a struggle for survival since colonization is now beginning to threaten the mainstream as well. Since indigenous societies have endured the threat for so long and against terrible odds, it is likely that the experience with what has become a global problem will have provided Native peoples with a keen perception of the situation. However, as astute as they may be with respect to the realities of global devastation, the solution must ultimately include the colonizer as well, in part because Aboriginal philosophy is founded upon the principle of relatedness, and as Harjo suggests, "everyone is ultimately a relative." More important, since the colonial mentality is the ultimate source of the devastating ideas and practices, any solution to the devastation that now grips the earth must speak to the colonizer as well. The devastation must be eradicated at its source, especially now that the colonial mentality is creeping even into Native communities. For this reason, Harjo's work is ever inclusive in its scope, including not only other peoples of color, but mainstream peoples as well: "I begin to draw maps of stars. / The spirits of old and new ancestors perch on my shoulders" ("We Must Call a Meeting" 14–15). Harjo's poetry confronts the present crisis facing all peoples of this world, opening up avenues into other realms where solutions might be discovered and discussed. However, she must meet with like-minded thinkers and activists in that realm, and the participants must come from all peoples if we are to overcome such terrible odds.

In a similar way, Harjo recognizes that any meeting must include people from all walks of life. For example, each of the poems in *The Woman Who Fell from the Sky* is followed by prose commentary. Following "Mourning Song," Harjo writes of the dilemma she often faces in confronting street people, not knowing whether to ignore them or enable their addictions. On one occasion she recognizes an old friend among the people of the street. The two of them share laughs and tears before they part:

> *I am still thinking of him and how each of us chooses our path daily, though our choices often appear limited by race, sex, and class.*
> *Knowing him the way I did I couldn't help but think he'd made a choice to be a modern warrior, and could gather more crucial knowledge from the streets of this city than he could have on a track called success by the colonizers.* (*Woman* 21)

Harjo has been criticized for discussing alcoholism in her work: "I was criticized for bringing [alcoholism] up, because some people want to present a certain image of themselves. But . . . part of the process of healing is to address what is evil. . . . When you are able to articulate something that is terrible that is inside you, that lives in you, and you no longer deny it, you are able to bring regeneration" (*Spiral* 139). Harjo suggests that alcoholism may be an alternative, if destructive, path to knowing, which raises the possibility for hope even in the midst of such devastation. The knowledge gained by all seekers must be included in the meeting of peoples to determine the path to the name of the enemy, and, since that which threatens the planet at present is a global addiction to profit, the knowledge gained by such frequently overlooked members of the community may be crucial. At any rate, alcoholism is not a Native problem; it is a contemporary human problem. Poverty simply makes addiction more apparent. Obvious addictions, however, are easier to admit, and, as Harjo suggests, admission (the ability to articulate) is the first step to recovery.

* * * *

> JOY HARJO: It seems that the Native American experience has often been bitter. Horrible things have happened over and over. I like to think that bitter experience can be used to move the world, and if we can see that and work toward that instead of killing each other and hurting each other through all the ways that we have done it . . .
>
> JOSEPH BRUCHAC: *The world, not just Indian people, but the world.*
>
> JOY HARJO: Sure, because we're not separate. We're all in this together. (*Spirals* 26–27)

* * * *

In "Inspired Lines: Reading Joy Harjo's Prose Poems," Robert Johnson notes Harjo's movement towards prose, specifically as marked by *In Mad Love and War* (1990). He notes that Harjo's adaptation of what is usually construed as a modernist and European form (prose poetry) is actually a natural evolution in the "Indian" quality of her work (20). While I would argue with Johnson concerning the peculiarly European nature of prose poetry, he is correct in the suggestion that the movement is a natural drift in Harjo's work. The movement is so pronounced in *A Map to the Next World* that the collection is subtitled *Poetry and Tales*. Certainly, this collection, as always, is permeated with tales—more correctly, it is a tale—yet it also never ceases to be poetry. The themes and formal tendencies that mark every stage of Harjo's work are crystalized in this most recent collection, in which she experiments freely with a fusion of genres. She merges fable, autobiography, essay, song, prayer, and more within this single collection (often within a single piece). The prose poem "the crow and the snake," for example, functions as a parable, while another prose piece, "there is no such thing as a one-way land bridge," reads much like a scholarly essay:

> The fault of that theory and so many others in the western world is that Indians are somehow less than human, or at least not as advanced as western European cultured humans. We are constantly being defined from the point of view of the colonizer. We are human and live complex and meaningful lives. I like the response given to an anthropologist when he asked a teacher in a particular Asian culture about ideology and theory. 'What ideology? We just dance.' (*Map* 38)

As genre theorist Carolyn Miller points out, the lines constructed between genres always and inevitably blur, making it ultimately possible to speak of genre only as social action: " . . . a rhetorically sound definition of genre must be centered not on the substance or the form of discourse but on the action it is used to accomplish" (151). The generic action of *A Map to the Next World* is, as with all Harjo's poetry, an effort to effect global transformation. The structure is tightly controlled; it conveys meaning and is charged with the transformative potential that exists at all levels of language. Regardless of the form and secondary genres that are suggested, each piece in the collection contributes to a unified structure and overall meaning. *A Map to the Next World* synthesizes into structural unity the various themes, formal tendencies, and discursive actions that have given Harjo's previous work such power: the tendency towards prose, the resolution of dualities into a regenerative whole, an emphasis on and performance of the relatedness characterizing all Creation, and a deepening movement into the spirit realm as a means of social action. In pulling these themes and tendencies into structural unity, the text describes reality in a heightened sense. The text maps our existence and performs the reality it describes. That is, *A Map to the Next World* recreates of the structure of our existence and, through that structure, taps into the "ongoing-ness" of our existence. In this collection (more so than the earlier texts), Harjo creates an opening into the creative spaces of human existence, and in this collection, she intensifies the discussion with those who choose to meet with her there.

With each successive volume of poetry, Harjo has increasingly worked with structure. Structure, like color, cannot help but convey meaning, and *A*

Spirals, Maps, and Poetry

Map to the Next World is as much architecture as poetry. Its structure has meaning and its structure is complex. Brenda Peterson's assistance with the arrangement is acknowledged in earlier volumes: *She Had Some Horses, In Mad Love and War,* and *The Woman Who Fell from the Sky.* Although her assistance is not acknowledged in this most recent collection, Harjo is clearly influenced by the pattern set by Peterson. That is, as in the earlier collections, threads of meaning are woven together through successive poems. Part I of *The Woman Who Fell from the Sky,* for example, in which Peterson assisted with the arrangement, begins with "The Creation Story." The next poem, "The Woman Who Fell from the Sky," is based on the Rotinohshonni (People of the Longhouse) Creation story. "The Naming," a poem on the birth of her granddaughter, follows and is yet another Creation story in microcosm. Prose commentary between the poems further tightens the thread of Creation running between the pieces. This collection begins with "Reconciliation: A Prayer" and ends with the Muscogee word MVTO (roughly, *thank you*), a common manner in Aboriginal languages of closing a prayer. These frame the two primary sections of the book, marking the beginning and end of an existence and pulling the collection together into structural unity as prayer. In this way, the collection structurally enacts the ideal of Aboriginal existence—life lived as prayer.

Threads of connection between the pieces are even more apparent in *A Map to the Next World.* The speaker addresses crows in "The Path to the Milky Way Leads Through Los Angeles": "So what are we doing here I ask the crow parading on the ledge of falling that / hangs over this precarious city?" (lines 25–26). In "the power of never," the prose poem that follows, the speaker again addresses crows and ends with a tribute to a human crow: "Last I heard he was evicted for selling drugs, this crow with manners and a taste for the fine things in life" (*Map* 47). The threading of themes is carried throughout the collection, between the lyric and adjacent prose poems and among the various pieces. The entire text is pulled together into a coherent thematic unity, much like a tightly woven fabric. The insistent connectedness of the text also performs the fundamental indigenous theory of connectedness. As Harjo notes in an interview, "A common belief to all tribal people is that the world is alive; absolutely everything is connected" (*Spiral* 134).

In accordance with such belief, Harjo's text not only discusses but suggests structurally a tribal worldview, in order that it may participate in the connectedness of absolutely everything including itself. The poems of *A Map to the Next World* are arranged in four parts: "Songline of Dawn," "Returning from the Enemy," "This is my Heart; it is a Good Heart," and

"In the Beautiful Perfume and Stink of the World." The sections are forty-three, forty-two, thirty-three, and five pages long respectively. A similar receding structure is enacted on a smaller scale in "Four Songs," in which the successive segments are eight, six, three, and one line(s) long. Structure, as mentioned, conveys meaning. For example, it has often been noted that the number four is a sacred number in Native traditions. Four is the number of the surface directions of the earth, the cardinal colors, the elements, and the seasons.[10] The number four also describes a circle, which is the (naturally) predominant and sacred shape. The sun, the moon, the earth (and their movement), the trunk of a tree, a bird's nest: all are circles. All of this has been noted in the earliest of anthropological studies on Native people. It is frequently taken as evidence of primitive thought. However, from another perspective, the importance of the circle becomes quite complex.

In suggesting that the number four describes a circle, for example, the circumferential aspect of a circle is being addressed. The Greek letter π in mathematical discourse represents the relationship between the circumferential aspect of a circle and its diametric aspect, a relationship which is represented mathematically by the number 3.14159 . . . , running off to infinity. Such a relationship corresponds to the Aboriginal understanding of God, or more correctly, *manitou*. For, as Viola Cordova points out, *manitou* (or *wakan tanka,* or *usen,* etc.) is the ultimate abstraction, that which cannot be reified. Cordova also suggests that the term *God* usually represents a reification, an anthropomorphic metaphor for this ultimate of abstractions (28–29). *Manitou*, then, is like a circle, which in its circumferential aspect encompasses all that is, and like a circle, which in its diametric aspect, also infuses all. The relationship between the constitutive (diametric) and encompassing (circumference) aspects of *manitou* can, like a circle, be expressed by π, a transcendent number that spirals off to infinity, though the expression π^∞ (*pi* to the power of infinity) would probably represent *manitou* more accurately.

With its four-part structure, *A Map to the Next World* therefore describes a circle, which implicitly suggests the sacred. The sacred is not only enacted structurally, it is overtly discussed as in the prose poem "ceremony":

> When considering ceremony the act of preparation is most crucial. Each day is a ceremonial progression in which every human takes part. We do so either consciously or unconsciously. You can prepare by setting the alarm clock and jumping into the world with anxiety, or you can still set the alarm clock, but take time to prepare for the day, by singing, by prayer, by a small acknowledgment of the gift of the day itself.

It has spirit, this creature called day, and will go on without us, dragging us behind it. Or, we can take part in the ceremony and walk (or run?) with grace into the momentum. . . . It's crucial we participate for the sun needs our song, prayers, acknowledgments. Too often the weight of humans has been carried by others who have not lost their original instructions on how to live with integrity in this system. (*Map* 58–59)

The poem concerns day as ceremony or sacred occurrence. (Being only *is* in occurrence.) *Day* is accorded being here, as elsewhere *never* ("the power of never"), *death* ("twins meet up with monsters in the glittering city"), *desire* ("traveling through the dark"), *event* ("The Ceremony"), *danger, fear,* and *story* are accorded being:

They wanted love, like we did, but did not know how to say it.
Humans were created by mistake, someone laughed and we came
crawling out. That was the beginning of the drama, we were hooked then.
What a wild dilemma, how to make it to the stars on a highway slick
with fear. The spirit of the story could smell the danger, climbed down
the clouds because things had gone too far. It breathed in life
from all directions, included the running boys in the beautiful pattern.
We followed. ("Holdup" 27–34)

This attribution of entity goes beyond the metaphorical. Elements that are usually understood as conceptual or emotional are accorded being, just as, in Aboriginal thought, vitality and reason are attributed to all aspects of Creation. If story and song have being, as Harjo's poetry suggests, then the collection's four-part structure and pervasive discussion of the spiritual allow for the text to fuse with the sacred. The collection, then, becomes a ceremony "to rid us of the enemy mind" that threatens to destroy us.

Among the disciplines, the sciences and technologies offer some wonderful answers to complex problems. They are able to outline, document, and (sometimes) ameliorate the threats to our existence. Nevertheless, they have proven themselves inadequate at finding ways to avert global devastation, possibly because the devastation is in some ways enabled by their findings. The pervasiveness and complexity of the problem make disciplinary universality the probable precondition to any solution, and since science and technology tend to be specialized and closed branches of knowledge, it is unlikely that they will spearhead the concerted effort required to avert the far-reaching threat, although they may make necessary contributions. The means of averting the threat and the inspiration to follow such a course will only be found through excursions into creative space, such as that offered by the arts. For example, among the insights that Harjo conveys is the suggestion that the problem is intellectual and spiritual in origin:

> Small winds tattoo my cheek.
> Soon they will bring mist,
> a small rain to clean the world
> send rainbows to dress us,
> for the ceremony
> To rid us of the enemy mind. ("Instinct" 8–13)

If the problem is intellectual and spiritual in origin, then the solution must involve a shift in worldview, and, as suggested in earlier chapters, Aboriginal literatures open up avenues of exploration of an alternative mode of thought and existence for non-Native as well as Native readers. However, since the value of literature as a potential means of intellectual and spiritual re-configuration cannot be proven in a Western epistemological sense—which tends toward specialization and closure rather than infinite connectivity—its value may well be overlooked.

It could be argued that Harjo did not intend her poetry to function as a means of spiritual transformation, that the collection only coincidentally has a four-part structure and is in no way designed to tap into *manitou*. However, the sacredness of four pervades indigenous thought systems, as does the concept of all-encompassing connectedness:

> The term [*Usen*] signifies a concept that may be 'pan-Indian.' That is to say, it may be more widespread through Native North America. . . . In all circumstances the term signifies something 'of a substance, character, nature, essence, quiddity beyond comprehension and therefore beyond explanation, a mystery; supernatural; potency, potential' (the description of Basil Johnston, an Anishinaabe writer) [*sic*]. The concept of this mysterious force also shares the notion of its being all-pervasive. It is everywhere and in all things, perhaps is all things. (Cordova, "European" 27)

Since such ideas are so pervasive in indigenous thought, it is very likely that Harjo did intend, at some level, to imbue the structure of the text with ceremonial meaning and to connect it to the field of infinite connectedness. The intention to connect with the sacred becomes evident in the subject matter which, as mentioned, is relentlessly ceremonial. Regardless, words have an energy of their own, and when placed in the proximity of other words, and when mapped onto larger structures (which have an energy of their own),

Spirals, Maps, and Poetry

meanings emerge which not even the poet could have anticipated. This is so whether or not the poet is aware of the lovemaking relationship that occurs between words, structures, stories, and other words. When the poet is aware, however—and Harjo seems fully aware—the potential is immeasurable:

> There is no world like the one surfacing.
> I can smell it as I pace in my square room,
> the neighbor's television
> entering my house by waves of sound.
> Makes me think about buying
> a new car, another kind of cigarette
> when I don't need another car
> and I don't smoke cigarettes.
> A human mind is small when thinking
> of small things.
> It is large when embracing the maker
> of walking, thinking and flying. ("Emergence" 20–31)

Poetry is likewise "large when embracing [the infinite]."

Several of the poems in *A Map to the Next World* concern the relation with the infinite that occurs during human lovemaking:

> You ask me what I am thinking when we make love
> and our eyes are closed and the sun is climbing halfway
> to the roof and the neighborhood dogs are all in love
> with the spirit dog who makes the rounds and tortures them
> with dreams of hills and running with the smell of heat
> and then the train adds to the song of progress
> making a web from city to city,
> backdoor to backdoor and I know it is possible to
> fly without the complications of metal and engineering
> and all the payoffs, paybacks and terrible holes
> in the earth and here we are in the territory of the wind,
> surrounded by devils and thieves, forgotten by a trickster god
> who has a wicked sense of humor
> yet there is something quite compelling
> about this skin we're in . . .
> . . . .
> We've been here before, thinking in skin and our pleasure
> and pain feed the plants, make clouds. I see it with my eyes
> closed. It's so beautiful. (1–15, 28–30)

Love, as mentioned, is Harjo's term for the connectedness of all that is. Human lovemaking is, therefore, a small part of *manitou*, and the poem describes the relationship with all things that occurs during such lovemaking.

Here, the lovers tap into all the universe as represented in the multifarious thoughts and images crowding the poem: the opening "sentence" of the poem takes sixteen lines to utter. As Harjo points out (noted previously), love is *"the very gravity holding each leaf, each cell, this earthy star together"* (*Woman* 10). That "very gravity" extends to encompass every aspect of creation, as suggested by the prose poem "earthly desire":

> Heading to the ocean is the Hanawi River dressed in flowers and bamboo who is also in love with the ocean. The story is complicated just as human stories can be complicated. The sky too is part of this story of attraction and yearning. The ocean and sky meet out on the horizon for the love of touch. To speak like this isn't simplification, or personification for the sake of making intimacy where there isn't—this is the truth of the matter. We are all here in this place because we desired it. Desired each other. (*Map* 115)

These illuminations may not be Harjo's alone—certainly they seem prevalent in indigenous thought and literature—but the fusion of structural and musical meaning with the lexical allow the poems to function on several levels as thoughts of the sacred.

The circle, as mentioned, is suggestive of *manitou* and is a prominent figure in *A Map to the Next World*. Likewise, the spiral, often noted as a prominent figure in Harjo's poetry, is important structurally and thematically in this collection. A spiral is a circle in motion heading into and out of infinity; it can be said to express *manitou* in the dynamic. While the circle is the predominant shape in nature, the spiral is the predominant motion: galaxies, hurricanes, tornadoes, whirlpools, the whorls of our fingertips, and the whorls of hair on a baby's head. All spirals are ultimately related, smaller spirals being parts of larger ones, and all of them connected in the grand spiral of existence. Spirals, as always in Harjo's poetry, populate *A Map to the Next World*. "Whirlwind" (quoted earlier) concerns the unhealthy spiral of an abusive relationship and performs its meaning in the poem's structure. The prose poem "kinetics of wind" expands the spiral structure thematically: "Each generation is a variation on the pattern. Eventually the pattern spirals toward a meaning that will reach to the other side of the sky" (*Map* 121).

Structurally, *A Map to the Next World* is a spiral in itself. As mentioned, the four parts are progressively smaller in page-length, not unlike the graphic image of four concentric circles dispersed throughout the book. This image also centers the painting *Four Directions* (by Hopi-Choctaw artist Linda Lomahaftewa) which is reproduced on the book jacket. Title poems from each of the four parts of the collection also spiral by their placement in the overall structure. "Songline of Dawn," for example, the title poem to the first section of the book, opens Part I. "Returning from the Enemy," the title poem to the second section, closes Part II. Continuing the spiraling motion, "This is my Heart" is the central poem of Part III, and "In the Beautiful Perfume and Stink of the World" is the only poem in the final section by the same name. The movement of successive title poems (front-back-center-all) within the respective sections recalls the motion of a spiral.

Structural dualism, which also characterizes *A Map to the Next World,* can likewise be said to describe a spiral motion. The poems of this latest collection alternate between prose and lyric pieces. Titles of the prose pieces are printed in lower case, while titles of the lyric poems are printed in upper case. This arrangement gives the collection an alternating movement between the prosaic and the lyrical and recalls the dualistic structure of *The Woman Who Fell from the Sky.* The pattern of dualism is performed in microcosm in "Returning from the Enemy," a poem in which fourteen numbered lyric pieces alternate with fourteen prose pieces, all of them contained within the single, long poem. The alternating movement that characterizes *A Map to the Next World* culminates in the final poem, "In the Beautiful Perfume and Stink of the World." This poem reads as two separate pieces, one with a prose rhythm and the other a lyric rhythm, which are arranged in counterpoint within the same poem:

> *As a newborn star shimmering there, and then I stopped counting and began to comprehend the view.*
>
> Sitting on the bed, blocking my view of the sleeping moon.
> If I get up to play my horn I'll awaken the neighbors.
>
> *My son was my dark-eyed baby again, kicking his legs after a bath, and then he was a man with fire in his hands.*
>
> If I get up to pee I'll lessen my chances
> of catching the wave of remembering and forgetting. (11–18)

The use of couplets and italicized font here distinguish between the two threads, a pattern that continues until the final two lines of the poem. There, one line of each thread joins with the other to form the final couplet, pulling the poem together into a single structural and thematic entity:

> *What is the meaning of all this? I asked, the wound in my heart still quivering with the knife. And I heard nothing but the dark.*

the terrified cling of marrow to teeth, to a lyric of beauty pushing through wind. And it is all here. Everything that ever was.

The cawing, flapping song of the beautiful dark

In the dark. In the beautiful perfume and stink of the world. (51–56)

That which I have called "counterpoint styling" is referred to by Harjo as songline, a device she continues to develop in a newly released collection:

> The original use of the word *songline* refers to the Australian Aboriginal concept of enforcing relationship to the land, to each other, to ancestors via the mapping of meaning with songs and narratives. Bruce Chatwin suggested in *The Songlines* (Penguin, New York, 1987) that the whole of Australia could be read as a musical score, where a musical phrase is like a map reference.
> All has been sung into existence. Every sunrise is sung and makes a continuous dawning all over the world. (*Became Human* 226)[11]

The device allows Harjo to enact structurally the dualism that has always figured prominently in her work: "She had some horses she loved. / She had some horses she hated. / These were the same horses."

To reconcile polarities is to infer a spiral pattern, though this is not always apparent. The reconciliation is a recognition, a mapping, of the dualities as the unified spiral that they constitute. The sets of horses, for example, seem irreconcilable but they are nevertheless the same horses. Likewise, day and night can be conceived as irreconcilable opposites, but, viewed from another perspective, they become parts of the same motion. Each day is a new creation; this day only *is* now because it is only happening now. (Being only *is* in its occurrence.) This day, however, is part of a larger movement encompassing all days and nights. The larger spiraling movement is most evident at the interstices of dualities, such as at dawn when a new arc of the spiral of (time) our existence is birthed. The motion between day and night, apparently irreconcilable opposites, forms a unified spiral within which we exist. The dawn is the point at which the poles are reconciled. The dawn is also the point at which we can enter our (occurring) being into the spiral motion that constitutes our existence. Our individual being constitutes a spiral. The dichotomous good times and bad times are part of the same spiral that is our life, just as kindness and cruelty can be part of the same relationship. To offer the spiral of our being to the larger spiral of all existence is to live life as participation in ceremony. As Harjo points out, "We do so either consciously or unconsciously" (*Map* 58).

Structure has meaning. Therefore, the meaning is in the structure, and by mapping the structure we understand the meaning:

> If I can locate the sense beyond desire,
> I will not eat or drink
> until I stagger into the earth
> with grief.
> I will locate the point of dawning
> and awaken
> with the longest day in the world. ("Emergence" 32–38)

If it were possible to get far enough above our existence, we would see the grand pattern. It would be a spiral and we would be part of it. If we could see the pattern, we would see that the negative aspects—the bad parts of relationships, the wars and murders, even the impending social-political-economic-environmental catastrophe—are all part of the same pattern, part of the "Beautiful Perfume and Stink of the World."

Joy Harjo's poetry works to get us above our existence, gets us looking at the grander patterns and seeing the spirals. Her most recent collection maps in a single canvas the spiraling motion that will carry us through the current devastation and into the, as yet undecided, next world: " . . . it's a very powerful moment and it could go either way" (*Spiral* 82). *A Map to the Next World* performs the structure of, discusses, and thereby fuses with the spiral of our existence. The text becomes a beautiful opening into a sacred space in which to consider the possibilities for survival. As Willie Ermine notes, Aboriginal epistemology is ancient and complex. He points out that the exploration of Native metaphysics was interrupted by the "relentless subjugation of Aboriginal people and the discounting of their ideas" (101). However, Joy Harjo and other indigenist artists are engaged in a renewal of these explorations of metaphysical truth. Their work functions as an invitation to enter into the exploration of an alternative and community-centered mode of thinking and being; their work becomes a place from which to embark.

Conclusion

> If, in order to admit the place of the other, we have to feel ourselves endangered, then we must have a very fragile sense of ourselves. To deny the past is to deny yourself, no matter how little you think you were a part of that past. To deny the past is actually to prepare the way for your own replacement because, after all, if you think you replaced somebody, then somebody will quite clearly replace you—and it won't be at the time of your choosing.
>
> —John Ralston Saul[1]

In his 1980 keynote address at the Conference on Contemporary American Indian Issues, Russell Thornton offered the suggestion that American Indian Studies had developed into a "reactive discipline," in that it tended to critique "existing bodies of knowledge . . . particularly those of anthropology and history [rather than] develop its own positive, unique directions" (6).[2] The suggestion, along with other aspects of this and Thornton's 1978 article "American Indian Studies as an Academic Discipline," seemed to signal a maturation of the discipline: Native Studies was beginning to examine itself critically. In retrospect, however, Thornton's assessment referred to a still nascent field, and his questions were only the first of many concerning the nature and function of Native Studies which have continued to plague the discipline. As discussed in chapters three and four, the function of formal education, insofar as Native students have been concerned (though the case is inherently generalizable), has always been assimilative. Furthermore, as M. Annette Jaimes (citing Thornton's work) points out, American Indian Studies has been not unrelated to the initial function of East Coast land-grant colleges, such as Harvard, Princeton, and Dartmouth, which was overtly assimilative: "It was the role of these institutions to 'civilize' the Indian, inculcating the perspective of Europe at the expense of indigenous worldview; Indian graduates were generally educated to become mental non-Indians" ("American Indian" 15).[3]

Its tendency to convert Native students into mental non-Indians has allowed the Western education system to assume the historical function of the United States Cavalry and the Royal Canadian Mounted Police with respect to Native people. Indian fighting, that is, after the introduction of widespread formal education, began to occur within the minds of indigenous students, who in turn tended to carry the virus of self-hatred back to their communities. Given that the more highly "educated" and more highly assimilated students have tended to acquire the more prestigious livelihoods, education-induced colonization has been especially potent. Note also that elite levels of the education system cannot presume to have functioned in isolation from the aggressively assimilative thrust of the system in general. However, as chapter three points out, it is possible and, I think, crucial to trace American Indian/First Nations intellectualism further back than is customary—into time immemorial. We need only make the radical gesture of suggesting that intellectualism did not begin with the abduction and indoctrination (inculcation) of Native children. It is crucial for any indigenist approach, indeed for any non-racist approach, to account for the antiquity of Aboriginal thought and to assert the antiquity of that intellectualism against more assimilative and dominant forms of inquiry. It is crucial, in other words, not to assume that indigenous thought began thirty years ago, nor even 200 years ago.

As noted in chapter three, radical movements on university campuses brought Native Studies into the academy in the late 1960s, and, as noted above, the discipline began to embark on a program of self-criticism over twenty years ago. William Willard and Mary Kay Downing, in their summary of the history of Native Studies, suggest that Native literature was a rather late addition to the discipline. At any rate, the discipline, specifically the criticism of indigenous literatures, continues to be dominated by non-Native scholars, in spite of the debate that continues to surround such domination. For example, again with specific reference to the sub-discipline of Native literary studies, in 1992 Daniel F. Littlefield, Jr. commented in his "American Indians, American Scholars and the American Literary Canon" on a "growing controversy between American Indians and American scholars" (95). Littlefield ended his essay, the 1992 MAASA Presidential Address, by noting: "Those of us who remain in the field of Indian studies and those who consider entering it should understand that the game we are now playing is a new one with rules that are constantly changing, that the Indians expect to be players, and that they know as much about the rules as we do" (108).[4] Arnold Krupat, however, in "Scholarship and Native American Studies: A Response to Daniel Littlefield, Jr.," took exception to what he perceived as Littlefield's disingenuous collegiality. Littlefield, a Cherokee scholar, had suggested that the "we" of his discussion referred to both Native and non-Native scholars: "By *we*, here and below, I mean American scholars, American Indian as well as non-Indian, who are products of Western educational philosophies and whose scholarly research and writing and teaching relate to American Indians" (Littlefield 108n). With this suggestion, Krupat disagreed: "This is what Littlefield says he means 'By we, here and below' . . . But this is not how he actually uses the pronoun. . . . Littlefield constructs the category of 'Indians' as a 'them' set against a non-Indian 'us'; he thus perpetuates exactly the opposition his remarks ostensibly seek to undo" (Krupat 81). Having dismissed Littlefield's brand of inclusivity, Krupat proceeded to dismantle the construction of social groupings he perceived as implicit in the arguments: "Neither Native scholars nor non-Native scholars can legitimately be represented as a singleminded, unified group with a consensual position on the issues in question" (81). As discussed at length in chapter one, Krupat also argued against his perception of Littlefield's position, and against Robert Warrior's 1991 argument against the inclusion of Native literature within the canon of American literature, and against several other sovereigntist writers, in his 1996 *The Turn to the Native* (Warrior, "A Marginal Voice" 30). While the debate is now over ten years old, events at recent Native American Literature Symposia (discussed in my introduction) suggest that the concerns of Native scholars have yet to be adequately addressed by their non-Native colleagues. There is still, after twenty or thirty years, nothing that could be called "rhetorical sovereignty" or "intellectual sovereignty" in Native Studies.

Throughout this book, I have argued from what might be termed a sovereigntist position. Nevertheless, I would like at this point to turn my argument against sovereignty. As noted in chapter three, "sovereignty" is one of those terms, like "democracy" and "Iraqi freedom," which stand in need of careful definition. Robert Warrior's use of the term, for example, differs markedly from Elizabeth Cook-Lynn's. Moreover, as Taiaiake Alfred points out, the term "is incompatible with traditional indigenous notions of power" (55). Alfred is careful to note that, "until now [the concept of sovereignty] has been an effective vehicle for indigenous critiques of the state's imposition of control; by forcing the state to recognize major inconsistencies between its own principles and its treatment of Native people, it has pointed to the racism and contradiction inherent in settler states' claimed authority over non-consenting peoples" (55). Likewise, I would suggest that sovereignty has proven useful as a vehicle for indigenous critique of colonization in literary studies; however, as Alfred also notes, "sovereignty" is tied to European notions of statehood. Etymologically, this much is obvious, and Alfred is certainly correct in his suggestion that the notion of "ruling over" a given land (or literature) is a distinctly non-traditional concept.

It is probably necessary to distinguish somewhat between "sovereignty" as a legal-political term and the use of the concept within indigenous literary studies; however, the usages are not unrelated. With respect to literature, this book has pointed out some difficulties with some prevailing scholarship and has argued for a corresponding need for a tribal-centered approach. This sounds very much like an argument in favor of sovereignty, and from such a position I do not wish to retreat. However, for the most part, I have used *sovereignty* uncritically, and I would like now to problematize the term, especially given the interminable nature of debates concerning the definition of the literature and peoples and concerning control over the discipline. Debates over control and definition have been unreasonably long-lived, and little if any movement has been made on the issues in spite of the validity and urgency of arguments in favour of sovereignty, and in spite of the increasing number of indigenous scholars working in the discipline. It seems likely, therefore, given that the concerns of indigenous scholars have been ignored almost altogether, that education does not eliminate racism. Education simply makes racism more subtle, more difficult to locate.

While some of the examples of colonialist criticism examined in this book may be deemed somewhat dated, similar tendencies can nevertheless be seen to operate among some of the most recent criticism as well. Education within a colonialist social structure (the academy being one) simply makes the more recent discourse of colonization more subtle. For example, in Arnold Krupat's most recent book *Red Matters,* he appears to have begun working in a genuine spirit of solidarity and support for Native literature and criticism: "Native materials continue to be badly neglected" (*vii*). This would seem to suggest that some progress has been made in the debates spawned in the early 1990s and fomented by Krupat. Politeness theory would support such a notion. As elaborated by Penelope Brown and Steven Levinson, politeness theory suggests that speakers across cultures consider certain contextual imperatives when (usually subconsciously) selecting linguistic strategies with which to perform a face-threatening act (FTA). "Face" concerns the speaker's wish to have his desires met (positive face), as well his wish to make his desires desirable to others (negative face) (62). Strategies for engaging in face-threatening acts, across cultures, depend on the "weightiness" of the FTA, which is determined by a combination of factors: the social distance between speaker and listener, the power relations between them, and the severity of the imposition. Since Krupat's most recent criticism is ostensibly more collegial, it can be assumed that the power he holds in the reader-writer relationship has decreased since his 1996 book *The Turn to the Native*. Nevertheless, while the more recent text seems, on the surface, quite supportive of indigenous concerns, the arguments are nevertheless fundamentally unchanged. On the first page of the book, Krupat makes the colonialist suggestion that "traditional" is synonymous with "non-combative": " . . . Native people, in particular the most traditional Native people, have generally avoided the sort of confrontational or performative politics on which the media thrive" (*vii*). The suggestion immediately defuses social action and prescribes a traditionalist subject position. It also ignores the fact that many traditional Native people—including Sitting Bull, Geronimo, Louis Riel, to name a few—have been quite political and have not worried about upsetting Romantic notions of noble savagery when the lives of their people have been threatened. Some may choose to focus on the qualifying adverb "generally" in the preceding quote—this is *generally*, not *absolutely*, the case about traditional people. The point is, Krupat is still presuming to define who and what a traditional Native person will be, and such people, he determines, are *generally* (as a rule, usually, for the most part) non-confrontational.

On the same page of the more recent text, Krupat goes on to suggest that those with genuine concern for Native people will enter into disciplines other than literature: " . . . given the horrendous situation of Indian people in terms of health, jobs, and education, one can readily understand why young persons, Native and not, interested in American Indians would choose to enter the fields of public health, medicine, and nursing, substance abuse and employment counseling, early childhood and adult education, rather than to go into cultural studies or literature" (*vii-viii*). Certainly, there is much work to be done in health and law, as elsewhere, but Linda Tuhiwai Smith notes a very similar set of "indigenous problems" in New Zealand to that in North America, which suggests quite strongly that the source of these devastating social problems is colonization. The problems result from the pervasiveness in indigenous life of colonial restraints and expectations, and the only way to eradicate the colonial habit of mind, from which colonial politics emerge, is to dismantle it at its source (153–54).

While such arguments as Krupat's may be seen to support the need for indigenous control of the literature, working towards "intellectual sovereignty" nevertheless involves the indigenist critic in an endless struggle to answer such colonialist arguments. Much time and effort must be expended unraveling the endless supply of increasingly subtle colonialist discourse and the increasingly twisted logic necessary to sustain the illogical paternalism. Furthermore, working within a sovereigntist paradigm confines the indigenist critic to the constraints of the statist system. With respect to Native Studies, the critic is bound by the inviolable disciplinarity of the academy while working in a discipline which is inherently interdisciplinary. Len Findlay makes this point in his recent "Always Indigenize! The Radical Humanities in the Postcolonial Canadian University" (312). Recall that the principle of connectedness in Aboriginal theory makes the interdisciplinary nature of Native Studies a justifiable orientation. Findlay argues for a radical humanities, but questions Tuhiwai Smith's affirmation in epigraph of Audre Lorde's caution against the use of "the master's tools [to] dismantle the master's house" (Tuhiwai Smith 19). He suggests rather that a concerted effort is required, one which uses "some of the master's most important tools" within a radical humanities to dismantle the house (310). While Findlay's article has all the sounds of radical indigenism—and it makes some important notes such as the co-dependent relationship of governments and elite institutions in maintaining "neo-paternalistic structures"—the article is nevertheless easily subjected to the same critique it levels against Geoffrey Hartman (307). That is, Findlay "combines radical textualism and cultural conservatism," albeit with more subtlety than Hartman (319). Findlay seems to work very hard in support of indigenization, yet he relies excessively on postmodern methodologies rather than indigenous. Even a radical (Western) humanities is bound into inefficacy by the (predominantly post-structuralist) tools available to it. For this reason, it is difficult to locate an exit from Findlay's text—let alone from humanities departments—through which to execute any transformation of social conditions. One is left, then, wondering whether the proposed radicalization of the humanities is not simply another ostensibly radical, but ultimately self-negating, exercise in academic discourse.

Since indigenous literature is tied to vital community interests and concerns, and since much of the prevailing criticism is colonialist in orientation, simply acquiescing to white domination of the discipline may not seem to be an option. As mentioned, sovereignty is only valid within a statist framework, one which assumes that land and literature can be "controlled"; sovereignty involves the critic in endless struggles against the colonizer at the expense of increased attention to the literature itself; and sovereignty ties the critic to the tools available within a statist framework. As noted in this book, however, in the Aboriginal worldview, land and story are alive, and any sense of control over such entities is foreign. What I am suggesting is that criticism, in order to be indigenist, must be infused so completely with the Aboriginal worldview that questions of sovereignty become irrelevant. That is, not only should the criticism recognize the interconnectedness of all that is and attempt to make connections to the infinite (and certainly extra-academic) community, it should also recognize the absurdity of, and refuse to engage any longer in, arguments over the control and definition of the land, literature, and people.

Those working from an indigenous worldview will assuredly comprehend the literature that issues from such a worldview at heightened levels. However, what is much more important than debates over control and definition of the literature is the literature itself. As repeated throughout my discussion, indigenous literatures contain the seeds of survival for humanity. As critics, therefore, we can no longer afford to engage in interminable debates when, first, we now have a sufficient number of scholars to carry on the discussion without any necessary recourse to academic sanction. That is, we are no longer in need of permission to study Native literature on Native terms. The indigenous-run (and, aptly, non-organizational) Native American Literature Symposium makes this point clear. Second, humanity finds itself in a crisis state at present, regardless of whether the academy will welcome political (activist) scholarship or not. The world needs (and a growing number are prepared) to hear what Native people are saying, especially in their literature, which, at its best, constructs an artistic rendering of the world infused with an Aboriginal worldview. However, as long as indigenist scholars of the literature are engaged in pointless debates over control of the uncontrollable, definition of the undefinable, the importance of Native literature will remain a rather minor academic concern.

* * * *

I would like to close by succinctly stating my sense of an indigenist criticism. Indigenist criticism is part of a larger movement in indigenous intellectualism, which extends to encompass the views and concerns of indigenous peoples around the globe. Indigenous intellectualism is connected, that is, to the struggles of the community in the expansive sense noted by Jace Weaver (*That the People xiii*). Therefore, indigenous intellectualism, of which indigenist literary criticism is a component, is concerned with the well-being of the land (environmentalism) and the well-being of the people (social justice). An indigenist criticism works to dismantle the barriers between the disciplines, and between the disciplines and the world, with or without the sanction of the academy. More correctly, it proceeds as if any such barriers were social constructs erected in the interests of the very few. An indigenist criticism does not limit its scope to the study and concerns of literature, because such a limitation is not possible except in theory, and an indigenist criticism consistently positions itself within an infinitely larger context. The criticism recognizes its own fundamental relatedness, as it does the expression of such relatedness in the literature, a relatedness which extends, as mentioned, to the larger community, and extends even to the spirit realm. Again, the criticism proceeds as if academic barriers between the sacred and the secular were social constructs: its sense of connectedness is without limit. An indigenist criticism is grounded in the recognition of the connectedness of everything and strives to enter into, rather than separate itself from, this fundamental reality.

Since, as Joy Harjo points out, "ultimately everyone is a relative," an indigenist criticism does not seek to exclude people based on "race." Entering into the indigenist project, however, has implications. To engage in an indigenist criticism is to begin working, at every juncture, in the interests of the community in the infinite sense of the word. When the non-Native indigenist critic looks outward to the community, she will likely recognize that white women and (to an even greater extent) poor whites are disenfranchised under the current system of white privilege. As such, the current system, which may be a source of privilege for the critic, must be dismantled; for the ways in which the present system oppresses particular EuroCanadians, based on class or gender, is very much related to how and why Native people are oppressed and dispossessed. Furthermore, the indigenist project implicitly, since it is based on relatedness, includes EuroCanadians and EuroAmericans, because diversity has always been crucial to survival from an Aboriginal perspective. An indigenist criticism, then, does not abandon non-Native scholars; it simply abandons the intensely isolating and increasingly prevalent dance towards death into which colonialism urges all peoples of the earth.

Migwetch.

Notes

NOTES TO THE INTRODUCTION

1. Cajete, *Look* 31.
2. Kenneth Roemer relates his experiences as a critic of American Indian literatures in the early 1970s: "One of my colleagues wittily announced that Indian literature was an oxymoron; another routinely called it 'shit lit'; another enjoyed giving me playful Hollywood war whoops as I entered the elevator; a fourth proclaimed, in a department newsletter, that I must have graduated from 'Bentnose U'" (17–18).
3. I refer here to discussions around the topic that dominated the American Literature Association Symposia on American Indian Literature in 1999 and 2000 in Puerto Vallarta, Mexico. Specifically, during a key Studies in American Indian Literatures (SAIL) session that was to serve as a retrospective of the discipline, several Native scholars wondered about the make-up of the panel, which included not one Native scholar. The general answer seemed to be that none could be found. The question was then raised as to why non-Native scholars were studying Native literature in the first place. Few answers were forthcoming, but the discussion became particularly heated at that point, with most non-Native scholars contending that the question was unfair. Following the 2000 symposium, the conference was moved to an American Indian-owned and -operated venue (Mystic Lake Casino) for 2002 and 2003, at which time the American Literature Association suspended its sponsorship. The name of the conference has since been changed to the Native American Literature Symposium (NALS). The 1999 symposium to which I refer was followed by a curiously sanitized re-telling of events at the conference, in which John Purdy reminded readers of Roemer's scare-quoted evaluation of Native literature (1–5). See above, note 2.
4. The alacrity with which Cherokees and Crees/Ojibwes have in separate instances adopted a syllabary or syllabic system suggests that the non-existence of written expression, if it is conceded, has little to do with "evolution" towards mental readiness.
5. Gregory A. Cajete (Tewa Pueblo) cites the work of Edwin J. Nicholls of the U.S. National Institute of Mental Health in arguing for *four* worldviews

181

among the peoples of the earth. At any rate, Cajete concurs that a strikingly similar worldview is evident among the Peoples of the Americas (*Igniting* 141). See also Dennis McPherson, "A Definition of Culture: Canada and First Nations," and Viola F. Cordova, "The European Concept of *Usen:* An American Aboriginal Text."

6. McPherson suggests the distinction occurred with seventeenth-century British (Lockean) philosophy (82); Cordova places the break earlier, in the immediate post-Classical period (31).

7. The discussion which follows borrows heavily from Marías, who notes three major themes of medieval philosophy, the third being reason; I focus only on the two that are pertinent to the present discussion. Other commentators enumerate the major themes of the Middle Ages differently. Heinz Heimsoeth, for example, finds six themes, with the universals covered under his fifth theme: the individual (193–205). However, Heimsoeth would concur with some of the argument I, following Marías, am advancing here: namely, that modern philosophical thought is rooted in an occurrence in the late Middle Ages, rather than, as is more commonly assumed, a Renaissance or Enlightenment flowering (33). David Knowles would agree with the inference that the synthesis achieved by Aquinas marked the "high point" of medieval thought (231–61). More recent thought on the matter, however, seems to favor the nominalist turn in general, and John Duns Scotus and William of Ockham (Occam) in particular, as the ultimate in medieval sophistication. See, for example, David Luscombe's introductory volume, *Medieval Thought,* or, for a more entertaining, while erudite, opposing view to my own, see Umberto Eco's *The Name of the Rose*. Louis Mackey, in the vein of St. Bonaventure and Duns Scotus, asserts a middle ground: the necessary coexistence of the universal and the singular (147–80). While some may object to the characterization of nominalism as a decline in medieval thought, and some may find the question of universals as more or less important than I have here indicated, the general consensus is that the issue is an important one with often overlooked implications for the present: " . . . and, at the same time, refreshing study of the enlightened monk Bede, rational comforts sought in Occam, to understand the mystery of the Sign where Saussure is still obscure" (Eco 511). At any rate, I am seeking not so much to situate myself in the context of serious debate over the importance of the question of universals in the Middle Ages, a context which would require years of serious study, than to suggest a source of the distinction between Aboriginal and Western epistemologies, a source that does not infer social Darwinism.

8. In this sense, perhaps Cordova is correct (n. 6), for the Classical period did not seek the answer for an assumed temporal genesis of Creation. The Creator is so inextricably a part of Creation that to ask the origin of Creation is as meaningless a question as to ask the origin of the Creator.

9. Cordova also mentions the appearance of such thinking in the work of Spinoza and Einstein.

10. Again in support of Cordova's contention, recall Parmenides' (b. 515? BC) notion of the Entity (Greek ον), or Being, which bears striking resemblance to *manitou* here discussed.

11. Paula Gunn Allen explains the distinction as follows:

> Another difference between these two ways [Western and Aboriginal] of perceiving reality lies in the tendency of the American Indian to view space as spherical and time as cyclical, whereas the non-Indian tends to view space as linear and time as sequential. The circular concept requires all "points" that make up the sphere of being to have a significant identity and function, while the linear model assumes that some "points" are more significant than others. In the one, significance is a necessary factor of being in itself, whereas in the other, significance is a function of placement on an absolute scale that is fixed in time and space. . . . the Indian universe moves and breathes continuously, and the Western universe is fixed and static. (59)

12. In addition to Weintraub's discussion of Orlan's work (77–83), see also the artist's website (*Orlan*).
13. The controversy brought the National Gallery of Canada before a House of Commons Committee to defend its budget ("National Gallery").
14. Note that Dempsey Bob also produces traditional regalia for ceremonial use in Northwest Coast communities.
15. While there are differences between Aboriginal writers from either side of the border, these, like the differences between writers of European ancestry, are incidental. That is, I wish to consider the fundamental epistemological orientations of the writers, which renders Canada-U.S. distinctions rather trivial.
16. Russell Means suggests, since India in 1492 was known as Hindustan, that the term "Indian" applied to Native people was actually a corruption of the Spanish "In Dios." Early Spanish commentators frequently noted the remarkable benevolence of the people they encountered in the "New World."
17. Tuhiwai Smith notes that she borrows the concept of "talking back," "writing back," etc., from others. See her note 10 (18).

NOTES TO CHAPTER ONE

1. Campbell, "It's the Job" 270.
2. On the sports mascot controversy, see Spindel. See also Phillip Deloria.
3. For Berkhofer's discussion of representations in literature in particular, see part 3 of his book-length treatment of images of the American Indian.
4. In addition to those mentioned, the reader may wish to consult the following sources on representations of Native people: Bataille (*Native American Representations*), Bellin, S. Elizabeth Bird, Churchill, Dumont, Durham, Jaimes-Guerrero, Jara and Spadaccini, Gordon Johnston, Owens, and Rock. See my bibliography.
5. "Two callow imperialists, seemingly far apart, would meet within a generation: the Castilians of Spain and the Aztecs of Mexico. Both were expanding states with tribal origins; both had quickly gained control over other peoples but had not absorbed them effectively. Of the two, Mexico

was by far the larger. The Aztec capital—today's Mexico City—held a quarter of a million people: four times more than Tudor London. The total population under its control was some 20 million" (Wright 11).
6. See titles listed above, note 4.
7. Interestingly, E. Pauline Johnston, born and raised in the Brantford, ON, area, is almost invariably included among Native American authors. Likewise, Mourning Dove, a great-aunt of Okanagan writer Jeannette Armstrong (born and raised in present-day British Columbia), is invariably included, while Armstrong herself is a relative unknown among American Native Literature specialists.
8. Note that Michaels' book includes an entire chapter on American Indians entitled "The Vanishing American," in which he seems to be arguing (in a rather convoluted way) that European immigrants actually were "vanishing Americans" during the 1800s and early 1900s. Much of this chapter is an analysis of Zane Grey's popular novel by the same title. Michaels writes: "If the Indians are the first Americans and the Americans are descended from the English, then the English become the 'forefathers' of the Indians and the Indians going off to fight for them are fighting as Americans for their ancestor and against the ancestors of the un-American missionaries. Or, to put this from the standpoint not of the Indians *about* whom Grey was writing but of the white Americans *for* whom he was writing, if the Indians are the "first Americans," then the Americans now going off to war are descended from them; the Indians, whose forefathers are the English, are themselves the forefathers of the Americans. Volunteering to fight and so proving themselves as American as the white man, they make it possible for the white man to become their descendant and so to become as American as the Indian" (40).

Duke University Press, publisher of Michaels' text, suggests in the advertisement for the book that Indian identity (specifically the destabilization thereof) is a key element of *Our America*: "Michaels's sustained rereading of the texts of the period—the canonical, the popular, and the less familiar—exposes recurring concerns such as the reconception of the image of the Indian as a symbol of racial purity and national origins, the relation between World War I and race, contradictory appeals to the family as a model for the nation, and anxieties about reproduction that subliminally tie whiteness and national identity to incest, sterility, and impotence."
9. Krupat's discussion of the topic in the first chapter ("Criticism and Native American Literature") of *The Turn to the Native* is a re-working of his 1993 response to Daniel Littlefield's "American Indians, American Scholars and the American Literary Canon." See Krupat's "Scholarship and Native American Studies: A Response to Daniel Littlefield, Jr."
10. The full name of this United States Statute at Large, commonly called the "Dawes Act" or the "Allotment Act," is An Act to Provide for the Allotment in Severalty to Indians on the Various Reservations, and to Extend the Protection of the Laws of the United States and the Territories over the Indians, and for Other Purposes.

11. For further reading on this aspect of indigenous thought, see Kimberly Blaeser's *Gerald Vizenor: Writing in the Oral Tradition* and Jeannette Armstrong's "Land Speaking." As with notions of "memory in the blood" and fundamental connectedness, such discussions of orality are widespread.
12. The Warrior work to which Krupat objects is a review of his [Krupat's] earlier book, *The Voice in the Margin* (Warrior, "A Marginal Voice" 29–30).
13. See Hulan, "Some Thoughts."
14. At the same convention (New York, 2002), Ruoff became just the third recipient of the Modern Language Association's Award for Lifetime Scholarly Achievement.

NOTES TO CHAPTER TWO

1. Cordova, "Doing Native" 14.
2. Two other edited collections of note are *(Ad)dressing Our Words: Aboriginal Perspectives on Aboriginal Literatures*, edited by Armand Garnet Ruffo, and *Creating Community: A Roundtable on Canadian Aboriginal Literatures*, edited by Renate Eigenbrod and Jo-Ann Episkenew. The only book-length treatment of indigenous literature in Canada is Helen Hoy's previously mentioned work.
3. In 1999 the UN Human Rights Committee expressed its concern that Canada had failed to implement the recommendations of the 1996 Royal Commission on Aboriginal Peoples. The UN report suggested that "Canada's treatment of aboriginals is in violation of international law and the social situation of first nations 'is the most pressing human rights issue facing Canadians'" (Gordon A4). More recently, the UN Committee on the Elimination of Racial Discrimination suggested that Canada continues to tolerate racism against Native people and other minorities. Kurt Herndl, the Austrian rapporteur on the reports submitted by Canada, noted "a disproportionately high proportion of indigenous people in detention—and [that] the same, of course, is true for people of African and Asian descent." The committee was also concerned about the high rate of "violence against and deaths in custody of Aboriginal and people of African and Asian descent" (Schlein). Such reports suggest that the following events have not gone unnoticed by the international community: the highly suspicious killing of Dudley George by the Ontario Provincial Police in 1995 ("What Does the United Nations?") and the complaint filed by an Aboriginal man that in January 2000 two Saskatoon police officers arrested him without cause and drove him outside the city, where they left him alone in light clothing. The latter incident was alleged to have occurred shortly after two other Aboriginal men were found frozen to death in the same area ("Canadian Oversight").
4. Carter Revard is an Osage poet, medievalist, and, significantly, a Rhodes Scholar.
5. Regarding polyvocality, Wong builds on P. N. Medvedev and Mikhail Bakhtin (14). See also the related discussion of heteroglossia in Mikhail M. Bakhtin's "Discourse in the Novel" (299–300).

6. Some examples: "Sometimes the warriors had their wives come forward and assist them in acting out their coups. (We must hope that they were as skilled in pulling their punches as they were in pantomime.)"; "One is reminded of the deconstructionist literary critics who argue, as does J. Hillis Miller, that undecidability 'is always thematized in the text itself in the form of metalinguistic statements' (1975:30–31)—and so the Hero Critics call our attention not to the text but to their own forthrightly subjective play with the text" (Brumble 25, 93).
7. In functional grammar, modality refers to the speaker's opinion as to the truth value of a statement; i.e., it locates the statement somewhere in the area between "yes-ness" and "no-ness." The phrase "it is said" lowers the truth value of the statement on indigenous perceptions of identity. Likewise, on page 39 of *Sending My Heart Back*, Wong uses a low modality configuration in referring to another aspect of indigenous knowledge: "language *is thought to reconfigure* reality" (emphasis added). A high modality configuration (language *reconfigures* reality) would omit the passive verbal phrasing, which recasts the statement as belief rather than fact and denies responsibility for the proposal, attributing it instead to an other. See M.A.K. Halliday's *Introduction to Functional Grammar*.
8. For a particularly lucid elaboration of nominalism and of medieval philosophy as it relates to this discussion, see Marías.
9. For a discussion of "residual orality" with respect to writers of the period, see Ong (93–98). See also Janel M. Mueller's chapter "Prose in the Later Fourteenth and Fifteenth Centuries," in which she notes the dismissal of medieval prose style in English among literary historians employing the evolutionary myth. Mueller notes, for example, George P. Krapp (1915), who remarks on the absence in medieval writing of the "more mature manner of modern English," and finds instead that the "sentences are short and direct, never complex. Few connectives are used, and those of the most obvious kind. . . . The whole tone of the expression is naive, the language of a grown-up child" (93).
10. Methot cites eleven articles in the previous year in *The Globe and Mail* alone. Grey Owl is also included in a government sponsored website on national heroes of Canada ("Grey Owl").
11. For further reading on Grey Owl, see texts by Brower, Donald B. Smith, Anahareo, Billinghurst, Ruffo, and Dickson.
12. *Smoke Signals* was released June 26, 1999; *Grey Owl* was released October 1, 1999.
13. See Krupat (*Voice* 13). See also Brumble (173–74). For an opposing view, see Womack (26). See also Tuhiwai Smith (72–74).

NOTES TO CHAPTER THREE

1. This story, taken from James Redsky's *Great Leader of the Ojibway: Mis-quona-queb*, was told by Mis-quona-queb to his children (65). "Nene-bush" is one of various spellings/pronunciations for the Anishinaabe (Ojibwe) trickster-figure. Nanabush, Nanabozho, and Waynaboozhoo are others.

Notes to Chapter Three

2. See Dickason, *Canada's First Nations*, and Francis, *Native Time*. Concerning the deaths of Poundmaker, Big Bear, and One Arrow, Dickason notes that "Prison terms were virtual death sentences" (286). All three had to be released early and died within a year. Dickason also points out that the legality of the trials was highly irregular. One Arrow, for example, spoke no English and received little translation (285–86).
3. Remarks during MLA session, Washington, DC, 2000. For further reading, see Warrior (*Tribal Secrets* 5–14).
4. "A request from American Indian high school seniors—backed by their parents—to wear traditional dress at graduation ceremonies has met with resistance from Albuquerque School District officials. Students, parents, teachers, attorneys and tribal leaders are preparing to protest the school's policy requiring caps and gowns only at the next school board meeting on April 16" (C5). The school board's reasoning for its refusal of permission was that if Native students were allowed to wear traditional regalia, then gang members, neo-Nazis, and KKK members must likewise be permitted to wear their preferred clothing.
5. See the discussion of the mayor of Pau's use of the same strategy in addressing a Béarnais crowd in Béarnais rather than French (Bourdieu 68–69).
6. See, for example, Adamson.
7. By "traditional," I refer to anything that springs from a worldview that emphasizes community and understands community as encompassing the entire temporal and spatial universe including the spiritual realm, which constitutes and infuses the physical. The traditional, then, looks outward and includes ultimately everything, while the non-traditional worldview obsesses over the self, looks inward, and ultimately implodes in solipsism. From this view, a traditional story can be told today, or it can be written and read into existence. The worldview from which it issues is what makes it traditional, rather than where or when it was written. Concerning the widespread acknowledgement of the transformative potential of language, see Brill de Ramirez: "Within American Indian traditions of oral storytelling, there is a power that actually transforms the listener through her or his engagement with the story" (6). See also Wiget: " . . . the transformative power of compelling language, a historical sense of place, and the political dimensions of poetry are especially evident in Simon Ortiz's most recent work, a cycle of poems entitled *from Sand Creek*." Finally, see LaLonde, who cites Lincoln: "Time and again, Native American traditions tell us, the first people turned and turn to ceremony and artistic utterance for celebration and healing. Both are intimately connected to place and are transformative. Kenneth Lincoln writes that for Native Americans 'Words carry their essential meanings' and songpoems 'sing the origins of people, creatures, things, in local revelations, exactly where they exist. The people hear and glimpse truths unexpectedly, out of the corner of the eye, as nature compresses and surprises with rich mystery. All things are alive, suggestive, sacred, and in common' (46). The act of articulation, then, of giving breath to and jointing together, is revelatory, celebratory, and transformative" (15).

8. Castro makes the same point with respect to the indigenous image in non-Native literature: "Since first contact, the literary treatment of the Native American by white writers has, in fact, been more revealing of white culture than red . . . When the [brutish] image persisted into the nineteenth century, it served to reinforce one of the driving myths of our culture—the myth of progress—as well as the social Darwinism that often supported it" (xiv-xv).
9. Regarding Ong's influence on Vizenor, see Blaeser (*Vizenor* 28–31).
10. Some examples: "One further comment on my intentions for this book is essential. I write for Indian people. . . . This is the audience that I first and foremost imagine reading my work. I see their faces as I write. This is not to say that I do not think about the non-Indian people who might also pick up this book. I hope that some of these readers will come to know this Indian person (and my ideas) a little better" (Monture-Angus, *Journeying* 17–18); "I also mean to make it clear that my primary audience is Native people. We have so much work to do. As a powerful woman once wrote, 'If we do not define ourselves, we will be defined by others for their use and to our detriment.' I agree, and so I write" (Bird, "Breaking" 48); "My purpose in writing *Red on Red* is to contribute, probably in a small way, toward opening up a dialogue among Creek people, specifically, and Native people, more generally, regarding what constitutes meaningful literary efforts" (Womack 1); "Though I hold no animosity toward the Europeans in this land, I did not intend to write for them. My voice is for those who need to hear some truth. It has been a long time since I had an intimate discussion with my own people and those other people who are not offended by our private truth. If you do not find yourselves spoken to, it is not because I intend rudeness—you just don't concern me now" (Maracle, *I Am Woman* 10).
11. HAARP, the High-Frequency Active Auroral Research Program, is a joint initiative of the US Navy and the US Air Force, based in Gakona, Alaska. According to the official website, "HAARP is a scientific endeavor aimed at studying the properties and behavior of the ionosphere, with particular emphasis on being able to understand and use it to enhance communications and surveillance systems for both civilian and defense purposes" (*HAARP*). The system will beam (probably is already beaming) 3.6 Gigawatts into the earth's ionosphere, heating and therefore destabilizing the earth's protective shield (and disturbing the Northern Lights) for such "civilian and defense purposes" as the disruption and control of weather patterns and communication systems. Interaction with the "Star Wars" defense shield is also anticipated.
12. For a collection of his newspaper articles and more recent attacks on AIM and its leaders, see Vizenor's *Crossbloods*.
13. See Weaver (*That the People* 26–29) and Warrior (*Tribal Secrets* xvii). Both bow unnecessarily to Vizenor; for their work is easily among the most sophisticated of Aboriginal theory and yet retains a community-centered focus.
14. See note 1 above.
15. I address the issue of essentialism more fully in Chapter Four.

16. For further examples of verbal-centered nature of indigenous languages, see Clements.
17. Whitehead's father was a vicar of the Church of England, and one of the major attractions of process thought has been the way it can be read into Christianity (Cobb and Griffin 162). However, when the process philosopher-theologian speaks of God and Christ, she is not referring to the "God" and "Christ" of popular or theological traditions. For her, God is process itself, as well as the "primordial envisagement of the pure possibilities" in which process occurs (28). To be "holy," then, is to enter fully into the process of existence and the realization of possibility.
18. The water droplet metaphor is my own. Whitehead's term for the becoming of existence is "concrescence." Process (my series of water droplets) is a "serially ordered society" of "occasions of experience." See Cobb and Griffin (13–29).
19. Note that "enjoyment" in process philosophy refers, roughly, to the experience (conscious or not) of actuality.
20. The review is entitled "Red Matters" and is elaborated upon in Krupat's subsequent text-length study *Red Matters: Native American Studies*.
21. On Andrew Jackson and Cherokee Removal, see Wright (214–21). Wright notes two Supreme Court cases, *Cherokee Nation v. Georgia* (1830) and *Worcester v. Georgia* (1832), which formed the basis of American Indian political status in the United States. Jackson's response to Chief Justice John Marshall's unequivocal decision was, "Marshall has rendered his decision; now let him enforce it." Cherokee removal, in which one quarter of the people perished, proceeded several years later in contravention of the Supreme Court decision. On the Burnt Church lobster dispute, see "Burnt Church News." The dispute concerns a Supreme Court decision of September 17, 1999, which upheld a 1760s treaty and permitted Native bands in the area to fish beyond the legal season: " . . . nothing less would uphold the honour and integrity of the Crown in its dealings with the Mi'kmaq people to secure their peace and friendship. . . ." Nevertheless, the RCMP and the Department of Fisheries and Oceans under the Chrétien government, in violation of the Supreme Court decision, began arresting Native fishers, confiscating and destroying boats and equipment, and ramming occupied boats at sea. Alarmingly graphic video footage of one ramming incident was made public and was instrumental in forcing a settlement of the lengthy dispute.
22. "Two-thirds of all North American uranium is located on or adjacent to Indian reservations. In aboriginal Australia, the figures are the same. Millions of acres of Canadian reserves are under lease for mining exploration" (LaDuke 64). See also Bird, "Breaking the Silence."

NOTES TO CHAPTER FOUR

1. Quoted in Whitt, 146. The introduction to the present chapter owes a great deal to Whitt's insightful and well documented essay.
2. The HGDP is a sub-project of the larger Human Genome Mapping Project. As Whitt points out, the HGDP is concerned with mapping the cell lines of Aboriginal Peoples for that which can be added to the understanding of

European cell lines and also because Aboriginal Peoples are considered "dying races."
3. I think here of Krupat's discussion in the introduction to *Voice in the Margin,* in which he all but erases Indian essence. See Chapter One of the present work for a fuller discussion.
4. This use of "story" as a verb is borrowed from Lee Maracle's *Ravensong.* Gregory Cajete also employs the usage (*Look* 138).
5. Although a 1939 Supreme Court case later ruled that the Inuit are "Indians" under the Constitution Act (1867), the Inuit, like the Métis, remain excluded from the 1876 Indian Act. See Chartier (48–49).
6. For more on the Indian Act, see *Henderson's Annotated Indian Act.* The site is an excellent source of Aboriginal law and contains links to other pertinent pieces of legislation. Henderson summarizes the progression of various acts and amendments to this remarkably persistent piece of colonial legislation as follows: "The first federal legislation about Indians after Confederation was the 1868 Secretary of State Act, soon followed by An Act for the Gradual Civilization and Enfranchisement of Indians. These statutes were consolidated in the Revised Statutes, 1876. Amendments can be traced through succeeding editions of these consolidations to about 1990. After 1990, it is necessary to consult the volumes of the Statutes of Canada or a current bills service for proposed and enacted amendments." See also Bartlett and *The Indian Act and Amendments, 1970–1993: An Indexed Collection.*
7. In 1998, an Ontario trial court judge dismissed 1993 charges against Steve Powley, a Métis from Sault Ste. Marie, ON, and his son of hunting moose without a license contrary to the Ontario Game and Fish Act. The landmark ruling, which would give Métis people the same rights as Indians in this regard, was upheld in February 2001, by the Ontario Court of Appeals. The Ontario government was subsequently granted permission to have the case heard at the Supreme Court of Canada. A decision was expected in 2003. Jean Teillet, counsel for the defense, is a great-grandniece of Louis Riel (Bailey).
8. See also Dickason (*Canada's* 145–46).
9. Mawedopenais also requested that his relatives south of the new border be included in the treaty. He was unsuccessful in securing this provision (Morris 68).
10. These reserves were later re-identified by the Canadian government as "Indian Reserves."
11. On Métis history and interactions with early Canada, see (in addition to Dickason) works by George F. G. Stanley, Grant MacEwan, Joseph Kinsey Howard, A. S. Lussier, and Don McLean.
12. On residential schools, see Milloy: "In particularly stubborn cases, the agent might consider withholding 'from unwilling parents all help that you have at your disposal, provisions, tea, tobacco, etc.'" (70). On treaty negotiations, see Dickason: "As Big Bear laboured to unite Amerindians, Edgar Dewdney, lieutenant-governor of the North-West Territories, 1881–8, worked to divide them. He did this by the differential distribution of

Notes to Chapter Four

rations, using food as an instrument to keep the people quiet whenever a situation threatened to get out of hand" (*Canada's* 278).

13. On the Canadian government's allotment of "$350 million to support community-based healing initiatives for Métis, Inuit and First Nations people on and off reserve who were affected by the legacy of physical and sexual abuse in Residential Schools," see the Indian and Northern Affairs Canada Internet site ("Aboriginal Healing").

14. From *Shell Shaker*: "*Dear Isaac: I am a Choctaw teenager, age eighteen. My boyfriend is twenty-five, and a Crow. He has asked me to marry him. . . . ' Dear Uncertain: Choctaws don't marry birds'*" (64). From *Keeper 'n Me:* "Or they'll be sharing deer hunting stories around a campfire one night and an Ojibway will describe a deer running through the bush faster'n the east end of a westbound Sioux" (6).

15. I borrow the terms from Monture-Angus (*Journeying* 17).

16. Flanagan received the prestigious and lucrative ($25,000) Donner Prize, awarded for a book on Canadian social policy, for his efforts.

17. Note the prominent pan-Indian movements that have issued from Native people themselves. For example, Pontiac (Odawa) (1712/25–69), Nescambiouit (Abenaki) (1660–1722), Kiala (Fox) (c. 1733–34), and other great chiefs argued for the importance of a pan-Indian alliance in maintaining indigenous freedom and homelands in North America. The Ghost Dance and the Native American Church have represented pan-Indian religious movements. The difficulty with pan-Indianism is not with the natural and ongoing intertribal exchange of ideas and practices, but with the external and ossifying imposition of definitions of being.

18. See also text by William M. Clements.

19. Ermine's discussion is the most detailed and concise exposition in writing of the Aboriginal worldview of which I am aware. For further reading, see, among many others, works by Leroy Little Bear, Gregory Cajete (esp. *Native Science* and *Look to the Mountain*), Jace Weaver, Dennis McPherson, Viola Cordova, Rebecca Tsosie, and Vine Deloria, Jr.

20. For an extended performance of such an infusion of Aboriginal reality through English, see Maria Campbell's *Stories of the Road Allowance People*. The book is a collection of traditional stories, translated by Campbell into a form of Rez English, and illustrated in painting by Sherry Farrell Racette. Regarding her fitness for the project, Campbell writes, "I am a very young and inexperienced storyteller [she was fifty-four at the time] compared to the people who teach me. And although I speak my language I have had to relearn it, to decolonize it or at least begin the process of decolonization. This has not been an easy task and the journey has taken me eighteen years. I have paid for the stories by re-learning and re-thinking my language and by being a helper or servant to the teachers. I have also paid for the stories with gifts of blankets, tobacco and even a prize Arab stallion" (2).

21. I allude here to Jane Elliott's work, captured in several films including *Blue Eyed* (1996). Elliott discusses and conducts workshops on the overwhelming pressure on people of colour to "act white."

22. Although it is considered prudent to distinguish between the writer (even the writer of an autobiography) and the first-person singular voice, I have decided to avoid forcing the distinction. My use of "Maria" and "Campbell" will be motivated primarily by stylistic considerations.
23. An excellent resource and compelling reading is Milloy's *"A National Crime": The Canadian Government and the Residential School System, 1879 to 1986.*
24. See above, note 6, regarding the Indian Act, 1876, and amendments. See also Dickason's *Canada's First Nations*.
25. On the image of the Métis, see article by Patricia Riley.
26. For further reading on Aboriginal pedagogical theory, consult any of the texts by Gregory A. Cajete noted in my bibliography, especially *Igniting the Sparkle*.

NOTES TO CHAPTER FIVE

1. Cajete, *Look* 42.
2. A quick search of the MLA Bibliography uncovers fifty records.
3. *Secrets from the Center of the World* is a collaborative work with photographer Stephen Strom.
4. See articles by Geary Hobson and Elaine Jahner ("Indian Literature").
5. For further reading on language poetry (in addition to Rasula), see edited collections by Ron Silliman and by Bruce Andrews and Charles Bernstein.
6. Harjo began her artistic career as a painter.
7. For Harjo's own discussion of the confluence of persons in this poem, see *The Spiral of Memory*, particularly her interview with Sharyn Stever (80–81).
8. The concerted effort to eliminate indigenous languages is well documented. Again, I refer the reader to John Milloy's work.
9. Asked by Laura Coltelli who her audience is, Harjo replied, "Who I saw when I closed my eyes and wrote this poem were women, mostly Indian women, those who survived and those who weren't strong enough (whose words we'll always have to carry), the ones who speak through me, and even those who hate me for speaking. I saw women who were holding many children, others embracing lovers, some dancing the stomp dance, and others swinging hard out on some spinning dance floor. . . . I think I always write with especially these women in mind because I want us all to know as women, as Indian people, as human beings that there is always hope, that we are whole, alive, and precious" (*Spiral* 18).
10. Seven is also considered a sacred number. There are seven directions, taking into account *up*, *down*, and *within*.
11. See, for example, Joy Harjo, "Letter (with songline) to the Breathmaker" (*How We Became* 177–78).

NOTES TO THE CONCLUSION

1. Saul, "Canada: A Layering."
2. Quoted *sic* in Jaimes, "American Indian" 15.

Notes to the Conclusion

3. In 1862, the Morrill Act (also known as the Land Grant Act) was passed, approving the "donation" of [Indian] lands for Colleges of Agriculture and Mechanic Arts. Today, most state colleges and universities in the USA are land grant institutions. On the history of private colleges, see article by Rogers.
4. Mid-America American Studies Association (MAASA).

Bibliography

"The Aboriginal Healing Foundation–Backgrounder." *Indian and Northern Affairs Canada Online.* 4 May 1998. Indian and Northern Affairs Canada. 28 Feb. 2003 <http://www.ainc-inac.gc.ca/nr/prs/m-a1998/may4bk.html>.

An Act for the Better Protection of the Lands and Property of the Indians in Lower Canada. S. Prov. C. 1850. 42.

An Act Respecting Civilization and Enfranchisement of Certain Indians. S.C. 1859. 9.

An Act to Provide for the Allotment in Severalty to Indians on the Various Reservations, and to Extend the Protection of the Laws of the United States and the Territories over the Indians, and for Other Purposes (General Allotment Act or Dawes Act). 8 Feb.1887. Stat. 24. 388–91.

Adamson, Joni. *American Indian Literature, Environmental Justice, and Ecocriticism.* Tucson: U of Arizona P, 2001.

Akpaliapik, Manasie. *Respecting the Circle.* Art Gallery of Ontario, Toronto.

Alexie, Sherman. *Indian Killer.* New York: Atlantic Monthly P, 1996.

Alfred, Taiaiake. *Peace, Power, Righteousness: An Indigenous Manifesto.* Don Mills, ON: Oxford UP, 1999.

Allen, Paula Gunn. *The Sacred Hoop: Recovering the Feminine in American Indian Traditions.* Boston: Beacon, 1986.

Althusser, Louis. "Ideology and Ideological State Apparatuses." *Lenin and Philosophy, and Other Essays.* London: New Left, 1971. 149–73.

Anahareo. *Devil in Deerskins: My Life with Grey Owl.* Toronto: New, 1972.

Anderson, Rufus. *Memoir of Catharine Brown.* Boston: Crocker and Brewster, 1825.

Andrews, Bruce, and Charles Bernstein, eds. *The L=A=N=G=U=A=G=E Book.* Carbondale: Southern Illinois UP, 1984.

Armstrong, Jeannette C. "Land Speaking." *Speaking for the Generations: Native Writers on Writing.* Ed. Simon J. Ortiz. Tucson: U of Arizona P, 1998. 174–94.

———, ed. *Looking at the Words of Our People: First Nations Analysis of Literature.* Penticton, BC: Theytus, 1993.

———. *Whispering in Shadows.* Penticton, BC: Theytus, 2000.

Awiakta, Marilou. *Selu: Seeking the Corn Mother's Wisdom.* Golden, CO: Fulcrum, 1993.

Bailey, Sue. "Top Court Will Hear Landmark Case in Hunting, Fishing Rights of Métis." *metisnation.ca*. 9 Oct. 2001. Métis National Council. 4 March 2002 <www.metisnation.ca/POWLEY/powley3.html>.

Bakhtin, Mikhail M. "Discourse in the Novel." *The Dialogic Imagination: Four Essays*. Ed. Michael Holquist. Trans. Caryl Emerson and Michael Holquist. Austin: U of Texas P, 1981. 259–422.

Barthes, Roland. *Mythologies*. Trans. Annette Lavers. New York: Hill and Wang, 1984.

Bartlett, Richard H. *The Indian Act of Canada*. Saskatoon: Native Law Centre, U of Saskatchewan, 1980.

Bataille, Gretchen M., ed. *Native American Representations: First Encounters, Distorted Images and Literary Appropriations*. Lincoln: U of Nebraska P, 2001.

Bataille, Gretchen M., and Kathleen Mullen Sands. *American Indian Women: Telling Their Lives*. Lincoln: U of Nebraska P, 1984.

Baudrillard, Jean. *Simulacra and Simulation*. Trans. Sheila Glaser. Ann Arbor: U of Michigan P, 1995.

Bellin, Joshua. *The Demon of the Continent: Indians and the Shaping of American Literature*. Philadelphia: U of Pennsylvania P, 2001.

Bentley, D.M.R. "Savage, Degenerate, and Dispossessed: Some Sociological, Anthropological and Legal Backgrounds to the Depiction of Native Peoples in Early Long Poems on Canada." *Canadian Literature* 124–25 (1990): 76–90.

Berkhofer, Robert F., Jr. *The White Man's Indian*. New York: Knopf, 1978.

Berryman, Charles. "Critical Mirrors: Theories of Autobiography." *MOSAIC* 32 (1999): 71–84.

Bill C-31. An Act to Amend the Indian Act. 28 June 1985. Indian Act. R.S.C. 1985. 1–5.

Billinghurst, Jane O. *Grey Owl: The Many Faces of Archie Belaney*. Vancouver: Greystone, 1999.

Bird, Gloria. "Breaking the Silence: Writing as 'Witness.'" *Speaking for the Generations: Native Writers on Writing*. Ed. Simon J. Ortiz. Tucson: U of Arizona P, 1998. 26–48.

———. "The Exaggeration of Despair in Sherman Alexie's *Reservation Blues*." *Wicazo Sa Review* 11.2 (1995): 47–52.

———. "Searching for Evidence of Colonialism at Work: A Reading of Louis Erdrich's *Tracks*." *Wicazo Sa Review* 8.2 (1992): 40–47.

———. "Towards a Decolonization of the Mind and Text 1: Leslie Marmon Silko's *Ceremony*." *Wicazo Sa Review* 9.2 (1993): 1–8.

Bird, S. Elizabeth. *Dressing in Feathers: The Construction of the Indian in American Popular Culture*. Boulder: Westview, 1996.

Blaeser, Kimberly M. *Gerald Vizenor: Writing in the Oral Tradition*. Norman: U of Oklahoma P, 1996.

———. "Native Literature: Seeking a Critical Center." *Looking at the Words of Our People: First Nations Analysis of Literature*. Ed. Jeannette Armstrong. Penticton, BC: Theytus, 1993. 51–62.

Bob, Dempsey. *Eagle Woman 1/3*. Susan Whitney Gallery, Regina, SK.

Bibliography

———, perf. *The Smart One: Dempsey Bob.* Dir. Gary Madder. Videocassette. Seaton Productions, 1995.

Bourdieu, Pierre. *Language and Symbolic Power.* Ed. John B. Thompson. Trans. Gino Raymond and Matthew Adamson. Cambridge: Harvard UP, 1991.

Bowering, George. "Indian Summer." *15 Canadian Poets X 2.* Ed. Gary Geddes. 2nd ed. Don Mills, ON: Oxford UP, 1990. 348–49.

Brill de Ramirez, Susan. *Contemporary American Indian Literatures and the Oral Tradition.* Tucson: U of Arizona P, 1999.

Brower, Kenneth. "Grey Owl." *The Atlantic Monthly* Jan. 1990: 74—84.

Brown, Penelope, and Steven Levinson. *Politeness: Some Universals in Language Usage.* Cambridge, Eng.: Cambridge UP, 1987.

Brumble, David H., III. *American Indian Autobiography.* Berkeley: U of California P, 1988.

"Burnt Church News." *Assembly of First Nations Online.* 28 Oct. 2002. Assembly of First Nations. 10 Jan. 2003 <http://www.afn.ca/BurntChurch/burnt_church_news.htm>.

Byrd, Don. "Learned Ignorance and Other Defenses." *Sulfur* 11 (1984): 168–77.

Cajete, Gregory A. *Igniting the Sparkle: An Indigenous Science Education Model.* Skyland, NC: Kivaki, 1999.

———. *Look to the Mountain: An Ecology of Indigenous Education.* Skyland, NC: Kivaki, 1994.

———. *Native Science: Natural Laws of Interdependence.* Santa Fe: Clear Light, 2000.

Campbell, Maria. *Halfbreed.* Toronto: McClelland and Stewart, 1973. Rpt. Halifax: Goodread, 1983.

———. Interview with Hartmut Lutz and Konrad Gross. *Contemporary Challenges: Conversations with Canadian Native Authors.* Ed. Hartmut Lutz. Saskatoon: Fifth House, 1991. 41–65.

———. "It's the Job of the Storyteller to Create Chaos." Interview with Beth Cuthand. *The Other Woman: Women of Colour in Contemporary Canadian Literature.* Ed. Makeda Silvera. Toronto: Sister Vision, 1995. 264–270.

———. *Stories of the Road Allowance People.* Penticton, BC: Theytus, 1995.

———. "Strategies for Survival." *Give Back: First Nations Perspectives on Cultural Practice.* Ed. Maria Campbell et al. North Vancouver: Gallerie, 1992. 5–14.

Canada Act 1982 (U.K.). 1982.

Canadian Oversight Agencies. "Speaking Notes for CACOLE Conference." *Office of the Police Complaint Commissioner Online.* September 2000. Office of the Police Complaint Commissioner. 2 November 2000 <http://www.opcc.bc.ca/CACOLEPapers/CanadianOversightAgencies.html>.

Carney, Ginny. "Native American Loanwords in American English." *Wicazo Sa Review* 12.1 (1997): 189–203.

Carney, Sarah. "A Review on *Mean Spirit* by a Native Reviewer." *The Oklahoma Project.* 1997–98. English Dept., U of Toronto. Ed. Christopher Douglas. 3 Sept. 2002 <http://www.furman.edu/~cdouglas/oklahoma/nreviews.html>.

Castro, Michael. *Interpreting the Indian: Twentieth-Century Poets and the Native American.* Albuquerque: U of New Mexico P, 1983.

Chartier, Clem. "Aboriginal Rights: The Métis Perspective." *Aboriginal Rights: Toward an Understanding*. Proc. of the Conf. on Aboriginal Rights. Jan. 1983. Ed. Anthony J. Long, Menno Boldt, Leroy Little Bear. Lethbridge: U of Lethbridge, 1983. 46–52.

Churchill, Ward. *Fantasies of the Master Race: Literature, Cinema, and the Colonization of American Indians*. San Francisco: City Lights, 1998.

Clements, William M. *Native American Verbal Art: Texts and Contexts*. Tucson: U of Arizona P, 1996.

Cobb, John B., Jr., and David Ray Griffin. *Process Theology: An Introductory Exposition*. Philadelphia: Westminster, 1976.

Coltelli, Laura. *Winged Words: American Indian Writers Speak*. Lincoln: U of Nebraska P, 1990.

Constitution Act, 1867 (U.K.). S.C. 1867. 91.24.

Cook-Lynn, Elizabeth. "American Indian Intellectualism and the New Indian Story." *Natives and Academics: Researching and Writing about American Indians*. Ed. Devon A. Mihesuah. Lincoln: U of Nebraska P, 1998. 111–38.

———. "How Scholarship Defames the Native Voice . . . and Why." *Wicazo Sa Review* 15.2 (2000): 79–92.

Cooper, James Fenimore. *The Last of the Mohicans*. New York: Washington Square, 1963.

Cordova, Viola. "Doing Native American Philosophy." *From Our Eyes: Learning from Indigenous Peoples*. Ed. Sylvia O'Meara and Douglas A. West. Toronto: Garamond, 1996. 13–18.

———. "The European Concept of *Usen*: An American Aboriginal Text." *Native American Religious Identity: Unforgotten Gods*. Ed. Jace Weaver. Maryknoll: Orbis, 1998. 26–32.

Crawford, John C. "What Is Michif?: Language in the Métis Tradition." *The New Peoples: Being and Becoming Métis in North America*. Ed. Jacqueline Peterson and Jennifer S. H. Brown. Winnipeg, MB: U of Manitoba P, 1985. 231–41.

Cruikshank, Julie, Angela Sydney, Kitty Smith, and Annie Ned. *Life Lived like a Story: Life Stories of Three Yukon Elders*. Lincoln: U of Nebraska P, 1990.

Dauenhauer, Nora. Personal interview. 29 Dec. 1999.

Davin, Nicholas Flood, comp. *Report on Industrial Schools for Indians and Half-Breeds, 14 March 1879*. MG 26A, vol. 91, 35428–45. Ottawa: NAC, 1879.

Deloria, Phillip. *Playing Indian*. New Haven: Yale UP, 1998.

Deloria, Vine, Jr. *God is Red*. New York: Dell, 1973.

Derrida, Jacques. "Différance." *Margins of Philosophy*. Chicago: U of Chicago P, 1982. 1–28.

Dewar, Elaine. *Bones: Discovering the First Americans*. Toronto: Random House, 2001.

Dickason, Olive P. *Canada's First Nations: A History of Founding Peoples from Earliest Times*. 2nd ed. Toronto: Oxford UP, 1997.

———. *The Myth of the Savage and the Beginning of French Colonialism in the Americas*. Edmonton: U of Alberta P, 1984.

Dickson, Lovat. *Wilderness Man: The Amazing True Story of Grey Owl*. Toronto: MacMillan, 1973.

Bibliography

DiNova, Joanne. "Seventh Fire." *This Bridge We Call Home: Radical Visions For Transformation.* Ed. Gloria E. Anzaldúa and AnaLouise Keating. New York: Routledge, 2002. 104.

Duchemin, Parker. "'A Parcel of Whelps': Alexander Mackenzie among the Indians. *Canadian Literature* 124–25 (1990): 49–74.

Duke University Press. Rev. of *Our America: Nativism, Modernism, Culturalism,* by Walter Benn Michaels. *Books at Duke University Press.* 2003. Duke UP. 5 May 2003 <http://www.dukeupress.edu/books/M_bk_authors.shtml>.

Dumont, Marilyn. "Popular Images of Nativeness." *Looking at the Words of our People: First Nations Analysis of Literature."* Ed. Jeannette Armstrong. Penticton, BC: Theytus, 1993. 45–49.

Dupee, F. W. Introduction. *Selected Writings of Gertrude Stein.* 1962. Ed. Carl Van Vechten. New York: Vintage, 1990. ix–xvii.

Durham, Jimmie. "Cowboys and . . . Notes on Art, Literature, and American Indians in the Modern American Mind." *The State of Native America: Genocide, Colonization and Resistance.* Ed. M. Annette Jaimes. Boston: South End, 1992. 423–38.

Eakin, Paul John. Foreword. *For Those Who Come After: A Study of Native American Autobiography.* Arnold Krupat. Berkeley: U of California P, 1989. *xi–xxxi.*

Eco, Umberto. Postscript. 1983. *The Name of the Rose.* 1980. Trans. William Weaver. Harvest-Harcourt: San Diego, 1994.

Eigenbrod, Renate, and Jo-Ann Episkenew, eds. *Creating Community: A Roundtable on Canadian Aboriginal Literatures.* Brandon, MB: Bearpaw; Penticton, BC: Theytus, 2002.

Elliot, Jane, perf. *Blue Eyed.* Dir. Bertram Verhaag. Videocassette. DENKmal-Films, 1996.

Ermine, Willie. "Aboriginal Epistemology." *First Nations Education in Canada: The Circle Unfolds.* Ed. Marie Battiste and Jean Barman. Vancouver: U of British Columbia P, 1995. 101–12.

Fairclough, Norman. *Language and Power.* London: Longman, 1989.

Fanon, Franz. *The Wretched of the Earth.* Trans. Constance Farrington. New York: Grove, 1968.

Findlay, Len. "Always Indigenize! The Radical Humanities in the Postcolonial Canadian University." *ARIEL* 31.1–2 (2000): 307 26.

Flanagan, Tom. *First Nations? Second Thoughts.* Montreal: McGill-Queen's UP, 2000.

Francis, Lee. *Native Time: A Historical Time Line of Native America.* New York: St. Martin's, 1996.

Fuss, Diana. *Essentially Speaking: Feminism, Nature, and Difference.* New York: Routledge, 1990.

Giese, Paula. "Dibaajimowin: From Birchbark Designs to Computers: Looking at Anishinaabemowin Word-Roots." *Native American Indian: Art, Culture, History, Education, Science.* 11 Jan. 1997. Ed. Paula Giese. 10 Feb. 2003. <http://www.kstrom.net/isk/stories/words.html>.

Goldie, Terry. *Fear and Temptation: The Image of the Indigene in Canadian, Australian and New Zealand Literatures.* Kingston: McGill-Queen's UP, 1989.

———. "Semiotic Control: Native Peoples in Canadian Literature in English." *Studies on Canadian Literature: Introductory and Critical Essays.* Ed. Arnold Davidson. New York: MLA, 1990. 110–23.

Gordon, Sean. "UN Panel Condemns Canada's Treatment of Aboriginals." *Vancouver Sun* 10 April 1999: A4.

Grant, Agnes. "Contemporary Native Women's Voices in Literature." *Canadian Literature* 124–25 (1990): 124–32.

"Grey Owl." *Heroes of Yore and Lore: Canadian Heroes in Fact and Fiction.* 13 Nov. 2002. National Library of Canada. 6 May 2003 <http://www.nlc-bnc.ca/2/6/h6-230-e.html>.

HAARP Home Page. 21 June 2003. High Frequency Active Auroral Research Program. 22 June 2003. <www.haarp.alaska.edu>.

Hall, Stuart. "When Was 'the Post-Colonial'? Thinking at the Limit." *The Post-Colonial Question: Common Skies, Divided Horizons.* Ed. Iain Chambers and Lidia Curti. London: Routledge, 1996. 242–60.

Halliday, M.A.K. *An Introduction to Functional Grammar.* 2nd ed. London: Edward Arnold, 1994.

Harjo, Joy. *How We Became Human: New and Selected Poems, 1975—2001.* New York: Norton, 2002.

———. *In Mad Love and War.* Hanover: Wesleyan UP, 1990.

———. *The Last Song.* Las Cruces, NM: Puerto Del Sol, 1975.

———. *A Map to the Next World: Poetry and Tales.* New York: Norton, 2000.

———. *She Had Some Horses.* New York: Thunder's Mouth, 1983.

———. *The Spiral of Memory: INTERVIEWS.* Ed. Laura Coltelli. Ann Arbor: U of Michigan P, 1996.

———. *The Woman Who Fell From the Sky.* New York: Norton, 1994.

Harjo, Joy, and Gloria Bird, eds. *Reinventing the Enemy's Language: Contemporary Native Women's Writings of North America.* New York: Norton, 1997.

Harjo, Joy, and Stephen Strom. *Secrets from the Center of the World.* Tucson: Sun Tracks-U of Arizona P, 1989.

Harper, Phillip Brian. *Framing the Margins: The Social Logic of Postmodern Culture.* New York: Oxford UP, 1994.

Hart, Jonathan. "Images of the Native in Renaissance Encounter Narratives." *ARIEL* 25.4 (1994): 55–76.

Heimsoeth, Heinz. *The Six Great Themes of Western Metaphysics and the End of the Middle Ages.* Trans. Ramon J. Betanzos. Detroit: Wayne State UP, 1994.

Hejinian, Lyn. "Writing Is an Aid to Memory #28." *In the American Tree.* Ed Ron Silliman. Orono: National Poetry Foundation, 1986. 55–56.

Henderson's Annotated Indian Act. 11 Feb. 1996. Ed. Bill Henderson. 27 Feb. 2003 <www.bloorstreet.com/200block/sindact.htm>.

Hobson, Geary. "The Rise of the White Shaman as a New Version of Cultural Imperialism." *The Remembered Earth: An Anthology of Contemporary Native American Literature.* Ed. Geary Hobson. Albuquerque: U of New Mexico P, 1980. 100–08.

Hoover, Paul, ed. Introduction. *Postmodern American Poetry: A Norton Anthology.* New York: Norton, 1994. *xxv–xxxix.*

Howard, Joseph Kinsey. *Strange Empire.* New York: Morrow, 1952.

Howe, LeAnne. *Shell Shaker.* San Francisco: Aunt Lute, 2001.
Hoy, Helen. *How Should I Read These?: Native Women Writers in Canada.* Toronto: U of Toronto P, 2001.
Huffstetler, Edward. "'And All Things European Will Eventually Disappear . . .': The Spiritual Context for a Political Manifesto in Silko's *Almanac of the Dead.*" ALA Symposium on Native American Literature. Presidente Inter-Continental Hotel, Puerto Vallarta, Mex. 13 Nov. 1999.
Hulan, Renée. "Some Thoughts on 'Integrity and Intent' and Teaching Native Literature." *Essays on Canadian Writing* 63 (1998): 210–30.
Hulan, Renée, and Linda Warley. "Comic Relief: Pedagogical Issues Around Thomas King's *Medicine River.*" *Creating Community: A Roundtable on Canadian Aboriginal Literatures.* Ed. Renate Eigenbrod and Jo-Ann Episkenew. Brandon, MB: Bearpaw; Penticton, BC: Theytus, 2002. 125–46.
———. "Cultural Literacy, First Nations, and the Future of Canadian Literary Studies." *Journal of Canadian Studies/Revue d'études canadiennes* 34.3 (1999): 59–86.
Indian Act, 1876. S.C. 1876. 18. 3.3.
Jahner, Elaine. "Indian Literature and Critical Responsibility." *ASAIL Newsletter* 1:1 (1977): 3–10.
———. "Knowing All the Way Down to Fire." *Feminist Measures: Soundings in Poetry and Theory.* Ed. Lynn Keller and Cristanne Miller. Ann Arbor: U of Michigan P, 1994. 163–83.
Jaimes, M. Annette. "American Indian Studies: An Overview and Prospectus." *Wicazo Sa Review* 1.2 (1985): 15–21.
Jaimes, M. Annette, and Theresa Halsey. "American Indian Women: At the Center of Indigenous Resistance in North America." *The State of Native America.* Ed. M. Annette Jaimes. Boston: South End, 1992. 311–44.
Jaimes-Guerrero, Marianette. "Savage Erotica Exotica: Media Imagery of Native Women in North America." *Native North America: Critical and Cultural Perspectives.* Ed. Renée Hulan. Toronto: ECW, 1999. 187–210.
Jara, Rene, and Nicholas Spadaccini, eds. *Amerindian Images and the Legacy of Columbus.* Minneapolis: U of Minnesota P, 1992.
Jaskoski, Helen. "'A terrible sickness among them': Smallpox and Stories of the Frontier." *Early Native American Writing: New Critical Essays.* Ed. Helen Jaskoski. Cambridge: Cambridge UP, 1996. 136–57.
Johnston, Gordon. "An Intolerable Burden of Meaning: Native Peoples in White Fiction." *The Native in Literature.* Ed. Thomas King, Cheryl Calver and Helen Hoy. Oakville: ECW, 1987. 50–66.
Johnson, Robert. "Inspired Lines: Reading Joy Harjo's Prose Poems," *American Indian Quarterly* 23.3–4 (1999):13–23.
Knowles, David. *The Evolution of Medieval Thought.* 1962. Ed. D. E. Luscombe and C. N. L. Brooke. London: Longman, 1988.
Kroetsch, Robert. "Seed Catalogue." *15 Canadian Poets X 2.* Ed. Gary Geddes. 2nd ed. Don Mills, ON: Oxford, 1990. 258–76.
Krupat, Arnold. *Ethnocriticism: Ethnography, History, Literature.* Berkeley: U of California P, 1992.

———. *For Those Who Come After: A Study of Native American Autobiography.* Berkeley: U of California P, 1985.

———. *Native American Autobiography: An Anthology.* Madison: U of Wisconsin P, 1994.

———. "Native American Autobiography and the Synecdochic Self." *Ethnocriticism: Ethnography, History, Literature.* Berkeley: U of California P, 1992. 201–31.

———. "Red Matters." Rev. of *Red on Red*, by Craig Womack. *College English* 63.5 (2001): 655–61.

———. *Red Matters: Native American Studies.* Philadelphia: U of Pennsylvania P, 2002.

———. "Scholarship and Native American Studies: A Response to Daniel Littlefield, Jr." *American Studies* 34.2 (1993): 81–100.

———. *The Turn to the Native: Studies in Criticism and Culture.* Lincoln: U of Nebraska P, 1996.

———. *The Voice in the Margin: Native American Literature and the Canon.* Berkeley: U of California P, 1989.

LaDuke, Winona. "They Always Come Back." *A Gathering of Spirit: A Collection by North American Indian Women.* Ed. Beth Brant. 3rd ed. Toronto: Women's, 1988. 62–67.

LaLonde, Chris. "New Stories and Broken Necks: Incorporating Native American Texts in the American Literature Survey." *Studies in American Indian Literatures* 8.2 (1996): 7–20.

LaRocque, Emma. "Here Are Our Voices—Who Will Hear?" Preface. *Writing the Circle: Native Women of Western Canada.* Ed. Jeanne Perreault and Sylvia Vance. Edmonton: NeWest, 1990. xv–xxx.

———. "Teaching Aboriginal Literature: The Discourse of Margins and Mainstreams." *Creating Community: A Roundtable on Canadian Aboriginal Literatures.* Ed. Renate Eigenbrod and Jo-Ann Episkenew. Brandon, MB: Bearpaw; Penticton, BC: Theytus, 2002. 209–34.

Lee, A. Robert. Introduction. *Shadow Distance: A Gerald Vizenor Reader.* By Gerald Vizenor. Hanover, NH: Wesleyan UP, 1994.

Lincoln, Kenneth. *Native American Renaissance.* Berkeley: U of California P, 1983.

Little Bear, Leroy. "Jagged Worldviews Colliding." *Reclaiming Indigenous Voice and Vision.* Ed. Marie Battiste. Vancouver: U of British Columbia P, 2000. 77–85.

Littlefield, Daniel F., Jr. "American Indians, American Scholars and the American Literary Canon." *American Studies* 33.2 (1992): 95–111.

Livesay, Nora. "Understanding the History of Tribal Enrollment." *American Indian Policy Center Online.* 4 Dec. 2002. American Indian Policy Center. 23 Jan. 2003 <http://www.americanindianpolicycenter.org/pubs/enroll.html>.

Lundgren, Jodi. "'Being a Half-breed': Discourses of Race and Cultural Syncreticity in the Works of Three Metis Women Writers." *Canadian Literature* 144 (1995): 62–77.

Luscombe, David. *Medieval Thought.* Oxford: Opus-Oxford UP, 1997.

Lussier, A. S., ed. *Louis Riel and The Métis.* Winnipeg: Métis Federation, 1979.

Bibliography

Lutz, Hartmut. *Contemporary Challenges: Conversations with Canadian Native Authors*. Saskatoon: Fifth House, 1991.

Lyman, John, perf. *Modern and Abstract Painting in Canada*. Dir. George Mully. Videocassette. Prod. National Gallery of Canada. National Film Board, 1991.

Lyons, Scott Richard. "Rhetorical Sovereignty: What Do American Indians Want from Writing?" *College Composition and Communication* 51:3 (2000): 447–68.

MacEwan, Grant. *Métis Makers of History*. Saskatoon: Western Producer, 1981.

MacEwen, Gwendolyn. *The Poetry of Gwendolyn MacEwen*. Ed. Margaret Atwood and Barry Callaghan. 2 vols. Toronto: Exile, 1993–94.

Mackay, J. *Quebec Hill; or, Canadian Scenery. A Poem In Two Parts*. Ed. D. M. R. Bentley. London, ON: Canadian Poetry, 1988.

Mackey, Louis. *Peregrinations of the Word: Essays in Medieval Philosophy*. Ann Arbor: U of Michigan P, 1997.

Maddox, Lucy. *Removals: Nineteenth-Century American Literature and the Politics of Indian Affairs*. New York: Oxford UP, 1991.

Mankiller, Wilma, and Michael Wallis. *Mankiller: A Chief and Her People*. New York: St. Martin's, 1993.

Maracle, Lee. *I Am Woman: A Native Perspective on Sociology and Feminism*. Vancouver: Press Gang, 1996.

———. Personal interview. 28 Dec. 1999.

———. *Ravensong*. Vancouver: Press Gang, 1993.

Marías, Julián. *History of Philosophy*. Trans. Stanley Appelbaum and Clarence C. Strowbridge. New York: Dover, 1967.

Martin, Calvin, ed. *The American Indian and the Problem of History*. New York: Oxford UP, 1987.

McLean, Don. *1885: Métis Rebellion or Government Conspiracy?* Winnipeg: Pemmican, 1985.

McNab, David T. *Circles of Time: Aboriginal Land Rights and Resistance in Ontario*. Waterloo: Wilfrid Laurier UP, 1999.

———. "Metis Participation in the Treaty-Making Process in Ontario: A Reconnaissance." *Native Studies Review* 1.2 (1985): 57–79.

McPherson, Dennis. "A Definition of Culture: Canada and the First Nations." *Native American Religious Identity: Unforgotten Gods*. Ed. Jace Weaver. Maryknoll: Orbis, 1998. 77–98.

Means, Russell. Interview with Linda Brookover. "The Existential Indian." *First Nations Issues of Consequence*. 18 October 2000. Ed. Jordan S. Dill. 28 December 2002 <http://www.dickshovel.com/intermeans.html>.

Medvedev, P. N., and Mikhail Bakhtin. *The Formal Method in Literary Scholarship: A Critical Introduction to Sociological Poetics*. Trans. Albert J. Wehrle. Baltimore: Coucher College Series, 1978.

Methot, Suzanne. "Belaney Baloney Sends All the Wrong Signals." *Globe and Mail* [Toronto] 18 Oct. 1999: D4.

Michaels, Walter Benn. *Our America: Nativism, Modernism, Pluralism*. Durham: Duke UP, 1995.

Miller, Carolyn R. "Genre as Social Action." *Quarterly Journal of Speech* 70 (1984): 151–67.

Modern and Abstract Painting in Canada. Dir. George Mully. Videocassette. Prod. National Gallery of Canada. National Film Board, 1991.

Momaday, N. Scott. *The Man Made of Words: Essays, Stories, Passages.* New York: St. Martin's, 1997.

Montgomery, Malcolm. "The Six Nations and the Macdonald Franchise." *Ontario History* 57 (1965): 13–25.

Monture-Angus, Patricia. *Journeying Forward: Dreaming First Nations' Independence.* Halifax, NS: Fernwood, 1999.

———. *Thunder in My Soul: A Mohawk Woman Speaks.* Halifax, NS: Fernwood, 1995.

Morris, Alexander. *The Treaties of Canada with the Indians of Manitoba and the North-west Territories Including the Negotiations on Which They Were Based and Other Information Pertaining Thereto.* 1800. Saskatoon: Fifth House, 1991.

Murray, David. *Forked Tongues: Speech, Writing, and Representation in North American Indian Texts.* Bloomington: Indiana UP, 1991.

Napier, David. "Sins of the Father." *Anglican Journal.* May 2000. Anglican Church of Canada. 20 July 2003 <http://www.anglicanjournal/126/rs>.

"National Gallery of Canada—Information and Services." *National Gallery of Canada Online.* 22 Nov. 2002. National Gallery of Canada. 21 Dec. 2002 <http://national.gallery.ca/info_services/about/index_e.html>.

Native Law Centre. *The Indian Act and Amendments, 1970–1993: An Indexed Collection.* Saskatoon: U of Saskatchewan, 1993.

Newlands, Anne. *Canadian Art: From Its Beginnings to 2000.* Willowdale, ON: Firefly, 2000.

Nichols, Roger L. *Indians in the United States and Canada. A Comparative History.* Lincoln: U of Nebraska P, 1998.

Ong, Walter J. *Orality and Literacy: The Technologizing of the Word.* London: Routledge, 1982.

Orlan Online. Ed. Orlan and Jeriko. 8 November 2002. CIVC Pierre Shaeffer. 21 December 2002 <http://www.orlan.net>.

Owens, Louis. *Mixedblood Messages: Literature, Film, Family, Place.* Norman: U of Oklahoma P, 1998.

Peterson, Jacqueline. "Many Roads to Red River: Métis Genesis in the Great Lakes Region, 1680–1815." *The New Peoples: Being and Becoming Métis in North America.* Ed. Jacqueline Peterson and Jennifer S. H. Brown. Winnipeg: U of Manitoba P, 1985. 37–71.

Pound, Ezra. "In a Station of the Metro." *The Selected Poems of Ezra Pound.* New York: New Directions, 1957. 35.

———. "A Retrospect." *Literary Essays of Ezra Pound.* Ed. T. S. Eliot. 1918. New York: New Directions, 1968. 3–14.

Pratt, E. J. "Newfoundland." *15 Canadian Poets X 2.* Ed. Gary Geddes. 2nd ed. Don Mills, ON: Oxford, 1990. 1–3.

Purdy, Al. "The Cariboo Horses." *15 Canadian Poets X 2.* Ed. Gary Geddes. 2nd ed. Don Mills, ON: Oxford, 1990. 192–93.

Purdy, John. Editorial. *Studies in American Indian Literatures* 11.4 (1999): 1–5.

Rasula, Jed. *The American Poetry Wax Museum: Reality Effects, 1940–1990*. Urbana, IL: NCTE, 1996.

Redsky, James. *Great Leader of the Ojibway: Mis-quona-queb*. Toronto: McClelland and Stewart, 1972.

Revard, Carter. "History, Myth, and Identity Among Osages and Other Peoples." *Denver Quarterly* 14 (1980): 84–97.

Riley, Patricia. "'That Murderin' Halfbreed': The Abjectification of the Mixedblood in Mark Twain's *Adventures of Tom Sawyer*." *Native North America: Critical and Cultural Perspectives*. Ed. Renée Hulan. Toronto: ECW, 1999. 174–86.

Roberts, Leslie. "A Gentic Survey of Vanishing Peoples." *Science* 252 (1991): 1614–17.

Rock, Roger. *The Native American in American Literature: A Selectively Annotated Bibliography*. Westport: Greenwood, 1985.

Roemer, Kenneth. "A Retro-Prospective on Audience, Oral Literatures, and Ignorance." *Studies in American Indian Literatures* 9.3 (1997):17–18.

Rogers, Jay. "God's Target for Revival: The Schools of the Northeast." *Media House International Online*. April 1990. Media House International. 26 Feb. 2002 <www.forerunner.com/forerunner/X0372_Schools_of_the_North.html>.

Rothenberg, Jerome. *Shaking the Pumpkin: Traditional Poetry of the Indian North Americas*. Garden City: Doubleday, 1972.

Ruffo, Armand Garnet, ed. *(Ad)dressing Our Words: Aboriginal Perspectives on Aboriginal Literatures*. Penticton, BC: Theytus, 2001.

———. *Grey Owl: The Mystery of Archie Belaney*. Regina, SK: Coteau, 1996.

Ruoff, A. LaVonne Brown. "Gerald Vizenor: Compassionate Trickster." *Studies in American Indian Literatures* 9.2 (1985): 52–63.

Saltzstein, Katherine. "Albuquerque Schools Fight Traditional Dress." *Indian Country Today* 21 Apr. 1997: C5–6.

Saul, John Ralston. "Canada: A Layering of Mythologies." Whelen Lecture. U of Saskatchewan. Delta Bessborough Hotel, Saskatoon. 22 Sept. 1998.

Saussure, Ferdinand de. *Course in General Linguistics*. 1916. Ed. Wade Baskin. 8 New York: McGraw-Hill, 1966.

Sayre, Gordon M. *Les Sauvages Americains: Representations of Native Americans in French and English Colonial Literature*. Chapel Hill: U of North Carolina P, 1997.

Schlein, Lisa. "UN Committee Tells Canada to Work Harder to Eradicate Racial Discrimination." *Yahoo! News*. 26 August 2002. Canadian Press. 12 Sept. 2002 <http://ca.news.yahoo.com/020826/6/ok6f.html>.

Scott, Duncan Campbell. "The Onondaga Madonna." *The Poems of Duncan Campbell Scott*. Toronto: McClelland and Stewart, 1926. 230.

Scott, F. R. "Laurentian Shield." *15 Canadian Poets X 2*. Ed. Gary Geddes. 2nd ed. Don Mills, ON: Oxford, 1990. 44–45.

Silliman, Ron, ed. *In the American Tree*. Orono: National Poetry Foundation-University of Maine at Orono, 1986.

———. *Tjanting*. Excerpt. Silliman, *In the American*. 134–46.

Smith, Donald B. *From the Land of the Shadows: The Making of Grey Owl*. Saskatoon, SK: Western Producer Prairie, 1990.

Smith, Mel. *Our Home or Native Land?: What Governments' Aboriginal Policy is Doing to Canada*. Victoria, BC: Crown Western, 1995.
Spindel, Carol. *Dancing at Halftime: Sports and the Controversy over American Indian Mascots*. New York: New York UP, 2000.
Spivak, Gayatri Chakravorty. *The Spivak Reader*. Ed. Donna Landry and Gerald MacLean. New York : Routledge, 1996.
Stanley, George F. G. *The Birth of Western Canada: A History of the Riel Rebellion*. 1936. Toronto: U of Toronto P, 1960.
Stein, Gertrude. *Tender Buttons*. 1914. Rpt. in *Selected Writings of Gertrude Stein*. 1962. Ed. Carl Van Vechten. New York: Vintage, 1990. 459–509.
Stevenson, Winona. "Colonialism and First Nations Women in Canada." *Scratching the Surface: Canadian Anti-Racist Feminist Thought*. Ed. Enakshi Dua and Angela Robertson. Toronto: Women's, 1999. 49–80.
St. Germain, Jill. *Indian Treaty-Making Policy in the United States and Canada: 1867—1877*. Toronto: U of Toronto P, 2001.
Stillar, Glenn F. *Analyzing Everyday Texts: Discourse, Rhetoric, and Social Perspectives*. Thousand Oaks: Sage, 1998.
Thompson, John B. Introduction. *Language and Symbolic Power*. By Pierre Bourdieu. Trans. Gino Raymond and Matthew Adamson. Cambridge: Harvard UP, 1991. 1–34.
Thornton, Russell. "American Indian Studies as an Academic Discipline." *American Indian Culture and Research Journal* 2.3–4 (1978): 10–19.
———. "American Indian Studies as an Academic Discipline: A Revisit." *American Indian Issues in Higher Education*. American Indian Studies Center. 1980. Los Angeles: UCLA, 1981.
Tompkins, Jane. "'Indians': Textualism, Morality, and the Problem of History." *"Race," Writing and Difference*. Ed. Henry Louis Gates, Jr. Chicago: U of Chicago P, 1986: 59–77.
Tsosie, Rebecca. "Surviving the War by Singing the Blues: The Contemporary Ethos of American Indian Political Poetry." *American Indian Culture and Research Journal* 10.3 (1986): 25–51.
Tuhiwai Smith, Linda. *Decolonizing Methodologies: Research and Indigenous Peoples*. London: Zed; Dunedin: U of Otago P, 1999.
Tyler, Stephen A. "PostModern Ethnography: From Document of the Occult to Occult Document." *Writing Culture: The Poetics and Politics of Ethnography*. Ed. James Clifford and George Marcus. Berkeley: U of California P, 1986. 122–40.
Venne, Sharon Helen. *Our Elders Understand Our Rights: Evolving International Law Regarding Indigenous Rights*. Penticton, BC: Theytus, 1998.
Vizenor, Gerald. *Crossbloods: Bone Courts, Bingos, and Other Reports*. Minneapolis: U of Minnesota P, 1990.
———. "Crows Written on the Poplars: Autocritical Autobiographies." *I Tell You Now: Autobiographical Essays by Native American Writers*. Ed. Brian Swann and Arnold Krupat. Lincoln: U of Nebraska P, 1987. 101–09.
———. *Darkness in St. Louis Bearheart*. Minneapolis: Truck, 1978.
———. *Manifest Manners: Postindian Warriors of Survivance*. Hanover: Wesleyan UP, 1994.

———. "Rev. of *Mean Spirit*, by Linda Hogan." *World Literature Today* 65 (1991): 168–69.

———. "Socioaccupuncture: Mythic Reversals and the Striptease in Four Scenes." *Crossbloods: Bone Courts, Bingo, and Other Reports*. 1976. Minneapolis: U of Minnesota P, 1990.

———. "Trickster Discourse: Comic Holotropes and Language Games." *Narrative Chance: Postmodern Discourse on Native American Indian Literatures*. Ed. Gerald Vizenor. Norman: U of Oklahoma P, 1993 (1989). 187–211.

Wagamese, Richard. *Keeper 'n Me*. Toronto: Doubleday, 1994.

Warrior, Robert Allen. "A Marginal Voice." *Native Nations* 1 (1991): 29–30.

———. *Tribal Secrets: Recovering American Indian Intellectual Traditions*. Minneapolis: U of Minnesota P, 1995.

Weaver, Jace. "From I-Hermeneutics to We-Hermeneutics: Native Americans and the Post-Colonial." *Native American Religious Identity: Unforgotten Gods*. Ed. Jace Weaver. Maryknoll: Orbis, 1998. 1–25.

———. *That the People Might Live: Native American Literatures and Native American Community*. New York: Oxford UP, 1997.

Weintraub, Linda. *Art on the Edge and Over: Searching for Art's Meaning in Contemporary Society, 1970s-1990s*. Ed. Lesley K. Baier. Litchfield: Art Insights, 1996.

Weis, L.P. "D.C. Scott's View of History and the Indians." *Canadian Literature* 111 (1986): 27–40.

"What Does the United Nations Human Rights Committee Say about Ipperwash?" *The Truth Must Come Out*. 2 March 2000. Coalition for a Public Inquiry into the Death of Dudley George. 6 May 2003 <http://www.web.net/~inquiry/nault2.htm>.

Whitehead, Alfred North. *Religion in the Making*. New York: Macmillan, 1926.

Whitt, L. A. "Cultural Imperialism and the Marketing of Native America." *Natives and Academics: Research and Writing About American Indians*. Ed. D. Mihesuah. Lincoln: U of Nebraska P, 1998. 139–71.

Whorf, Benjamin. *Language, Thought, and Reality*. Cambridge: MIT P, 1956.

Wiget, Andrew. "Simon Ortiz." *The Heath Anthology of American Literature*. 4th ed. Ed. Paul Lauter. *Houghton Mifflin Online*. 26 Nov. 2002. Houghton Mifflin. 2 Mar. 2003 <http://college.hmco.com/english/lauter/heath/4e/students/authorpages/contemporary/ortizacomapueblo_si.html>.

Willard, William, and Mary Kay Downing. "American Indian Studies and Inter-Cultural Education." *Wicazo Sa Review* 7.2 (1991): 1–8.

Wilson, Terry P. "Custer Never Would Have Believed It: Native American Studies in Academia." *American Indian Quarterly* 5.1 (1979): 207–27.

Womack, Craig. *Red on Red: Native American Literary Separatism*. Minneapolis: U of Minnesota P, 1999.

Wong, Hertha Dawn. *Sending My Heart Back Across the Years: Tradition and Innovation in Native American Autobiography*. New York: Oxford UP, 1992.

———. "First-Person Plural: Subjectivity and Community in Native American Women's Autobiography." *Women, Autobiography, Theory: A Reader*. Ed. Sidonie Smith and Julia Watson. Madison: U of Wisconsin P, 1998. 168–78.

Wright, Ronald. *Stolen Continents*. Toronto: Viking, 1991.

Young, Robert C. *Colonial Desire: Hybridity in Theory, Culture and Race*. London: Routledge, 1995.

Young-Ing, Greg. "Aboriginal Peoples' Estrangement: Marginalization in the Publishing Industry." *Looking at the Words of Our People: First Nations Analysis of Literature*. Ed. Jeannette Armstrong. Penticton, BC: Theytus, 1993. 177–87.

Index

A

Aboriginal Healing Foundation, 114–115
Aboriginal theory; *see* indigenous theory
Academic credentials, 88–89
Academy as Western institution, 52–53
Akpaliapik, Manasie, 9
Alexie, Sherman, 36
Alfred, Taiaiake, 175
Allen, Paula Gunn, 7n.11
Althusser, Louis, 131, 135
America as idea, 38–39, 126
American Indian Movement, (AIM) 79, 81, 90–91
American Indian Studies, 80–81, 85, 173–175, 178
American Poetry Wax Museum, 142
Anthropology, 83–84
Appropriation, 109–110
Aquinas, Thomas, 65–66
Aristotle, 5, 65
Armstrong, Jeannette, 34, 50, 53, 84–85, 105, 123–127, 140
Assimilation, 38–39, 47, 60–61, 98
Atwood, Margaret, 129, 134–135
Aull, Bill, *et al.*, 153
Autobiography theory, 53–54

B

Bakhtin, Mikhail, 82
Banks, Dennis, 90
Baraka, Amiri, 143, 144
Barthes, Roland, 77
Bataille, Gretchen M., and Kathleen Mullen Sands, 55, 59–61
Belaney, Archibald, *see* Grey Owl
Bentley, D. M. R., 26, 31
Bering Strait Theory, 51
Berkhofer, Robert F., Jr., 23, 49
Berryman, Charles, 53–54, 63
Big Bear, 79
Bird, Gloria, 17, 97, 103, 139
Blaeser, Kimberly, 19, 54, 75, 76, 93–94, 139, 145
Boarding schools, 97–98; *see also* Residential schools
Boas, Franz, 53–54
Bob, Dempsey, 9–10
Bodily Harm, 134–135
Bonnin, Gertrude, 80
Bourdieu, Pierre, 51–52, 82–83, 147
Bowering, George, 29
Brown, Catherine, 98
Brown, Penelope, and Steven Levinson, 176
Bruchac, Joseph, 154
Brumble, David H., III, 55, 58 -59
Byrd, Don, 143

C

Cajete, Gregory, 1, 4n. 5, 92–93, 136, 138, 139, 140, 145
Campbell, Maria, 16, 21, 54, 60–61, 110–111, 114, 115, 119–120, 122, 126, 128–138, 140
Canada
   United Nations, 51, 51n. 3
   Aboriginal policy as flawed 119
Carabi, Angels, 154
Carney, Ginny, 32
Carney, Sarah, 90
Chiapas, 106
Chona, Maria, 60

209

Chrétien, Jean, 104
Christianity, 98
Circles, 164, 168
Collective autodestruction, 114
Coltelli, Laura, 47, 50, 148, 152
Columbian discourse, 24–25
Communitism, 92, 140
Community, 6, 62–63, 71–72, 92, 93, 140, 171
Connectedness, 6, 53, 64, 70–71, 139–140, 145, 155
Constitution Act (Canada), 112
Cook-Lynn, Elizabeth, 45, 89, 128, 175
Cooper, James Fenimore, 49
Copway, George, 32, 80
Cordova, Viola, 4nn. 8–10, 49, 53, 92
Cortez, Jayne, 144
Crawford, John, 127
Creation, 66, 71–72, 142
  as universal relatedness 149–150, 162, 163
  language of 148–149; *see also* Land Speaking
Creator, 66, 82, 123
Cruikshank, Julie, 47
Culture as social practice, 33–35
Curtis, Edward 77

D

Dauenhauer, Nora, 89, 92
Davies, Robertson, 129
Davin, Nicholas Flood, 131
Dawes Act, 36–37, 36n. 10, 79
Day as ceremony, 165
Deep ecology, 92
Deloria, Vine, 46
De Man, Paul, 57
Derrida, Jacques, 82
Dewar, Elaine, 50–51
Dickason, Olive, 24, 82, 127
Différance, 82
Discourse analysis, 49, 52
  indigenous theory, 52
Doctrine of discovery, 104
Duchemin, Parker, 25
Dumont, Gabriel, 79, 131, 135, 137

E

Eakin, Paul John, 55

Eastman, Charles, 80
Education, 45, 79–81, 92–93, 97–98, 131–134, 174
  traditional 135–138
Eigenbrod, Renate, and Jo-Ann Episkenew, 34
Encounter narratives, 24–26
Environmental destruction, 105–107, 160, 171
Epistemology, 5–6
Ermine, Willie, 6, 53, 64–65, 92, 124, 140, 155, 171
Essentialism, 35–38, 43, 46, 73, 96–97, 100–102, 103, 110–111, 117–123
Ethnocritical approach, 37, 122–123
Eurocentrism, 2
Evolutionary model, 2, 58, 59, 63, 72–73, 85, 100
  economics, 26–27
  language, 29

F

Fairclough, Norman, 31–32, 39–40, 102, 147
Fanon, Frantz, 114
Findlay, Len, 178
First Nations? Second Thoughts, 119
Flanagan, Tom, 119
Foucault, Michel, 31, 51–52
Four as sacred number, 164
Fragmentation, 5–6, 65–67
Functional grammar, 64n. 7
Fuss, Diana, 96–97, 102, 120, 121

G

Genre theory, 162
Geronimo, 79
Ghost Dance, 79, 97–98
Ginsberg, Alan, 144
Giorno, John, 144
Globe and Mail, 67–68
Goldie, Terry, 16, 23, 29, 32, 49
Goodread Biographies, 129
Grant, Agnes, 111, 130
Greek letter *pi,* 164
Greek philosophy, 4–5
Grey Owl, 67–68

Index

indigenous identity, 67–68
Pierce Brosnan, 67–68

H

HAARP, 87n. 11
Halfbreed, 110–111, 128–138
   blanket metaphor 137–138
   first song 129
Hall, Stuart 122
Harjo, Joy 12–13, 16, 17, 140–171, 180
   audience, 159n. 9
   concept of love, 13, 150, 167–168
   horses, 154–155
   indigenous theory, 140–141, 145, 146
   lyric form,152
   politics, 144–145
   prose style, 152
   storytelling, 152
   structure, 162–164, 168–171
   theme of alcoholism, 160–161
   transcendence, 155–156
Harper, Phillip Brian, 84
Hart, Jonathan, 24
Hartman, Geoffrey, 178
Hartshorne, Charles, 98
Hejinian, Lyn, 11
Heteroglossia, 82
Hodgins, Jack, 130
Hogan, Linda, 89–90, 93, 146–147
Howe, LeAnne, 116
Hoy, Helen, 49
Huffstetler, Edward, 50
Hulan, Renée, 34, 46, 50
Hulan, Renée, and Linda Warley, 19, 21,146
Human Genome Diversity Project (HGDP), 109–110, 109n. 2
Hybridity theory, 120–122

I

Identity, 33–34, 62–63, 68, 71–72, 77–79, 95, 96, 110, 117
   cultural theorists, 117
   destabilization, 33–39
   marketing of Indian, 127–128
   performance, 78–79, 127–128
Ideological state apparatus (ISA), 51, 88, 134–135
Indian Act (Canada), 111

Métis people, 112
   women, 112
Indian Affairs (Canada), 27–28, 79–80
Indian Arts and Crafts Act, 37
Indians, definition of, 111–112, 131
Indigenist criticism, 179–180
Indigenous image, 21–32, 77–78, 93
   compared to European image, 26
   nostalgia concerning, 27, 29
Indigenous intellectual tradition, 93–94, 96–98, 100, 174
Indigenous people, global, 2, 66, 92, 103–104, 105
Indigenous theory, 6, 32, 52, 64–65, 66–67, 84, 87 -88, 92–94, 99, 100, 104, 105, 116, 123–128, 139, 166, 171, 179–180
   discourse analysis, 64–65
   language, 84–85, 99, 123–128, 166–167
   tradition, 69–70
Individuality, 6
In Mad Love and War, 152, 161
Internal criticism, 95
Intertribal rivalry, 116

J

Jackson, Andrew, 104
Jaimes, M. Annette, 173–174
Jaskoski, Helen, 47
Johnson, E. Pauline, 32
Johnston, Gordon, 32
Jones, David, 60

K

Keeper'N Me, 116
Kincheloe, Joe, and Ladislaus Semali, 122–123
King, Thomas, 75
Kitschymen, 90
Klein, A. M., 30
Kroetsch, Robert, 30–31
Krupat, Arnold, 16, 35–39, 35n. 9, 41–47, 49, 50, 55–58, 73, 175–178
   rhetoric versus logic 44–46

L

Land Speaking, 84–85, 123–127, 130–131
   Manitou, 124–125

Land-grant colleges, 173–174
Language
   Aboriginal worldview transmitted through English, 125
   indigenous theory, 52–53, 155
   Rez English, 126, 126n. 20
   thought, 158
   transformative potential, 147–148
   Western theory of, 52
Language use
   as political, 147
   as social practice, 51
LaRocque, Emma, 34
Last Song, 150 -152, 153
Legal system, 104–105
Levertov, Denise, 143
Liddle, John, 109–110
Linguistic capital, 51–52
Literary theory, 31, 94
   definition of, 7–8
   identity, 118
Little Bear, Leroy, 92
Littlefield, Daniel F., Jr., 174–175
Loanwords, 32
Logic, 49–50
Lorde, Audre, 178
Lundgren, Jodi, 110
Lurie, Nancy, 60
Lutz, Hartmut, 47, 50, 131
Lutz, Hartmut, and Konrad Gross, 119–120, 126, 128
Lyons, Scott, 33

M

MacDonald, Sir John A., 79
MacEwan, Gwendolyn, 50
Mackay, J., 26
Mackenzie, Alexander, 25–27
MacPherson, Dennis, 92
Maddox, Lucy, 23, 47, 50
Manitou, 6, 124, 130–131, 150, 166, 168
Mankiller: A Chief and Her People, 68–74
Mankiller, Wilma, 16, 54–55, 68–74
Map to the Next World, 152, 154, 161–171
Maracle, (Bobbi) Lee, 60–61, 82, 85
Marías, Julián, 4n. 7
Master narrative, 38–39

Mathews, John Joseph, 46
Mawedopenais, 112–114
Mayan people, 106
McClelland and Stewart, 129–130, 131
McNab, David, 131
Medieval period, 65–66
Medieval thought, 4–7, 4n. 7, 92
   Creation and, 4–6
   Creator and, 4–6
   as primitive, 5–6
Memory in the blood, 37, 73–74, 117
Methot, Suzann, 67–68
Métis, 16
   as First Nations, 111, 115–117, 127
Michaels, Walter Benn, 33, 35, 35n. 8, 78
Michif, 127
Miller, Carolyn, 162
Milloy, John, 79–80
Misogyny, 30–31
MLA Bibliography, 141
Momaday, N. Scott, 37, 54
Montezuma, Carlos, 80
Monture-Angus, Patricia, 53, 119
Morris, Alexander, 112–114
Mountain Wolf Woman, 60
Munro, Alice, 129

N

NAFTA, 106
Nanabush (Nanaboozhoo, Nene-bush, Naanabozho, etc.), 75, 75n. 1, 81–82, 94
Native autobiography
   autobiography theory, 53–54, 63–64
   compared to classical, 63
   genre, 55, 58, 59, 61, 130
Native literature
   academy, 1, 3nn. 2, 3, 43–44, 50
   Canada-U.S. border and, 22–23, 34–35
   canon and, 33–35
   control of, 63
   inclusion in canon, 56–57, 63, 146
   literary theory and, 54, 61, 76, 82–83, 84, 91, 101, 137, 140
   Native criticism and, 95–96
   ownership of, 41–44, 56–57, 59–60, 83–84, 104

Index

publishing industry and, 85, 129–130
Negative presence, 28–29
Newman, Barnett, 8
Nominalism, 65–66
Northwest Angle Treaty, *see* Treaty Three
Northwest Territories, 113–114

O

Object-text approach, 22–23, 49–50
Occam, William of, 65–66
Ondaatje, Michael, 130
One Arrow, 79
Ong, Walter, 16, 39–41, 85
Orality and oral culture, 40–41
Order of discourse, 31–32, 51–52, 83
Orlan, 7–8
Our Home or Native Land, 119

P

Pan-Indian movements, 119n. 17
Peterson, Jacqueline, 114
Plato, 5
Poetic Justice, 144
Poetry
    comparison between Western and Aboriginal, 7–14
    language poetry, 11–12, 144
    performance poetry, 143–144
    politics and, 142–144
    protest lyric, 143
Politeness theory, 176–177
Postindian, 78
Pound, Ezra, 10
Poundmaker, 79
Pratt, E. J., 28
Principle of connectedness, 66
Principle of individuation, 65–66, 99
Process philosophy, 98–101, 100n. 17
Purdy, Al, 30

R

Race as social construct, 33–35
Radicalism, 80–81, 85, 96, 97, 100–102, 150, 174, 179
Rasula, Jed, 142, 143
Ravensong, 82, 85–88
Red Matters, 176

Report on Industrial Schools for Indians and Half-Breeds, 131
Residential schools, 78–79, 114n. 13, 131–134; *see also* Boarding schools
Revard, Carter, 57
Rich, Adrienne, 143
Riel, Louis, 79, 131
Rothenberg, Jerome, 144
Ruoff, A. LaVonne Brown, 46–47, 50, 80
Rupert's Land, 113–114

S

Said, Edward, 23
Sanapia, 60
Sanders, Ed, 144
Saul, John Ralston, 173
Sayre, Gordon, 23
Scott, Duncan Campbell, 27–28, 29
Scott, F. R., 28–29
Scotus, John Duns, 65
Secrets from the Center of the World, 142
Sekaquaptewa, Helen, 60
Self, indigenous notions of, 57
    synechdochic self, 57
Serrano, Andres, 7
Settler Nations, 17, 122, 126
Shaw, Anna Moore, 60
She Had Some Horses, 152, 154, 156
Shell Shaker, 116
Silko, Leslie Marmon, 54
Silliman, Ron, 11–12
Sitting Bull, 79
Smith, Mel, 119
Social constructionists, 97, 117–123, 127
Social Darwinism, 26–27, 29, 59
Social order, 31–32, 51–52, 83
Social sciences, 83–84
Sovereignty, 33, 35, 38–39, 43, 56, 63, 98, 104, 118–119, 120, 159, 175-179
    intellectual sovereignty, 94–95, 100–101, 104
    rhetorical sovereignty, 33
Spirals, 168–171
Spivak, Gayatri, 102
Sports mascots 22, 106

St. Catherine's Milling v. The Queen, 114
Stein, Gertrude, 10–11
Stevens, Wallace, poetry of, 146
Stevenson, Winona, 112
Storytelling, 130
    education, 131
Strom, Stephen, 142
Subject position, 25–26
Syllabary or syllabic system, 3n. 4
Symbolic capital, 44, 82–83
    scholarly profit as, 32–33

T

Terminology, use of, 16–19
Thornton, Russell, 173
Thunderbird, Margo, 109, 111
Thure, Karen, 60
Tradition, 54, 60–61, 63, 85n. 7, 130
Treaty Three, 112–114
Trickster discourse, 75, 81–82, 88, 91, 141
Tuhiwai Smith, Linda, 18, 53, 101–102, 104, 105

U

Udall, Louise, 60
Underhill, Ruth, 60
Universals, 5, 13, 65–66

V

Vampire Project, 109–110
Vanderhaeghe, Guy, 129
Visual art
    avante garde, 7
    comparison between Western and Aboriginal, 7–14
    modernist and abstract movements in painting, 7–8
Vizenor, Gerald, 54, 75–94, 95, 96, 101, 121
    humor and, 76–77
    Striptease and, 76–78

W

Wagamese, Richard, 116
Wallis, Michael, 54–55
Warrior, Robert, 41–42, 46, 53, 56, 75, 92, 93–94, 94–101, 103, 175
Weaver, Jace, 53, 92, 93–94, 118–119, 121–122, 128, 140
What Moon Drove Me to This, 152
Whispering in Shadows, 105–107
Whitehead, Alfred North, 98–99
Whitt, Laurie Anne, 53, 109–110
Whorf, Benjamin, 125
Wild Man figure, 24
Willard, William, and Mary Kay Downing, 174
Wilson, Terry, 80
Womack, Craig, 43, 53, 102–103
Woman Who Fell from the Sky, 152
Wong, Hertha Dawn, 55, 58, 61–66
Worldview, Aboriginal, 2, 4n. 5, 6–7, 52, 53, 84, 92, 127, 140, 145, 179;
    see also indigenous theory
    compared to Western worldview, 2, 6–7, 13–14, 42, 66–67
    in visual art, 9–10
Worldview, Western, 6, 12
Wounded Knee, 79

Y

Young, Robert, 120–121
Young-Ing, Greg, 129–130

Z

Zubiri, Xavier, 66

For Product Safety Concerns and Information please contact our EU representative GPSR@taylorandfrancis.com
Taylor & Francis Verlag GmbH, Kaufingerstraße 24, 80331 München, Germany

www.ingramcontent.com/pod-product-compliance
Lightning Source LLC
Chambersburg PA
CBHW052040300426
44117CB00012B/1900